RESTORING THE CHAIN OF
MEMORY

T.G.H. Strehlow standing next to an Aboriginal man at Henbury
Station, Central Australia, 1935 (courtesy of the State Library of
South Australia, PRG 1218/34/97)

RESTORING THE CHAIN OF
MEMORY

T.G.H. Strehlow and the Repatriation of Australian Indigenous Knowledge

James L. Cox

SHEFFIELD UK   BRISTOL CT

Published by Equinox Publishing Ltd.

UK: Office 415, The Workstation, 15 Paternoster Row, Sheffield, South Yorkshire, S1 2BX
USA: ISD, 70 Enterprise Drive, Bristol, CT 06010

www.equinoxpub.com

First published 2018
First printing in paperback 2022

British Library Cataloguing-in-Publication Data
A catalogue record for this book is available from the British Library.

Library of Congress Cataloging-in-Publication Data
 Names: Cox, James L. (James Leland), author.
Title: Restoring the chain of memory : T.G.H. Strehlow and the repatriation
    of Australian indigenous knowledge / James L Cox.
Description: Bristol : Equinox Publishing Ltd., 2018. | Includes
    bibliographical references and index.
Identifiers: LCCN 2017036786 (print) | LCCN 2017047964 (ebook) | ISBN
    9781781797037 (ePDF) | ISBN 9781781793374 (hb)
Subjects: LCSH: Strehlow, T. G. H. (Theodor George Henry), 1908-1978. |
    Aranda (Australian people)--Religion. | Aboriginal Australians--Religion.
    | Australia--Religion.
Classification: LCC BL2630.A68 (ebook) | LCC BL2630.A68 C69 2018 (print) |
    DDC 299/.9215--dc23
LC record available at https://lccn.loc.gov/2017036786

ISBN: 978 1 78179 337 4 (hardback)
        978 1 80050 311 3 (paperback)
        978 1 78179 703 7 (ePDF)

Typeset by CA Typesetting

DEDICATION

To Dr T. Jack Thompson, a close colleague and friend

CONTENTS

List of Illustrations

ACKNOWLEDGEMENTS

I am indebted to the many individuals and organizations that have made this book possible. I start with Western Sydney University, which has generously funded numerous research trips I have made to Australia, particularly to Alice Springs and surrounding areas in Central Australia. Adam Possamai, Professor of Sociology and Director of Research and Higher Degree Research in the School of Social Sciences and Psychology at Western Sydney University, has been an invaluable support, both as a colleague and fellow researcher and as one who has worked with me to attain funding for my trips to and within Australia. Professor Possamai also promoted my appointment as Adjunct Professor in the Religion and Society Research Cluster at Western Sydney University, which made it possible for me to have access to facilities in the University and to participate in numerous research seminars. Without his help, none of this would have been possible.

I also want to mention the support given to me by David Moore, a linguist and translator in Central Australia, who assisted me in my research, engaged me in discussions about the theme of this book and helpfully answered questions I needed for clarification. The Strehlow Research Centre in Alice Springs has provided vital assistance in this project, first by making the resources of the library available to me, including some of Strehlow's notes and unpublished material, and then by guiding me to important source material. In particular, I want to thank Graeme Shaughnessy, former Librarian at the Strehlow Research Centre, and Michael Cawthorn, former Director of the Centre, who helped me during my earlier research visits to Alice Springs. More recently, I want to thank Adam Macfie, the Repatriation Anthropologist at the Strehlow Research Centre and the Indigenous Researchers, Mark Inkamala and Shaun Angeles, for their helpful comments and advice as the project unfolded. Anna Kenny, a postdoctoral fellow at the Australian National University and a consultant anthropologist who has been based in Alice Springs for the past 20 years, offered me helpful insights on the theme of this book. I extend special appreciation to David and Margaret Hewitt and Olga Radke, as well as David and Susan Moore, who have worked to develop the Friends of the Strehlow Research Centre, which has facilitated several one day conferences in Alice Springs to which I have been invited to present papers and participate in the discussions. I am grateful to Dr Steve Bevis, an independent researcher in Central Australia, whom I first met when he was still a

PhD candidate in the University of Sydney in 2009, for his continued interest in my work. I acknowledge also the help provided to me by John Strehlow, T.G.H. Strehlow's son, who gave me important insights when we first met in London and then invited me to the important conference he organized in Alice Springs in 2014. The Lutheran Archives in Adelaide were made available to me in 2014, for which I express my appreciation. Still in the Australian context, I want to express my thanks for the support and encouragement provided to me over the last eight years by the Department of Studies in Religion in the University of Sydney, and particularly to Professor Carole Cusack and Dr Christopher Hartney, who have made it possible for me to present papers and test my ideas during seminars held at the University of Sydney.

In the UK, in my capacity as Honorary Professorial Fellow in the School of Divinity at the University of Edinburgh, I have had access to the facilities of the University, including the library and information technology. I am grateful to the Religious Studies Subject Area for supporting me in this capacity and for the encouragement provided by the Head of the School of Divinity, Professor Paul Foster. I also want to thank the Royal Society of Edinburgh for providing support for this project in its early phases by awarding me an Auber Grant in 2014. I am grateful to Janet Joyce of Equinox Publishing for accepting this manuscript for publication and to her and her staff for working with me towards its completion.

I would be extremely negligent if I did not express my gratitude for the many insights into Australian Indigenous Religions I have discovered through the writings of the subject of this study, T.G.H. Strehlow. I can only hope that this book does justice to his immense contribution to promoting understanding of the complex and immensely rich religious life of the Indigenous people of Central Australia.

Finally, I want to express my thanks to my wife, Valerie, who has not only provided unending support and encouragement, but also has exhibited enormous patience, as I have worked to complete this book in my 'retirement'.

James L. Cox
Cupar, Fife, Scotland

Preface

I first became interested in T.G.H. Strehlow in 2009 when I visited the Strehlow Research Centre Museum in Alice Springs, Australia. I studied with interest the displays indicating events in Strehlow's life and while there watched *Mr Strehlow's Films* (2001), written and directed by Hart Cohen of Western Sydney University. I was particularly impressed by Cohen's depiction of Strehlow's story, which began with his years growing up among Arrernte children as the son of the missionary-linguist Carl Strehlow during the early part of the twentieth century. He was the only non-Indigenous child on the Lutheran Mission at Hermannsburg, located approximately 130 kilometres west of Alice Springs. I followed Cohen's account further through T.G.H. Strehlow's years as a young researcher who returned to Central Australia in 1932 and then served as Native Patrol Officer appointed by the Commonwealth Government. During these years Strehlow gained the trust of Aboriginal Elders and, as one who knew the language of the region from childhood, recorded on film numerous Indigenous ceremonies and produced tapes of secret-sacred songs, while at the same time documenting genealogical information that he coordinated with painstaking constructions on maps.

Near its conclusion, Cohen's film devotes considerable time to the controversy that surrounded the years immediately prior to Strehlow's death in 1978, including his decision to sell photos of sacred ceremonies to *Stern* magazine in Germany on the understanding that these would never be published in Australia. After they appeared in the Australian magazine, *People*, he was accused of betraying his Aboriginal informants. In addition, he and his second wife, Kathleen, claimed to be the owners of the secret-sacred objects, photographs, recordings and films that had been entrusted and revealed in confidence to him by Elders. At the time I viewed Cohen's film I wondered if the controversies that surrounded the final years of Strehlow's life had overshadowed and diminished his immense contribution to promoting widespread understanding of the Indigenous Religions of Central Australia.

Following my initial visit to the Strehlow Research Centre, I embarked on a project to delve into Strehlow's own writings about the Arrernte people and other Indigenous groups in Central Australia. I wanted to investigate if his writings not only confirmed his personal significance as an interpreter of the traditional religious beliefs, rituals and social organization of central desert Indigenous peoples but if his material could be used as a means of encouraging an empathetic understanding of Indigenous Religions in general. I soon discovered that the impact of Strehlow's research extended beyond his contribution to the academic study of Indigenous Religions, and was increasingly becoming important to Indigenous peoples themselves. This is confirmed by the attention currently being devoted to his copious notes, photographs, films, recordings and genealogies by local Aboriginal people, who are increasingly consulting his Collection housed at the Strehlow Research Centre to restore knowledge of their ancient traditions, stories and ceremonies that has been lost or forgotten. In this book, I pursue these themes as I discovered them over a period of seven years by studying and analysing Strehlow's writings and by my research in Central Australia that included helpful contacts with the staff and researchers at the Strehlow Research Centre, which I visited every year between 2009 and 2016.

The Organization of This Book

I begin my study of T.G.H. Strehlow in Chapter 1 by setting the context for the chapters that follow. After providing biographical background on Strehlow and situating his work among the Arrernte, the Indigenous people among whom he primarily worked in Central Australia, I review and evaluate the writings of three of his principal biographers and critics, whom I refer to as Strehlow's 'detractors'. In Chapter 2, I explain that I have placed my study of Strehlow within a theoretical model I have been developing and refining over the past 15 years, which has resulted in an increasingly narrow, socio-cultural working definition of religion and Indigenous Religions. I demonstrate how the theoretical framework through which I am interpreting Strehlow's writings leads to my discussion later in the book of the significance of his collected works for contemporary events aimed at the 'repatriation of knowledge' among the Arrernte-speaking peoples of Central Australia.

With the theories that inform this study explained, I turn in the next four chapters to presenting a detailed analysis of Strehlow's own writings. I begin in Chapter 3 by describing his accounts of the stories and myths about totemic ancestors on which the Arrernte have built their entire religious worldview and on which their social structures traditionally were based. This will involve a discussion of how Strehlow has corrected common misconceptions about 'Dreamtime' as promoted in popular literature and how his studies demonstrate that the adoption of the Indigenous word *altjira* as equivalent to the Christian God is equally erroneous. In Chapter 4, I analyse how Strehlow related the stories about totemic ancestors to the complex Arrernte social organization he called 'personal monototemism in a polytotemic community'. I then draw together in Chapter 5 the mythic and social

dimensions of traditional Arrernte religion by providing an in-depth description and analysis of Arrernte ceremonies as Strehlow presented them in his
monumental achievement, *Songs of Central Australia* (1971). I conclude my
analysis of Strehlow's own writings in Chapter 6 by interrogating his claim
that by 1970 virtually all knowledge of traditional Arrernte stories, ceremonies, locations of ceremonies, meanings associated with secret-sacred objects
and genealogical records had been forgotten by the Indigenous Elders to
whom the sacred memory had been entrusted. I also discuss his claim that
Indigenous knowledge among the Arrernte peoples was preserved only in the
records he obtained and documented over the 40 years he had been accumulating material that formed his considerable Collection, which was in his possession at his death.

After having outlined in detail Strehlow's descriptions and interpretations of Indigenous Religions in Central Australia, in Chapter 7 I consider
the theoretical methodology Strehlow employed while conducting his field
research and which informed the subsequent presentation of his findings in
his numerous publications. I argue that Strehlow employed methods that
were fully consistent with principles broadly associated with the phenomenology of religion. I present evidence that although he never called himself
a phenomenologist of religion, Strehlow is best understood for students of
religion precisely in this way. In order to document this, in Chapter 7, I outline the main tenets in the phenomenological method and demonstrate in
what ways Strehlow pursued these aims vigorously.

In the concluding two chapters I relate Strehlow's writings to contemporary events. In Chapter 8, I focus on repatriation movements and discuss
how conventional understandings of repatriation have been transformed by
the concept called the 'repatriation of knowledge'. It is at this point that
Strehlow's work has become fundamental for the attempts by contemporary
Arrernte Elders to restore knowledge of their traditional stories, ceremonies
and social structures. In Chapter 9, I return to the discussion which I began
in Chapter 2 where I restricted religion to an authoritative tradition that
is preserved and transmitted from generation to generation. I argued that
Indigenous Religions refer exclusively to traditions that are bound to ancestors and operate in strictly delineated geographical locations. I demonstrate
how my research on Strehlow and the contemporary repatriation of knowledge movement confirms my theoretical starting-points and encourages an
empathetic understanding of Indigenous Religions in Central Australia in
ways consistent with the principles advocated by the phenomenology of
religion. At the same time, I discuss contemporary movements in the context of issues surrounding two main theoretical categories: types of knowledge and the relationship between tradition and modernity. I conclude by
arguing that the collected work of T.G.H. Strehlow functions not only as
a dynamic source for Indigenous communities as they respond creatively

and positively to the changing circumstances occurring within Australian society but also that his extensive research on Central Australia, although concluded more than 50 years ago, can make a significant contribution to contemporary global studies in Indigenous Religions.

As a point of clarification, I should note that Strehlow generally used diacritical marks throughout his writings to indicate pronunciation of Arrernte words. Normally, he did not use these in publications aimed at international audiences, such as in his contribution to a book edited by C.J. Bleeker and Geo Widengren dealing with religions around the world (Strehlow, 1971b: 609–28). I have chosen in this book not to replicate Strehlow's diacritical marks, apart from 'ŋ', which carries an ng sound. For purposes of consistency, I have used 'ŋ' throughout the book when Strehlow included it in spelling Arrernte words. This is because Strehlow employed two spellings for traditional secret-sacred objects: *tjurunga* when he referred to sacred objects made of stone or wood on which secret totemic symbols were engraved, and the phonetic spelling *tjuruŋa*, which implied the entire totemic tradition.

Sensitive Issues Addressed in This Book

I am aware that I am an outsider not only to Australia but particularly to the cultural and social situation in Central Australia. I have undertaken this study not as one who thinks it is possible in a short period to speak with authority on issues that have impinged on the circumstances of people, both Indigenous and non-Indigenous, who have lived in Central Australia for all or most of their lives. At the same time, I am aware that as an outsider, I risk offending Australian researchers, whose knowledge of the wider historical and social contexts within Australia has formed part of their growing up, and which they have honed through many years of studying the varied societies and cultures found throughout Australia. In one sense, I am giving the authority to speak as an insider to T.G.H. Strehlow by presenting his findings on Central Australian religions in as fair and as unbiased a way as I can. Of course, it is my interpretation of Strehlow that will emerge, but I believe that by returning to his own writings I can bring a fresh perspective that suggests how Strehlow's insights can contribute in contemporary times to promoting understanding of the religions and cultures of Central Australia. In the context of the global study of Indigenous Religions, I am interpreting Strehlow's contribution through the lens of my own theories of religion and Indigenous Religions and, in the process, I hope to introduce new material into the debates over the nature of Indigenous Religions and their place within the larger field of Religious Studies.

One of the most sensitive issues that will emerge as I present Strehlow's writings relates to the extreme secrecy which surrounds the traditional religious and cultural practices in Central Australia. Strehlow described in detail ceremonies in which participation was restricted exclusively to initiated males and he related songs associated with them that were closely guarded secrets maintained and transmitted to the next generation by Indigenous Elders. He did so, on one level, to preserve for posterity knowledge that he thought was rapidly being lost, but also as a means of promoting understanding among outsiders of the common human religious sentiments expressed in the ceremonies and songs of the people native to Central Australia. The aim of encouraging such understanding was to counter the widespread assumption, promulgated by early scholars and researchers in Central Australia, that Aboriginal societies were among the most primitive and backward found anywhere in the world. By presenting the myths, social organization and rituals of the peoples of Central Australia in terms that could be compared with the same categories found among other religious communities throughout the world, Strehlow believed that his writings could have repercussions far beyond academic circles by informing public perceptions of Indigenous culture, encouraging enlightened choices among policy makers and ultimately fostering Indigenous pride.

In light of Strehlow's larger aims, I have chosen to present details of his descriptions of Indigenous myths, social organization and ceremonies. I am aware that my accounts derived from Strehlow potentially could offend current Indigenous people who are using Strehlow's Collection in Alice Springs to recover knowledge of lost or forgotten ancient traditions. I have two responses to this extremely sensitive issue. First, the material I am presenting is already in the public domain, not only in Strehlow's writings, but in numerous other anthropological accounts of Indigenous cultures in Central Australia and in many other parts of the continent. It does not seem appropriate to allow Strehlow's positive contribution to promoting understanding of Central Australian religion to remain overshadowed by the negative judgements of his critics through a superficial presentation of his research findings and by restricting my conclusions to broad generalizations divorced from empirical studies. Secondly, I have tried throughout this book to use the material Strehlow presented carefully and in full awareness of the delicate nature of the material described. I have not included any photographs of Indigenous ceremonies or secret-sacred objects, and I have tried to limit the ritual descriptions to the most essential parts so the reader can obtain an idea of what was occurring within the ceremonies in light of their significance for the age-old authority of the tradition that was being transmitted. I have limited my use of Indigenous terms to those that are almost universally used in the literature, such as *tjurunga*. I have not used Arrernte language in the songs associated with the ceremonies, as Strehlow did, but have limited them entirely to his translations into English.

I am also aware that I am exercising power by describing and interpreting beliefs and practices that are not my own. With this in mind, I have tried in every way, following my presentation of Strehlow as a phenomenologist of religion, to employ empathy based on the phenomenological mantra that nothing human ultimately is alien to other humans. In other words, by employing the practice of intense empathy, we gain an understanding of beliefs and practices that at first sight might appear totally alien to our own way of life. In this sense, I am asserting that at the most basic level, all humans think alike. Social, cultural and other related factors, such as geography or means of subsistence, produce different responses to the immediate environment resulting in a variety of religious understandings of the world. Nonetheless, I have found in my work in various cultures that differences can be understood and translated into terms to which I can relate if I adopt an empathetic, non-judgemental, approach and try through the process of interpolation to translate what appear as 'foreign' ways of thinking and acting into contexts that make sense to me based on my own cultural and social background. This is a method well established among researchers who follow the broad principles outlined within the phenomenological approach to the study of religions and cultures.

In the end, this book is dedicated to the principle of Indigenous agency. I am not refocussing attention on the writings of T.G.H. Strehlow to suggest that they can dictate how and for what ends the knowledge he has preserved will be used by Indigenous people in Central Australia. I am convinced, however, that the story I am telling can contribute to promoting what a recent Canadian Mennonite magazine has called the 'Quest for Respect', part of which involves movements by Indigenous people globally to reclaim the knowledge that originally was theirs (Friesen and Heinrichs, 2017). Nonetheless, I believe that outsiders also have a stake in this process. This point was made by Christopher Anderson, former Director of the South Australian Museum, in his important edited book, *The Politics of the Secret,* which addresses sensitive issues surrounding secrecy in Aboriginal societies in Australia. Anderson (1995: 13) acknowledged that 'some will say that these papers should not have been written or published'. In response to this, he argued that to refuse to discuss Indigenous secrecy in Australia 'ultimately is detrimental to Aboriginal culture and its place in Australian society' (1995: 14). He added that 'it also demeans and homogenises the location-specific cultural knowledge of places such as Central Australia' (1995: 14). I find Anderson's comments relevant to my aims in this book. By drawing attention to the significant place Indigenous knowledge in Central Australia occupies in the rich diversity of human cultures, and by outlining the contribution T.G.H. Strehlow has made to promoting understanding of Indigenous Religions generally, I believe I am contributing to the greater goal of encouraging universal respect for Indigenous ways of life and in the process helping to build a better, more humane world.

1

THE CONTEXT: CENTRAL AUSTRALIA, T.G.H. STREHLOW AND HIS DETRACTORS

Before describing and analysing in the following chapters the contribution of T.G.H. Strehlow to promoting understanding of Indigenous Religions in Australia, in this chapter I present a brief biographical summary of Strehlow and then provide an introduction to the Indigenous people among whom his life's work was devoted. I then review the work of three main writers who have given considerable attention, often highly critical, to documenting events in Strehlow's career and the various problems he encountered in his dealings with family members, academic colleagues, politicians and towards the end of his life with Indigenous people themselves. This review of some of Strehlow's chief detractors is undertaken to demonstrate how his substantial work on the religions of Central Australia has been overshadowed by nega‐tive judgements on his personal life. It also provides the context for a fresh examination of the principal themes he pursued in his writings.

Who Was T.G.H. Strehlow?[1]

In 1877, the Lutheran Church established a mission around 130 kilometres west of Alice Springs at what they called Hermannsburg, named after the theological institution where they trained ministers and missionaries in Ger‐many. The mission was abandoned by 1891 due to severe problems at the sta‐tion resulting from drought and disease. In 1894, the Reverend Carl Strehlow, who had already worked among the Dieri people in the northern part of South Australia, was assigned by the Immanuel Synod of the Lutheran Church in South Australia to take charge of the troubled mission station at Hermanns‐burg in the hope of reviving its work among Aboriginal people in the area. After marrying Frieda Keysser in 1895, to whom he had been engaged in Germany, the newly married couple began a ministry at Hermannsburg that

---

1.   I obtained the core of the information summarizing the main events of Strehlow's life from an Information Sheet provided by the Strehlow Research Centre (2000) and from Strehlow's biography appearing in the *Australian Dictionary of Biography*, writ‐ten by Philip Jones (2002), Senior Curator in Anthropology at the South Australian Museum in Adelaide. Other sources are cited and direct quotations acknowledged.

continued until Carl's death in 1922. They had six children, the youngest of whom, born in 1908, was named Theodor Georg Heinrich. In the light of anti-German feeling during World War II, in 1945 T.G.H. changed his name to Theodor George Henry (J. Strehlow, 2011: 46). As a child, he was called Theo and as an adult was known as Ted. In 1910–11, the family took missionary furlough in Germany, where they left their five oldest children to complete their education. Ted returned to Australia with his parents, where he grew up as the only white child on the Hermannsburg Mission, and where he remained until the age of 14, when his parents were forced to leave due to Carl's ill health. Carl died at Horseshoe Bend while en route to Oodnadatta in South Australia on a desperate journey to secure medical treatment.

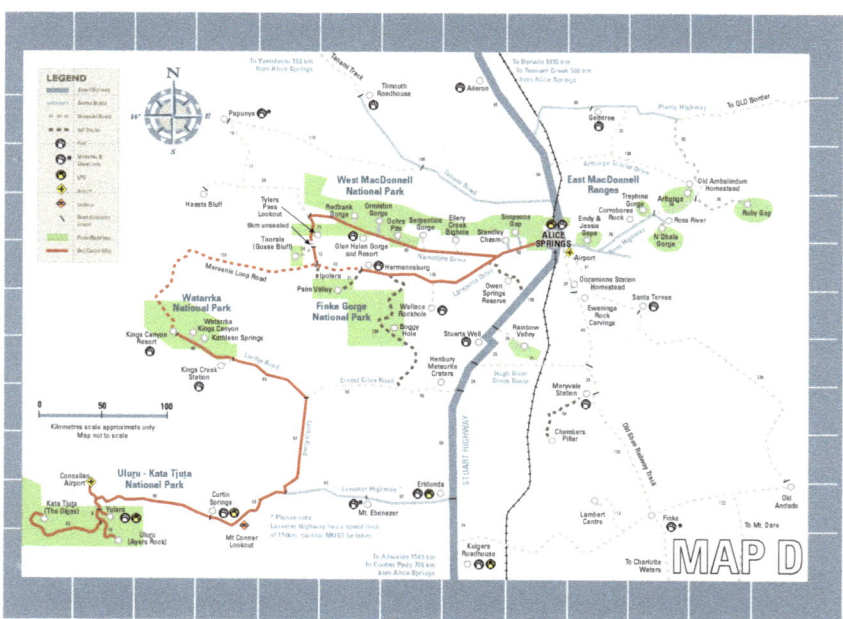

Figure 1. Map of Central Australia. Courtesy of Tourism Central Australia

Ted and his mother settled in Adelaide, where Ted was enrolled in Immanuel College before entering the University of Adelaide to study Classics and English, which resulted in his earning a Bachelor of Arts (Hons.) degree in 1931. Following the completion of his university degree, his mother returned to Germany. Ted remained in Australia and at the urging of his Professor in Classics at the University of Adelaide, J.A. FitzHerbert, undertook a study of Arrernte linguistics under a grant obtained from the Australian National Research Council. He arrived in Central Australia in March 1932 where he began researching, not only the language of the peoples of the central desert region, but also their culture, religion, social organization, stories, songs, sacred sites and ceremonies, which he recorded and documented over the next 40 years. He submitted his findings on Arrernte linguistics to the University of Adelaide, resulting in a Masters of Arts degree in 1938, which, after initially appearing as a series of articles in the journal *Oceania* from 1942 to 1944, was published under the title *Aranda Phonetics and Grammar* (1944), with an introduction by A.P. Elkin. His first major work outlining the cultural, social and religious life of the Arrernte, which was based largely on the research he conducted between 1932 and 1934, was published in 1947 as *Aranda Traditions*. During his initial research trips, partly because of his intimate knowledge of the language and also because he had grown up among Arrernte children, Strehlow gained the trust of Arrernte Elders who shared with him knowledge of their secret ceremonies, sacred sites and songs associated with ritual performances, as well as entrusting him with some of their most secret-sacred objects, called *tjurunga* in the Arrernte language.

In 1935, Strehlow returned to Central Australia under another grant from the Australian National Research Council. In December of that year, he married Bertha James, a school teacher from Adelaide. The couple began their life together by undertaking an arduous research trip by camel through parts of the Northern Territory. In 1936, with the assistance of the noted anthropologist at the University of Sydney, A.P. Elkin, Strehlow was appointed by the Commonwealth Government as Native Patrol Officer covering the southern half of the Northern Territory with responsibility for investigating charges of mistreatment of Indigenous peoples in the region. He and Bertha settled at Jay Creek, approximately 45 kilometres west of Alice Springs, a base from which they travelled extensively by camel as Strehlow carried out his duties. In a biography of Strehlow written for the *Australian Dictionary of Biography*, Philip Jones reports that as Patrol Officer Strehlow often opposed high-ranking officials in his attempt to increase the supply of rations that were distributed to needy Aboriginal families. Jones notes that 'Strehlow recommended that a number of European employers of Aboriginal labour be prosecuted for exploitation and physical abuse'. This resulted in Strehlow describing himself as 'the most hated man in Central Australia' (Jones, 2002).

Strehlow served six years as Native Patrol Officer, a period in which he was unable to conduct any significant further academic research. In 1942, at the height of the Second World War, he was recruited for full-time military service, during which time he performed clerical duties in several military units. In early 1945 he earned a commission as lieutenant and was posted to Canberra, where his primary job was to train servicemen to be colonial administrators (Jones, 2002). He was able to resume research following the war in 1946, when he was appointed research fellow in Australian linguistics and lecturer in English literature at the University of

Adelaide. Extensive field research was made possible a year later when he received a two-year post-graduate fellowship at the Australian National University in Canberra. During his visits to Central Australia over the next two years, he took copious notes, recorded songs and chants and was allowed to film in colour some of the most significant rituals within the Arrernte ceremonial cycle. During this period he began recording 'songs' and 'chants' associated with Arrernte ceremonies that resulted in a manuscript he entitled *Songs of Central Australia*. The book was accepted in 1956 by Angus and Robertson, a Sydney-based publisher (Berndt, 1979a: 231), but due to technical and financial difficulties, it was not published until 15 years later in 1971. Despite the delay in its publication, *Songs of Central Australia* represents Strehlow's most significant contribution to understanding Arrernte religious beliefs, cultural symbols and ceremonial life.

In order to establish his credentials as an anthropologist, at the urging of A.P. Elkin, in 1950 Strehlow travelled to England to work with the internationally recognized anthropologist, Raymond Firth, at the London School of Economics. This period, from mid-1950 until early 1952, was deeply disappointing to Strehlow, who, according to Jones (2002), regarded it as 'wasted'. Although Strehlow presented numerous papers in London and showed some of the films he had produced during his recent research trips, Jones reports that among his British audiences the 'response was lukewarm'. Strehlow returned to Australia, again according to Jones (2002), 'with a bitter sense of personal and professional alienation', and was 'convinced that he alone could interpret his data'. After being appointed Reader in Australian linguistics at the University of Adelaide in 1954, he continued to receive funding for further research on the peoples of Central Australia, which he pursued throughout the 1950s and 1960s. It was during this time that he most fully documented genealogical information of Indigenous groups and produced detailed maps of local areas showing important totemic boundaries and ceremonial sites, which he supported by further research notes, recordings and choreographed colour films.

Towards the end of his career, Strehlow was recognized for his academic achievements by the University of Adelaide, being awarded a Personal Chair in Linguistics in 1970, and two years after his retirement in 1973 was conferred an Honorary Doctor of Letters. During the same period, Strehlow's life changed dramatically. He divorced his wife Bertha in 1972 and married his research assistant Kathleen Stuart. Together, they worked to establish the Strehlow Research Foundation as an entity entirely independent from academic institutions. This was based, at least in part, on Strehlow's claim that the vast collection he had acquired over the many years of his research was his own personal property. Jones (2002) records that Strehlow's collection comprised:

4500 Aboriginal song verses and more than 100 myths (all written in Arrernte and Loritja dialects and languages in his notebooks), 800 ceremonial acts captured on tape and 26 hours of film, maps of several hundred ceremonial and mythical sites, 8000 photographs, 150 detailed genealogies, and, most controversially, a collection of 1200 artefacts.

Part of the agreement regarding the new Foundation included the clause that on his death Strehlow's collection would pass into the possession of his wife, Kathleen.

Strehlow suffered heart attacks in 1975 and 1976. He died in Adelaide on 3 October 1978, on the exact day and just a few hours ahead of the scheduled opening of the Strehlow Research Foundation at the State Library of South Australia. Justice M.D. Kirby, who was Chairman of the Australian Law Reform Commission, with whom Strehlow had worked as an advisor, had been asked to perform the official opening. Kirby and Ronald Berndt, Chair of the Strehlow Research Foundation Committee, had arranged to meet Strehlow and his wife Kathleen at Strehlow's rooms at the University of Adelaide to discuss final preparations before the official opening. Kirby (1980: 172) wrote later that as Strehlow 'ascended the stairs, I remarked to myself how radiant was his expression. A day long anticipated had arrived'. The four sat down and Strehlow explained the cover picture on the programme for the opening which featured the native bandicoot. Kirby describes what happened next: '"Ingkaia", the name of the furry-eared bandicoot in the Aranda tongue was the last word he said. He collapsed. Despite every effort of his wife, his colleagues, medical and other personnel, he died' (1980: 173). A decision was made to go ahead with the opening despite Strehlow's dramatic death. Ronald Berndt was asked by Kathleen Strehlow to read the notes Strehlow had prepared for his address at the inaugural event. In his obituary of Strehlow, Berndt (1979b: 232) relates that Strehlow had intended to tell the gathering that the chances of his surviving long enough to complete any further writing on central desert peoples were 'slim'. Berndt then quotes Strehlow's concluding remark: 'It is now five minutes before midnight and then will come that oblivion that has no end'. This comment referred to the decline in the knowledge of traditional culture in Central Australia, but Berndt used it with a dual meaning in which he also applied it to Strehlow himself.

During the four decades of his research on the Indigenous peoples of Central Australia, Strehlow had covered a total of 160,000 kilometres by camel and car. The extensive research documents and material that he accrued over the many years of conducting field studies beginning in 1932, after ten years of negotiating with Kathleen Strehlow, were purchased by the Northern Territory Government and now nearly all the Strehlow Collection is housed in the Strehlow Research Centre in Alice Springs, which opened in 1991.

The Arrernte Peoples

Strehlow's primary research in Central Australia focussed on the Arrernte peoples, although he included some references to neighbouring groups, principally the Luritja (Loritja) speakers to the west and south. The term Arrernte refers in the first instance to a language group, but it is also applied to groups of people who speak variations of Arrernte dialects. When Strehlow published his major works, he spelled Arrernte as Aranda, which was the conventional spelling of the word at the time. The most widely accepted current spelling is Arrernte, although variations exist such as Arrarnte or Arunta. The spelling as Arrernte emphasizes how the word is pronounced (UH rranda) with the double rr indicating that the r is rolled. Arrernte language dialects are commonly divided into Western, Eastern and Central (now commonly referred to as Upper Arrernte), and Southern regions, with Western Arrernte defining the language Strehlow learned as a boy at Hermannsburg. Eastern and Central Arrernte, or Upper Arrernte, is spoken in and around Alice Springs, with the Southern Arrernte dialect found along the Finke River south of Maryvale (http://ourlanguages.org. au/arrernte-language-map/, accessed 24 May 2017). In a map he inserted on the back inside cover of *Aranda Traditions,* Strehlow himself identi-fied more detailed linguistic divisions, classifying the Arrernte language groups as Western (near Hermannsburg), Northern (including the impor-tant ceremonial site at Krantji), Central (in and around Alice Springs), Eastern (near Kriŋka), Upper Southern Arrernte (near Imanda in the vicinity of the Hugh River) and Lower Southern Arrernte (bordered by the Finke River on the west and the Simpson Desert on the east). He con-structed these divisions not only according to the language dialects, but also to represent the lines of travel followed by the totemic ancestors as told in Arrernte myths. Some estimates suggest that today there are more than 3000 indigenous speakers of Arrernte languages (Amery and Bourke, 1994: 124), although the figure has been estimated as high as between 5000 and 6000 (Turpin, n.d.).

Myfany Turpin, writing on the website of the Central Land Council, explains that there are three principal language groupings in Central Aus-tralia: the Western Desert Language family, the Arandic and the Ngarrkic. Within each of these, she notes, 'overlapping dialects/languages share common vocabulary and grammatical features', adding that 'the distinc-tions between the dialects may be quite minimal' (Turpin, n.d.). According to Turpin, the Arandic language family is comprised of Eastern and Central Arrernte, spoken around Alice Springs, the Western Arrernte region mainly around Hermannsburg and Jay Creek and Southern Arrernte, which in ear-lier days was spoken south of Alice Springs, but today there are few speak-ers remaining. Other languages in the Arandic group are spoken primarily

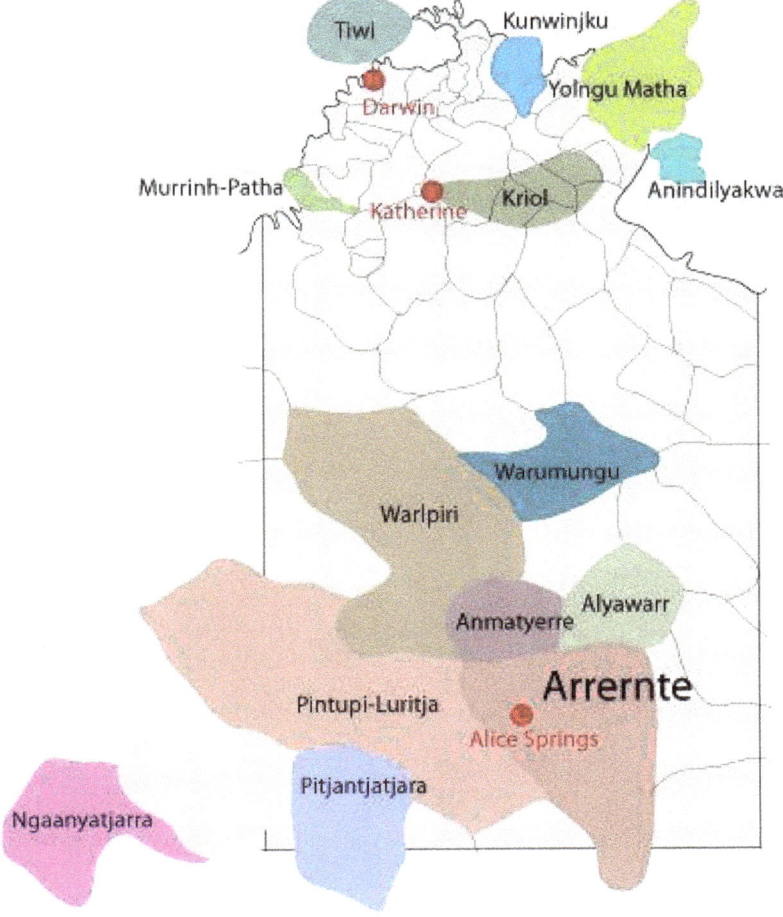

Figure 2. Language map of Central and North Central Australia. Courtesy of Italk Studios, Alice Springs

north of Alice Springs and include Central and Eastern Anmatyerr, Alyawarr and Kaytetye. Turpin places Luritja among the Western Desert languages, but suggests Luritja speakers originally covered a wide area, from Oodnadatta in South Australia moving northwards along the Finke River to Maryvale up to Jay Creek, with Pintupi Luritja spoken as far as the Western Australia border. For this reason, she suggests that Luritja has been used as a 'lingua franca' between Western Desert and Arandic speakers. This would explain why Luritja-speaking communities comprise the other main language group that T.G.H. Strehlow referred to in his writings. The

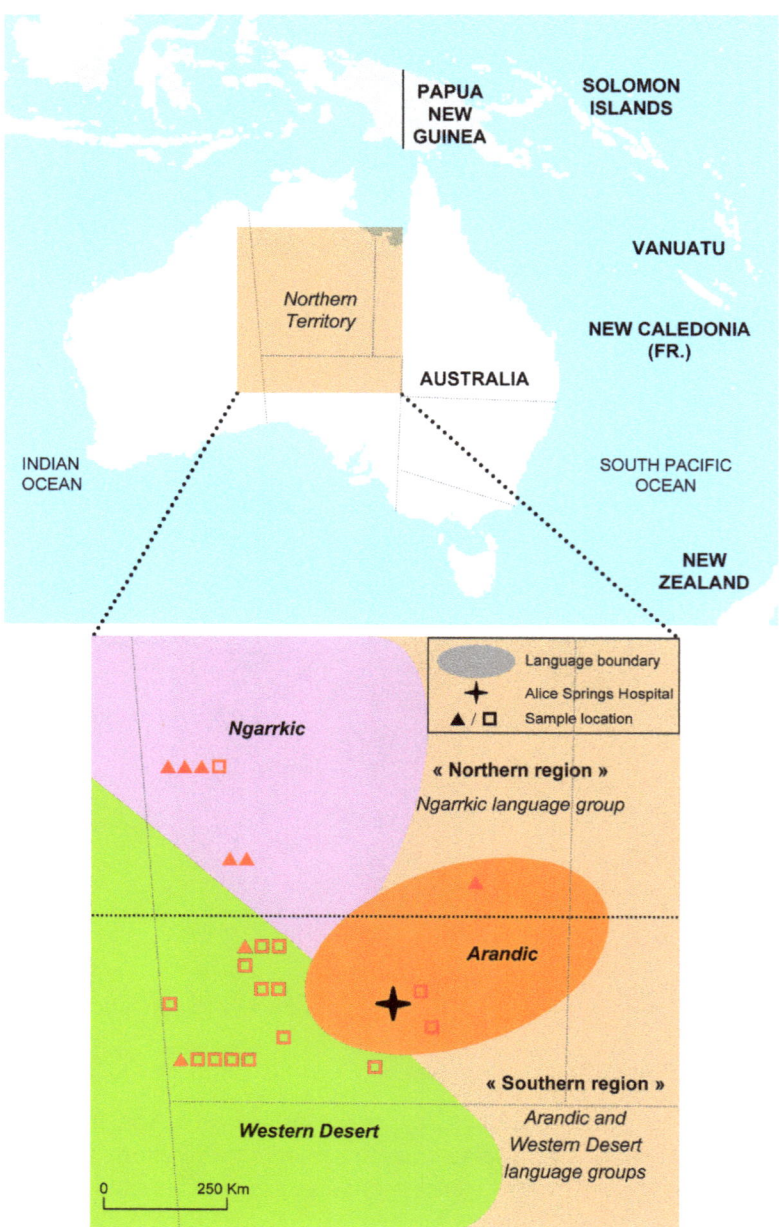

Figure 3. Arandic and Western Desert Language Groups. Source: O. Cassar, L. Einsiedel, P.V. Afonso, and A. Gessain (2013). 'Human T-Cell Lymphotropic Virus Type 1 Subtype C Molecular Variants among Indigenous Australians: New Insights into the Molecular Epidemiology of HTLV-1 in Australo-Melanesia'. *PLOS Neglected Tropical Diseases* 7(9): w2418. https://doi.org/10.1371/journal.pntd.0002418

Ngarrkic, the third language family on Turpin's chart, is comprised primarily of Warlpiri speakers, who live in an extensive geographical area northwest of Alice Springs. Turpin suggests that there are currently around 3000 people who speak Warlpiri as a first language, but many people speak Warlpiri as a second or third language. Due to the increased mobility of people living in the Northern Territory, numerous Indigenous languages and dialects can be heard in Alice Springs.

Most of T.G.H. Strehlow's research was conducted in the areas comprising the Arrernte-speaking regions. At the time of his initial research, the Arrernte population probably did not exceed 3000. Originally, the Arrernte would have been nomadic hunters and gatherers, but with very clear ideas of what constituted their homelands. In an article appearing in a book edited by R.M. Berndt, Strehlow (1970: 92) explained that 'the fact that the Aboriginal inhabitants did not live in towns, villages, or even fixed dwellings, did not turn them into aimlessly wandering bands of nomads who continually clashed with one another over disputed natural food supplies'. They travelled throughout the year along circuits and camped at places to which they gave names, usually near water holes. The size of the camps varied, sometimes being limited to an extended family, or at times of important ceremonial events, could swell to over 200 (https://tinyurl.com/places-aranda).

Much of the traditional Arrernte way of life had changed when Strehlow conducted his research due to the impact of colonial administrations, Christian missions and settlement of the land by white pastoralists, but, as we will see, during his research conducted between 1932 and 1934, many traditional Arrernte rituals and totemic symbols persisted. Strehlow's writings confirm that at the time of his original research in 1932, the locations of the camps and the ceremonies associated with them retained their close identification with myths about totemic ancestors as told in age-old songs and stories that had been transmitted through the generations. Writing in a volume edited by Berndt, he underscored this point: 'The operation of the concept of the totemic landscape ensured ... such things as the stability of tribal boundaries and of linguistic groups, the distribution of interlocking and intermarrying subgroups, and even the firm establishment of authority' (Strehlow, 1970: 93). As I discuss Strehlow's descriptions of Arrernte songs, ceremonies, stories, ritual centres and social organization in the chapters that follow, it will be important to keep in mind that Strehlow was writing originally from his knowledge of Western Arrernte language and culture, which he enlarged and extended after his return to Central Australia in 1932 to cover wider areas in which other Arrernte dialects prevailed. His descriptions of ceremonial centres, interactions between various totemic groups and the discussion of polytotemic communities need to be understood in the context of the relationships between Arrernte-speaking regions, including the occasional references in his writings to some Luritja language groups.

Strehlow's Principal Biographers and Critics: McNally and Hill

Two authors wrote lengthy biographies of T.G.H. Strehlow: Ward McNally and Barry Hill. Both were highly critical of Strehlow citing his arrogance with regard to his collection, his alleged betrayal of the trust given to him by his Aboriginal informants and his overestimation of the value of his own notes, records and films as a preserve of Aboriginal knowledge. The first biography of T.G.H. Strehlow was written by McNally (1917–1991) and published in 1981 under the title *Aborigines, Artefacts and Anguish*, three years after Strehlow died. Barry Hill's biography, first published in 2002, carries the title, *Broken Song: T.G.H. Strehlow and Aboriginal Possession*. The title is a play on words derived from Strehlow's *Songs of Central Australia* and clearly suggests that Strehlow's claims to personal ownership of his collection amounted to a break of trust with those Aboriginal Elders who freely shared knowledge of their ancient traditions with him. I will consider these two important books in turn.

McNally, who was born in New Zealand, moved to Australia in 1950, where he worked primarily as a journalist serving in the late 1960s as editor of *The Centralian Advocate* published in Alice Springs (https://tinyurl.com/9780195533811). He wrote numerous books on Australian public figures and society, one about the noted Australian aviator Sir Charles Kingsford-Smith, entitled *The Man on the Twenty Dollar Note*, published in 1976, that caught Strehlow's attention. In the preface to his biography of Strehlow, McNally quotes from a letter Strehlow sent to him when he agreed to meet with McNally and help him with the proposed book on his life:

> Thank you for your letter of March 1, 1978, regarding your proposal to write a biographical book about me along the lines of your The Man on the Twenty Dollar Note ... I ... feel honoured by your proposal, and I shall endeavour to make available to you all the material you need for writing the proposed book (McNally, 1981: Preface).

McNally then admits that his book 'has not produced the story the late Professor Strehlow would have desired' but he claims that his 'is an honest book', adding, 'I make no judgments' (McNally, 1981: Preface).

As the title suggests, McNally's aim was to appeal to a broad popular audience. His chapters present considerable information obtained in interviews with Strehlow and important figures who played significant roles throughout Strehlow's life, including his first wife Bertha and their son, Theodor. Yet, much of the information reported in the book is untraceable because the interviews are undocumented and read oftentimes as if they are anecdotal. The entire tenor of the book is written in a journalistic style, focussed primarily on sometimes intensely personal events in Strehlow's life, how he reacted to them and the impact these had on his relationships with family members, academic colleagues and Aboriginal informants. McNally includes in his accounts details of Strehlow's childhood growing up on the Mission in Hermannsburg, his acquiring the Arrernte language even before he knew English, the story of his father's tortuous journey that ended in his death at Horseshoe Bend and the subsequent bitterness towards the Lutheran authorities in Adelaide that Strehlow harboured for the remainder of his life. McNally spends considerable time supporting Strehlow's claim that after he returned to Central Australia in 1932 he earned the trust of Arrernte Elders who shared with him many of their secret ceremonies and later placed in his care the sacred objects, *tjurunga*, and the stories and chants associated with them. Evidence of McNally's journalistic style is found in his description of Strehlow's attitudes towards his children, which he describes as cold and harsh. He cites an interview he had with Strehlow's son, Theodor, who shared his feelings of exclusion as a child when his father found him looking through some boxes containing colour films and was strictly reprimanded for it (McNally, 1981: 100). The book is riddled with such examples aimed at exposing Strehlow's personality as one who was enigmatic, contradictory, intolerant of anyone who disagreed with him and later bitter towards many of his academic colleagues.

McNally devotes a chapter to describing Strehlow's role in the case of the Aboriginal man, Rupert Max Stuart, who was accused of raping and murdering a young white girl in December 1958 along a beach in Ceduna, South Australia. Stuart always maintained his innocence and claimed that his confession had been forced from him by violence from the police force. After Stuart had been convicted and sentenced to death at a trial held in Adelaide in April 1959, the defence lawyer appealed and, under the advice of the Catholic priest Thomas Dixon, who had worked among Indigenous people in the Northern Territory and Queensland, called on Strehlow as an expert witness to support Stuart's case. As a linguist and as one who understood Aboriginal culture, Strehlow argued that the confession allegedly made by Stuart could not have been the words of a man who could neither read nor write but instead was composed by the investigating officers who either forced or tricked Stuart into signing the statement. Strehlow also argued that because Aboriginal sense of time is quite different from European ideas of time, the fact that Stuart appeared unclear about his movements on the day of the crime represented cultural influences rather than indicating that Stuart was lying. After an appeal to the South Australia High Court was denied, under intense media pressure, a Royal Commission was established to investigate the case. Strehlow was heavily involved in the appeals and in the hearings of the Commission. The Commission never reached a conclusion because the Australian Premier, Thomas Playford, intervened and commuted Stuart's sentence from death to life imprisonment. McNally observes that 'many people were certain Playford's decision was generated by Strehlow's argument, and that it amounted to a triumph for Strehlow' (McNally, 1981: 123). Despite this, McNally adds that 'Strehlow always believed that his defence of Stuart damaged him professionally, and that because of it he was discriminated against within the hierarchy of Adelaide University and the power-brokers of South Australia' (McNally, 1981: 124).[2]

The issue of ownership of the Strehlow Collection plays an important role in McNally's assessment of Strehlow's academic judgement and casts doubt over his personal morality. McNally underscores the point that Strehlow was funded throughout his career from various grants, latterly from the University of Adelaide, but that he considered the vast material he collected over the years to be his own personal property and not that of the University nor of the research agencies that supported him. Early in the book McNally makes this clear when he quotes an unnamed academic with connections to the University of Adelaide as saying: 'Strehlow was the most overrated man I know... He had no moral right to hold on to the artefacts he claimed as his own!' (McNally, 1981: 88). McNally follows this by commenting that 'almost all his research expeditions to Central Australia were made possible by funding from Adelaide University and were expressly for and on its behalf' (McNally, 1981: 102). Later in the book, he reiterates his strong feelings about this subject when he recounts the dispute Strehlow had with Phillip Scherer, the Lutheran Pastor Strehlow employed as a research assistant with the primary aim of constructing the detailed map Strehlow planned to include in *Songs of Central Australia*. Scherer, who spent many months researching the details of the map, including visiting the sites mentioned on it, believed that rights to ownership of the map should at the very least be shared with Strehlow, but Strehlow refused. McNally comments on this point: 'Even in kindness, one has to believe that Strehlow applied two standards of conduct to his dealing with Scherer and the University. On the one hand, he denied Scherer any rights to the map; on the other, he denied the University any claims to what, by his own standards applied to the map, were the University's property' (McNally, 1981: 137).

The latter part of McNally's book focusses almost exclusively on Strehlow's personal life, including his betrayal of his first wife, Bertha, his divorce and his marriage to Kathleen Stuart and her entanglement in the controversy over the disposition of the Strehlow Collection. He devotes a chapter to Strehlow's misjudgement in selling photographs of secret Arrernte ceremonies to *Stern* magazine in Germany on the condition that they never be published in Australia, only to find that they appeared shortly afterwards in the Australian magazine, *People* (McNally, 1981: 188–91). He also underscores Strehlow's strained relationship with his children from

2.   For a detailed account of the Stuart case, see Inglis (2002).

his first marriage and claims he favoured his son, Carl, born to him and his second wife, Kathleen (McNally, 1981: 150). This interpretation is echoed also by T.G.H. Strehlow's son from his first marriage, John, who writes: 'This stalwart fighter for the disinherited black population had no compunction about totally disinheriting his own children, either, specifically excluding us from his will' (J. Strehlow, 2011: 44).

At the conclusion of Ward McNally's biography of T.G.H. Strehlow, the reader will have been led to a sense of discomfort with Strehlow's personality, his treatment of those who should have been closest to him, his disloyalty to his first wife, even a callous attitude towards her, and arguably his equal disloyalty to the Aboriginal people who entrusted him with their most precious secrets, the knowledge of which he maintained as his own private property. Although McNally contended at the outset of his book that he was not interested in passing judgements on Strehlow's personal life, the outcome inevitably causes the reader to pass judgements, admittedly at times, as in the case of the Rupert Max Stuart case, ones that are sympathetic to Strehlow's commitment to righting injustices done to Aboriginal people. Nonetheless, the author intended to produce emotional responses, either positive or negative, about Strehlow from his general readership.

By far the longest and in some ways most intensely researched biography of Strehlow was published in 2002 by Barry Hill.[3] At the time the book appeared, Hill was an Honorary Fellow at the Australian Centre at the University of Melbourne and Poetry Editor of a national newspaper, *The Australian*. The manuscript, including bibliography, index and numerous photographs extends to 818 pages. The biographical information at the front of the Vintage Books edition (Hill, 2003) refers to Hill, who was born in 1943, as a 'prize-winning poet and historian, who had 'exclusive access to Strehlow's diaries'. It calls the book 'a deeply layered intellectual recovery of Strehlow's life in translation, and, by implication, a placement of it in the context of contemporary anxieties about cultural degeneration and continuity'. In his introductory chapter, Hill states that the focal point of his study is Strehlow's *Songs of Central Australia*, which he describes as Strehlow's 'life work' (Hill, 2003: 6). Of course, Hill is interested in far more than *Songs of Central Australia*; he explains that his biography is primarily about 'the man who composed it' (Hill, 2003: 6).

As implied in the title of the book, 'Broken Song' and the sub-title, 'T.G.H. Strehlow and Aboriginal Possession', Hill's actual themes focus on Strehlow's alleged breaking of trust with Indigenous people and on the

---

3.   The first edition was published in 2002 by Knopf Australia and was followed by an edition published by Vintage Books a year later. The citations I am using are taken from the Vintage Books publication.

issue of legitimate 'ownership' of Indigenous knowledge. From the outset, Hill casts doubt in the reader's mind about Strehlow's character and moral judgement. After initially indicating that his book was about Strehlow's collection of Arrernte poetry in *Songs of Central Australia*, we are told almost immediately thereafter that 'by his own lights' Strehlow was 'a white custodian of Aboriginal culture' (Hill, 2003: 7). Hill even notes that Strehlow called himself *ingkata*, defined by Hill as the Arrernte word for 'ceremonial chief' (Hill, 2003: 7). Of course, these statements are true, but they are inserted at this point in his long book because Hill wants to set the tone for what follows. That Hill is concerned primarily to expose flaws in Strehlow's character is made clear when he asserts that Strehlow, 'after three decades of collecting songs and befriending Aborigines, after a life that ostensibly (some would say ostentatiously) honoured the sacred – acted sacrilegiously' (Hill, 2003: 7). Hill is referring to the sale of photographs of Indigenous ceremonies to *Stern* magazine, an act that he labels 'Strehlow's disgrace' (Hill, 2003: 7). This act, which was 'the result of a business deal about secret-sacred material ... mocked the care so often affirmed in the course of his life' (Hill, 2003: 7). 'What can we say', asks Hill, 'when, in good faith, a white chief is anointed as custodian of the black man's things, and such a fate befalls him?' (Hill, 2003: 7).

A case in point of Hill's aim to discredit Strehlow is found much later in the book where Hill discusses Strehlow's important description of Arrernte social and religious organization, which Strehlow called 'personal monototemism in a polytotemic community'. Strehlow first coined this phrase in a long article published in 1964, but it was reprinted in the year of his death, 1978, as *Central Australian Religion* by the Australian Association for the Study of Religions. I devote Chapter 5 in this book to analysing Strehlow's complex and detailed description of Arrernte religious and social life outlined in this publication because I believe it offers unrivalled insight into how totemic ancestors and ceremonies associated with them contribute to promoting understanding of traditional religion in Central Australia. Hill dismisses this important publication by trivializing it and personalizing it, suggesting at the outset, in accordance with his well-rehearsed theme of 'possession', that it helped 'justify the collection he [Strehlow] was accumulating' (Hill, 2003: 633). Although Hill suggests, at another level, that the publication is 'richly descriptive', he argues that it lacks a theoretical coherence, partly because Strehlow was 'a writer who compulsively wove his personal experience into the framing of his discussion' (Hill, 2003: 633). It is no coincidence that Hill follows this statement by arguing that *Central Australian Religion* is about 'sex, the carnality at the heart of the most secret-sacred men's ceremonies' (Hill, 2003) He cites Strehlow's description of the kangaroo totemic ceremony at the sacred ceremonial centre at Krantji, which Strehlow earlier described at length in *Songs of Central Australia*.

Hill suggests that in *Central Australian Religion* Strehlow has emphasized the 'sexual symbolism at the climax of the ritual' (Hill, 2003: 634; see, Strehlow 1978a: 32). That this relates to Strehlow's personal life at the time he first wrote the article in 1964, which coincided with the period in his life when he was about to begin his relationship with his research assistant and later second wife, Kathleen, is only implied in Hill's remark: 'Desire formed the heart of the rituals; the religion with which he was so intimate was fundamentally about that' (Hill, 2003: 634).

This comment is set in the context of what one can only regard as a contradiction in Hill's presentation. After claiming that Strehlow 'never argues from theory' (Hill, 2003: 633), Hill then outlines how Strehlow wrote *Central Australian Religion*, in part, to 'rebut the monotheistic, and Eurocentric construction' of the early twentieth century German Catholic missionary in Papua New Guinea, Joseph Winthuis, who interpreted the Supreme Deity of the Melanesians as a bisexual god and infused his descriptions of their rituals with sexual symbolism (Bischofberger, 1999: 745–46). Hill, who calls Winthuis a 'German Freudian' (Hill, 2003: 634), argues that although Strehlow disputed Winthuis's theological projection of a bisexual deity onto Melanesian religion, he never attempted 'to refute the general point about sexuality' (Hill, 2003: 634). Strehlow's own interpretation, as we will see later, was that the most critical idea found among the religions of Central Australia, what Spencer and Gillen had translated as 'the Dreaming', actually was best referred to as Eternity. This, Hill quickly asserts, is evidence of Strehlow's underlying commitment to Christian mysticism, and, as the son of a Lutheran missionary, to the Christian faith itself. Hill argues that this becomes evident in *Central Australian Religion* when towards its conclusion Strehlow claims that Arrernte myths, songs and ceremonies fuse 'transient time and timeless Eternity' (Strehlow, 1978a: 34). For someone who 'never argues from theory', a critique of Freudian-infused theories of religion in contrast to his own interpretation of myth, ritual and sacred time (reflective of the theories of the historian of religion, Mircea Eliade),[4] Hill appears to have stumbled into a web of contradictions.

Hill's discussion of *Central Australian Religion* is just one example of the many ways he undermines Strehlow's contribution to promoting understanding of the Indigenous peoples of Central Australia. Page after page is replete with direct and indirect challenges to Strehlow's intentions as a researcher and as an academic, achieved largely by reducing his scholarly work to personal terms. One final example can be given. As we have noted, Strehlow grew up on the Hermannsburg Mission and knew Western Arrernte as one of his native tongues. His original research was encouraged

---

4. See for example, Eliade (1959, 1964, 1973); for my discussion of Eliade, see Cox (2006: 177–87).

by his mentor at the University of Adelaide, J.A. FitzHerbert, which resulted in the manuscript for his Master's thesis on Arrernte phonetics and grammar. Hill attacks Strehlow for not acknowledging previous work on the languages of Central Australia, including that done by his father, nor for crediting A.P. Elkin with his help in securing funding for his research in the 1930s. Hill makes the rather odd statement that his failure to acknowledge his father's contribution to the field was as if, in Hill's (2003: 402) words, 'he had been in prison in Central Australia, and unfamiliar with his father's work'. Hill concludes that 'Elkin gets no acknowledgement for his framing his work, either, nor any other Australian linguists' (Hill, 2003: 402). Here is another example in which Hill, rather than discussing Strehlow's grammar and its contribution to Central Australian linguistics, disparages Strehlow's character by depicting him as self-centred, ungrateful and mean-spirited. This is further confirmed by the concluding chapters in which Hill draws the reader's attention to the problems Strehlow had with academic colleagues in the Australian Institute for Aboriginal Studies (AIAS), with fellow academics in Adelaide University and particularly by focussing on the details about the deal made with *Stern* magazine for financial gain in total disregard for his obligations to the Indigenous people for whom he had declared himself custodian of their traditions.

I am not alone in finding Barry Hill's monumental volume to be lacking in fairness to T.G.H. Strehlow as a scholar, academic and contributor to the field of the scientific study of Indigenous Religions. In her article , 'Rereading Barry Hill's "Broken Song"', which appeared on the online blog 'Things German Australian', Silke Beinssen-Hesse (2013: 1) of Monash University asserts that Hill's book 'seemed to have set itself the task of destroying the credibility of a man who had spent his life proclaiming and furthering the recognition of the social, intellectual and cultural worth of the Aboriginal people of Central Australia'. Beinssen-Hesse marvels at the fact that *Broken Song* won wide recognition as a 'prize-winning biography', which she attributes, in part, to the fact that Hill 'is a gifted poet and word-smith who has no problems using the language for his own purposes and dazzling his readers with it' (Beinssen-Hesse, 2013: 1). She notes, as I pointed out in my brief examples, that although in many places in his text Hill acknowledges the value of much of Strehlow's work, he quickly qualifies any positive statements with negative or detracting comments. Beinssen-Hesse suggests that what appear to be points of commendation by Hill 'are all almost immediately devalued if not ridiculed, mostly from the superior perspective of a psychologist who hints at character problems' (Beinssen-Hesse, 2013: 1). In this way, Hill gives the impression of presenting a fair judgement on Strehlow's life and personality, but in the mind of the reader the demeaning comments that focus on Strehlow's weaknesses dominate. After presenting what she regards as her own fair and unbiased summary of Strehlow's life as a correction to Hill's distorted version, Beinssen-Hesse then summarizes what she sees as Hill's final picture of Strehlow: 'As Hill would have it, Strehlow ... showed a complaining and somewhat precious selfishness, paternalism towards the native, no sense of appropriate loyalty to the white men he encountered in the course of his work, tactlessness, an overestimation of his role as a white Arandan, and a German "mission boy's" underlying and conflicting loyalty to the archaic Christian cause' (Beinssen-Hesse, 2013: 4). In light of what I have extracted briefly from Hill's comments about Strehlow, Beinssen-Hesse would appear to have provided a highly accurate précis of Hill's work and intentions. This view was supported in a response to Beinssen-Hesse's blog by Adam Macfie, the current repatriation anthropologist working at the Strehlow Research Centre, to whom I return in Chapter 8. Writing on 5 July 2015, Macfie commented: 'This is the best and most accurate review of Hill's "Broken Song" I have ever read. I agree with every point you make' (https://tinyurl.com/2013-07-barry-hills).

Tim Rowse: An Academic Critique of T.G.H. Strehlow

Writers other than McNally and Hill have scrutinized Strehlow's claim to be a uniquely placed interpreter of Aboriginal culture in Central Australia, but one of the most critical and analytical has been developed by Tim Rowse, Emeritus Professor in the Institute of Culture and Society at Western Sydney University. Rowse wrote two important papers on T.G.H. Strehlow, both of which focussed on Strehlow's varying roles as a mediator between white Australians and Aboriginal peoples in Central Australia and as an exponent of Indigenous culture and religion in the region. The first, published in 1992 under the cleverly conceived title, 'Strehlow's Strap: Functionalism and Historicism in Colonial Ethnography', appeared in a collection of essays edited by Bain Attwood and John Arnold. The second, which was published in 1999 as an Occasional Paper by the Strehlow Research Centre, was entitled, 'The Collector as Outsider – T.G.H. Strehlow as "public intellectual"'.

The title of Rowse's 1992 article reflects the context of Strehlow's appointment as the first Commonwealth Patrol Officer in Central Australia. Rowse documents that Strehlow believed that corporal punishment was consistent with traditional Aboriginal ways of dealing with offenders of tradition. He used 'the strap' to inflict punishment on those who violated laws, immediately and forcefully. Rowse suggests that Strehlow believed if he failed to demonstrate force, he would lose the respect of the Elders who would regard him as weak. Rowse cites from Strehlow's monthly reports the case of an Aboriginal man called Archie, whom Strehlow described as 'a lad spoiled exceedingly by contact with miners' (Rowse, 1992: 88). As a result, Strehlow writes, 'I gave him a few cuts with the strap' (cited by

Rowse, 1992: 88). Rowse then provides an interpretation of Strehlow's use of physical force as a punishment that is not immediately apparent for those unfamiliar with Arrernte cultural traditions. He suggests that Strehlow's 'use of the strap and his inscription of the event as a properly motivated action … mark a turning point in the colonisation of Central Australia' (Rowse, 1992: 88). With Strehlow's appointment as Native Patrol Officer, Rowse argues, the neglect of Aboriginal welfare by the Australian government was replaced by 'a new philosophy and set of institutions which were more pacific, all-embracing and rehabilitative in intention' (Rowse, 1992: 88). The historical context and Arrernte cultural traditions explain this seemingly counter-intuitive conclusion.

Rowse notes that prior to Strehlow's appointment as Native Patrol Officer, local Aboriginal issues were dealt with by 'several mounted policemen and half a dozen telegraph workers' who over the years had persistently committed atrocities against Indigenous people (Rowse, 1992: 89). He describes the 'last of the region's known massacres' as occurring in 1928 among the Anmatyerr and Walpiri people (Rowse, 1992). An inquiry into this event followed, headed by J.W. Bleakley, Chief Protector of Aborigines in Queensland, who, according to Rowse, 'was critical of the state's undeveloped capacities to succour Aborigines' suffering, to supervise their dealings with whites and to educate those with potential to "improve"' (Rowse, 1992). Further reports of police violence in 1935 were investigated by a Board of Inquiry, which recommended the appointment of a patrol officer who would have the power to administer 'summary corporal punishment "on the spot"' (Rowse, 1992: 90). Because he was known to have been born on the Hermannsburg Mission and due to his knowledge of the language and the culture of the peoples of Central Australia, on the recommendation of A.P. Elkin, Strehlow was approached about taking the newly established position, which, as we have seen, he accepted. In the context of his knowledge of Aboriginal customs and way of dealing with offenders, Rowse argues that 'Strehlow saw the use of physical force as essential to his (masculine) authority among Aboriginal men' (Rowse, 1992: 91). This was based on the 'Aborigines' own high evaluation of physical force' (Rowse, 1992: 91).

In 1937, Strehlow set up a rationing programme from his settlement at Jay Creek. This was to provide for the needs of Aboriginal people by helping to alleviate hunger and starvation, as well as to provide them with other commodities, such as tobacco. In a talk delivered in 1957 to the South Australian Peace Committee of the Society of Friends in Adelaide, Strehlow explained that he had discovered on his return to Central Australia in 1932 that 'disease, under-nourishment, squalor, and hopelessness were gradually destroying the bodies and the minds of the natives' (Strehlow 1958: 32). Rowse (1992: 92) contends that Strehlow drew on his Hermannsburg experience as a model of 'an authoritarian "sanctuary" from punitive kill-ings and exploitation' and used it as an instrument to address the govern-ment's 'humanitarian outrage at frontier atrocities'. The backdrop for this, which Strehlow (1962b: 4; 1970: 112–21) documented in his writings, was the traditional Aboriginal method of capital punishment administered to those who violated traditional Law, including ceremonial protocols. By intervening in Aboriginal disputes with physical force, Strehlow could use his knowledge of Indigenous traditions to halt the widespread use of the death penalty for infringements of customary Law while at the same time administering immediate punishment to offenders in a way that was consis-tent with the Aboriginal sense of justice.

Thus far, Rowse appears to be offering an interpretation of Strehlow's role as Patrol Officer as an example of an enlightened and culturally sensitive approach to Indigenous relations in Central Australia. We soon see, how-ever, that Rowse's discussion of Strehlow's use of his knowledge of Indigenous ways of life when he was Native Patrol Officer was undertaken not primar-ily to document with approval Strehlow's actions as a government agent, but clearly to criticize what he called Strehlow's 'hubris' rooted in 'his claim to distinctive expertise' based on 'his gratuitous identification with aged male authority' (Rowse, 1992: 96). Strehlow's claim to have earned the trust of senior Arrernte men is an important point that I will refer to throughout the chapters that follow. Strehlow believed that the younger generation was rap-idly losing all knowledge of traditional practices, beliefs, ceremonies, songs, sacred sites and the meanings associated with *tjurunga*. The fact that many old men chose to reveal these closely guarded sacred secrets in Strehlow's mind established him as the guarantor and preserver of ancient traditions as opposed to the younger men who no longer were the trusted recipients of such knowledge. This was due in part to the intervention of colonial admin-istrators and missionaries and the result of fundamental changes in ways of subsistence which saw young Aboriginal men working in mines and for white pastoralists. The association with whites caused what Strehlow inter-preted as a lack of respect for Elders who in turn refused to pass on tradi-tional knowledge to them. What Strehlow seemed to overlook, according to Rowse, was that the Elders refused to transmit Indigenous knowledge to the young not because the young were rebellious and uninterested but because under the changing circumstances created by the 'new colonial order' the old men decided that it was preferable no longer to employ the powers they once had as enforcers of ceremony and tradition: 'they were better forgotten than passed on' (Rowse, 1992: 95).

Rowse's argument hinges on his interpretation of Strehlow as one who gratuitously cultivated the favour of selected Elders as his informants. On the one hand, according to Rowse, Strehlow used his knowledge functionally to implement strategies aimed at improving the quality of life of Aboriginal communities. On the other hand, and much more importantly, he exalted the authority of older men with the aim of establishing his own authority based on his knowledge of 'a cherished body of customary law whose contingent meanings were arbitrated by senior men with whom he could achieve understanding and legitimacy' (Rowse, 1992: 98). Rowse calls Strehlow's attempt to preserve for posterity the ancient traditions revealed to him by the Elders his 'historicist' tendency as opposed to the functionalist use of ethnographic research to affect the daily lives of those among whom he was working. Rowse explains: 'Strehlow postulated an "ancient native code" (a political/jural conception of authority), in others he conveyed a more contingent, negotiated and disorderly process of cultural transmission from old to young' (Rowse, 1992: 94). These contrasting tendencies, the historicist and the functionalist, can be found running throughout Strehlow's writings in ways, according to Rowse, that reflect a 'mutually destabilising presence' (Rowse, 1992: 102). This dual approach, he concludes, confirms Strehlow's 'endeavour both to record and to enact indigenous authority within a reforming colonial practice' (Rowse, 1992: 102–103).

Rowse's second major article on Strehlow, written in 1999 as a Strehlow Research Centre Occasional Paper, provides an in-depth study of the methods and changing aims of Strehlow's research in Central Australia beginning with his first ventures in the region as an academic in 1932 through his period as a Patrol Officer and culminating in his final years which Rowse characterizes as Strehlow's growing period of 'alienation' (Rowse, 1999: 75–78). Rowse's paper, which extends to nearly 60 pages, is based on research he conducted at the Strehlow Research Centre and features references to numerous personal journal entries by Strehlow and private letters he wrote in response to events occurring in his life. As such, Rowse provides an invaluable source for insight into Strehlow's thinking that would not be apparent by referring strictly to Strehlow's published books, articles and papers.

Rowse's starting point is based on a long autobiographical letter Strehlow wrote in 1971 to the Liberal politician Bill Wentworth, in which Strehlow, referring to the period beginning in 1932 up to and including his period as Native Patrol Officer, states that 'for ten years I had thrown in all my energies, all my money, and all my loyalties with the dark folk, and had stood up for their rights fearlessly against those white persons in Central Australia who had tried to exploit them' (cited by Rowse, 1999: 66). Strehlow continues: 'Out of gratitude they ... revealed to me their most treasured possessions – secret rites and sacred traditions' (Rowse, 1999: 66). Rowse concludes from this statement that Strehlow sought to create a relationship of emotional dependency of Indigenous peoples on him as the custodian of their most sacred ceremonies and customs. This leads to one of Rowse's most stinging criticisms of Strehlow: 'The bond between white man

and "dark folk" – his self-sacrifice, their gratitude – became Strehlow's transcendent moral base, the frame through which he judged the strivings of all
others – anthropologists, politicians and Indigenous people' (Rowse, 1999:
66).

Later in the paper Rowse urges the reader to consider and evaluate
Strehlow's involvement in the founding of the Australian Institute of
Aboriginal Studies (AIAS) and his subsequent alienation from its members resulting in his resignation from the Institute in 1973. Rowse notes
that 'Strehlow was involved in the Institute from its inception' and that
'he presented a paper at the inaugural conference in Canberra in 1961'
(cited by Rowse, 1999: 83). By the time he wrote his long autobiographical letter to Wentworth in 1971, Strehlow had become highly critical of the
AIAS asserting that the methods of contemporary anthropologists associated with the Institute were lax and careless in comparison to his own.
Strehlow writes:

> Instead of sitting down – in the manner of the Institute's modern research-
> ers – at some mission or government settlement, and working with infor-
> mants conveniently fed and maintained by such an institution, I bought a
> small string of camels and, with one middle-aged and very loyal aboriginal
> "camel boy", started traversing Central Australia in order to locate accu-
> rately the linguistic areas and the "tribal" boundaries' (cited by Rowse,
> 1999: 86).

Rowse then cites a four-page pamphlet written by Strehlow in which he
reviewed the first ten years of the Australian Institute of Aboriginal Studies. Strehlow complained that the AIAS 'encouraged short field trips by persons eager to gain easy fame through obtaining material for short papers and
theses' (cited by Rowse, 1999: 93). For Strehlow, this demonstrated the self-
interested aims of researchers associated with the AIAS who exploited the
knowledge of Indigenous informants for their own benefit. This meant that
the Indigenous voice largely had been silenced in contemporary research projects. Strehlow urged the AIAS to stop supporting the research of 'raw-city-
trained graduates' and instead support the 'small numbers of well-established
people whose work has already proved that they have won the full confidence
of some defined aboriginal group or groups' (cited by Rowse, 1999: 93).

Rather than affirming Strehlow's analysis of appropriate research methods in support of those worthy of receiving grants from the AIAS, Rowse
turned the tables on Strehlow by suggesting that these critical comments
were the result of his annoyance at the failure of the AIAS to fund his own
research projects, particularly by refusing to finance the publication of *Songs
of Central Australia* during the complicated process of negotiation with the
publisher. Rowse calls Strehlow's dismissal of the AIAS and its anthropological methods an instance of autobiographical 'self-championing' (Rowse,

1999: 66: 94). He also suggests that Strehlow's bitterness with the Institute originated in conflicts he provoked almost immediately with the original Board appointed in 1961, particularly when the post of Deputy Chairman and Executive Officer was awarded to the noted anthropologist based at the Australian National University in Canberra, W.E.H. Stanner. Rowse asserts that Strehlow maintained a grudge against Stanner 'with whom he had quarrelled in the 1950s over the ANU's claims to some of Strehlow's ethnographic films and recordings' (Rowse, 1999: 92)

Rowse's two articles depict T.G.H. Strehlow as a man who cultivated trust from Indigenous Elders in exchange for his interventions aimed at protecting them from mistreatment at the hands of white police and settlers and for his rationing programme instituted when he was Native Patrol Officer. Senior Arrernte Elders showed their gratitude by sharing with Strehlow knowledge of their most secret ceremonies, myths and songs, which, in Strehlow's mind, made him a unique depository for recording ancient traditions that were rapidly dying out. According to Rowse's version of the story, this sowed the seeds for Strehlow's later alienation from his colleagues and eventually from the Indigenous communities who had entrusted him with their most sacred secrets. As a result, Rowse asserts that Strehlow elevated himself above other researchers and regarded his collection as his own private property.

Although Tim Rowse's presentation of the events of Strehlow's life are cast in terms of academic categories such as the contrast between functionalism and historicism in an attempt to evaluate Strehlow as a 'public intellectual', the conclusions he reaches and the picture he paints of Strehlow's personality are not far different from those presented by McNally and Hill: Strehlow was a man with great talents but was tainted by severe personality faults. The overall impact of Rowse's articles, when read in conjunction with the biographies written by McNally and Hill, leads the reader to conclude that Strehlow was the victim of his own pride and exaggerated sense of self-importance. He expected recognition, even adulation, from peers, the public and from the Indigenous communities among whom he worked.

Concluding Remarks

From my review of McNally, Hill and Rowse, each of whom devoted much attention to expounding views on Strehlow the man, I am led to conclude that each in his own way had a damaging impact on Strehlow's reputation in various sectors: among the general Australian public (primarily McNally), on the public and the academic world (Hill) and among the scholarly and political communities (Rowse). Each diminished the value of Strehlow's contribution to promoting understanding of Indigenous Religions in Central Australia and in the process detracted from Strehlow's potential importance as a scholar whose writings still can play a noteworthy role within the burgeoning academic field devoted to the international study of Indigenous Religions. By re-visiting Strehlow's works in the following chapters, I hope to clarify his important insights into Aboriginal religion and culture that currently are being re-discovered and appropriated by Indigenous people at the Strehlow Research Centre. I begin this process in the next chapter by outlining the theoretical approach I am taking in this book.

2

RESTORING THE CHAIN OF MEMORY:
A THEORY OF RELIGION AND INDIGENOUS RELIGIONS

This book explores the contribution of T.G.H. Strehlow to the preservation and restoration of Indigenous knowledge in Central Australia. Before I begin to analyse this theme, I need to set out the theoretical approach which gives rise to the title of this book. In numerous publications, I have developed a definition of religion based in part on the idea of religion as a 'chain of memory', which I derived in the first instance from two important publications written by the French sociologist Danièle Hervieu-Léger. The first was included as a contribution to a volume dealing with issues surrounding definitions of religion, edited by Arie Molendijk and Jan Platvoet (Hervieu-Léger, 1999: 73–92), and the second was her major work on this subject, first published in French in 1993 under the title, *La Religion pour Mémoir*, which was translated into English and appeared in 2000 under the title *Religion as a Chain of Memory*. I incorporated Hervieu-Léger's analysis into my own definition of religion in several stages beginning in 2007 with my book *From Primitive to Indigenous: The Academic Study of Indigenous Religions*, and then applied it gradually to my increasingly restricted and limited definition of Indigenous Religions.

In this chapter, I establish the backdrop for the study which follows by tracing the development of my definitions of religion and Indigenous Religions, and then by focussing on religion as 'memory' in ways that I have not done previously. By the conclusion of this chapter, I hope to have established the theoretical framework for the entire book, the application of which I will explore in the concluding chapter, where I examine the significance of Strehlow's extensive research, which he conducted principally between 1932 and 1970, for contemporary efforts by Indigenous peoples in Central Australia to re-discover their traditions, or to put it in terms of this book, to 'restore the chain of memory' on which the knowledge and persistence of their ceremonies, stories and kinship systems depend.

The Evolution of a Working Definition of Religion

If researchers construct definitions of a subject prior to the actual investigations being conducted, they run the risk of pre-determining the results and invalidating the conclusions they reach. This complaint is counterbalanced by the argument that if researchers have no clear idea of what constitutes the subject matter they are investigating, and thus leave the content entirely open, it becomes impossible to place any rational constraints or limitations on the research process itself. I have opted in my publications to begin by proposing working definitions of religion and Indigenous Religions. A working definition does not presuppose the findings of research but sets out practical boundaries within which the researcher operates in order to conduct empirical studies and eventually test theories. A working definition, moreover, is subject to change, modification and even rejection as the actual research is conducted. Without formulating a working definition at the outset, the researcher is prone to follow dead-ends and may never be able to formulate a reliable and testable set of research questions.

Yet, as the research project progresses towards its conclusions, the working definition is likely to become much more limited and precise than it was at the outset. There are two developments in the process of conducting research that produce a narrowing of an initial or working definition of religion. The first relates to theoretical considerations and the second results from the findings of the empirical investigations into the particular communities that are being described and interpreted. Either of these or both may cause the researcher to reduce the parameters of guiding definitions and arrive at conclusions that severely restrict the way, in our case, religion in general and Indigenous Religions in particular are defined.

Theoretical considerations, just like the guiding questions to be addressed by empirical investigations, must evolve during the research process. Initially, a hypothesis is formulated in order that the researcher knows what questions to ask and what the research is intended to test, but this should never be prescriptive, since during the investigations new findings must be allowed to alter or even re-direct the original research questions causing a shift in the theoretical framework of the project itself. The new questions may become paramount and point the researcher towards a hypothesis that outweighs in significance the original framework the researcher envisaged. If a working definition, which quite broadly sets out the scope of a research project, is not open to amendment and if the researcher does not engage with new theories as the investigations proceed, the conclusions presented at the end will be highly suspect and most likely will be flawed.

When seen as a process, or as an evolution of a research project, in my own work I have followed precisely these principles. I began my earlier publications on theory and method by constructing a guiding definition of religion and Indigenous Religions in order to conduct logical and testable empirical studies. As my research proceeded over the years, I demonstrated how a working definition operates pragmatically by becoming increasingly narrow in response to changes demanded by the empirical data, while at the same time modifying my approach in response to new theories. When I first developed a definition of religion in my publication, *Expressing the Sacred* (1992), I discussed various problems with prior definitions, including their being too broad or too narrow, too inclusive or too exclusive, or their being unwittingly biased in favour of Western, Christian interpretations. The problem of inclusive or exclusive definitions is sometimes coined in terms of substantive and functional definitions of religion, the former being too restrictive and the latter too broad. In my own contribution to the Platvoet and Molendijk volume, I argued for a working definition that favoured a substantive approach by insisting that religion must be focussed on a 'postulated non-falsifiable alternate reality' (later changed to 'alternate realities') (Cox, 1999: 268–72). This was an endeavour to move substantive definitions away from their tendency to restrict religion to beliefs in gods or supernatural agents. Nonetheless, my definition suffered from the same problem associated with all substantive definitions. By substituting 'a postulated non-falsifiable alternate reality' for supernatural entities, although I was trying to transform a substantive definition into a more open, non-restrictive and wide range of beliefs and practices, I still limited religion to beliefs in agents that are manifested for adherents exclusively in non-ordinary experiences.

As I developed this definition in *From Primitive to Indigenous* (Cox, 2007a), I added to my earlier definition Hervieu-Léger's emphasis on a chain of memory by arguing that religion always includes an overwhelming authoritative tradition that is transmitted among identifiable communities from one generation to the next generation in a chain extending back to the legendary times of beginnings. In my *Introduction to the Phenomenology of Religion* (Cox, 2010), I arrived at what I thought was an exemplary compromise between substantive and functional definitions by including both elements in my conclusion. At the same time, I insisted that this was still a working definition that operated as a pragmatic guide to what constitutes the field of religion. I defined religion as being comprised of:

> identifiable communities that base their acts of believing and resulting communal experiences of postulated non-falsifiable alternate realities on a tradition that they legitimate by appealing to its authoritative transmission from generation to generation (Cox, 2010: 21).

I argued that because this is a working definition, it can be tested empirically; it is embedded in socio-cultural contexts and avoids the error of searching for a theologically inspired 'essence' of religion. I contended that my working definition was both substantive and functional because it provided a content to religion (the beliefs and practices that identifiable communities hold in relation to 'postulated non-falsifiable alternate realities') but at the same time described the function of religion in social-cultural terms as transmitting a tradition with overwhelming authority from generation to generation.

As I read further into problems with defining religion, particularly in light of the conflicting methods represented by the academic study of religions and theology, I became uncomfortable with the substantive element in the definition because its focus on 'postulated non-falsifiable alternate realities' could easily be translated into a theology of religions derived from a liberal, Christian perspective. This led me to the next development in my quest to find a satisfactory definition of religion. I decided to limit my scope even further by removing altogether the necessity that for religion to be present, identifiable communities must have a primary focus on 'alternate realities'. This was partly because substantive definitions, which almost always include some reference to supernatural agents (even if these are called 'postulated, non-falsifiable alternate realities') are subject to the criticism that for religion to be religion it must primarily contain beliefs in and practices directed towards some extra-ordinary being or beings. A non-theological substantive definition thus seemed impossible, even on my very broad terminology that tried to make the 'alternate realities' applicable to a wide variety of communities.

In these ways, over a number of years, I adjusted and narrowed my initial, working definition of religion in response to the theoretical problem posed by the 'theologising' of the academic study of religion. I became convinced that theology had been imposed both theoretically and institutionally on Religious Studies, and that one way out of this problem was to remove the insistence that for religion to be religion it must contain some reference to supernatural agents. If a convincing alternative could be developed, the inevitable conclusion would follow that the academic study of religion has no intrinsic affinity with theology but belongs squarely within the social sciences. This would have a practical effect on institutions by disengaging the connection so long assumed, particularly in the Anglo-American world, between Theology and Religious Studies, or as it is now called universally in institutional and research networks in Britain, Theology and Religious Studies (TRS).[1] This challenge led me to pose the academic question, 'Is it

---

1. 'Theology and Religious Studies UK (formerly "The Association of University Departments of Theology and Religious Studies" or AUDTRS) was founded more than 20 years ago as a national forum for discussion amongst academics and teachers of theology and religious studies working in institutes of higher education at a time of change and in the face of growing governmental and European reviews and assessments of the work of colleges and universities as places of teaching and research' (http://trs.ac.uk/about-trs/).

possible to have religion without any reference to alternate realities at all?', which in turn prompted me to consider what constitutes the *sine qua non* of religion, that without which religion is not religion. I followed this by seeking a restricted and severely limited definition of Indigenous Religions in response to the empirical research I conducted initially in Alaska, followed by quite intensive studies of the Indigenous Religions in Zimbabwe, and most recently by case studies focussing on the Māori of New Zealand and Indigenous Christians in Australia.

The Sine Qua Non of Religion: Necessary and Sufficient Conditions

I first addressed the issue of the *sine qua non* of religion in my contribution to a *festschrift* in honour of Professor Ulrich Berner of the University of Bayreuth, published in 2013 under the title, *Alternative Voices: A Plurality Approach for Religious Studies*, edited by Afe Adogame, Magnus Echtler and Oliver Freiberger. My chapter was entitled, 'The Authoritative Transmission of Tradition: That Without Which Religion Is Not Religion' (Cox, 2013a: 308–23). This article was inspired by the work of the leading American scholar in Religious Studies, the late Walter Capps (1995: 1), who argued in his important textbook, *Religious Studies: The Making of a Discipline*, that the scholar of religion 'must adopt a kind of reductive analytical technique, probing one's way … to "that without which the subject would not be what it is"'. My aim in my chapter in the Berner *festschrift* was to disentangle the longstanding connection in many academic circles between Religious Studies and Theology, which I argued was linked to the idea that religion, like theology, must contain an emphasis on transcendent beings in some form. I suggested in the article that by identifying the *sine qua non* of religion, I was not limiting the many ways religions are expressed, but I was attempting to isolate the absolute rock-bottom factors without which religion could not be said to exist. I contended that beliefs in supernatural beings indeed were found in many religions, but such beliefs did not constitute a necessary element within religion (Cox, 2013a: 310–11).

I pointed out that the notion of the *sine qua non* of anything is related to the philosophical distinction between accidental characteristics and the necessary and sufficient conditions for something to be what it is. In their helpful introduction to philosophy, Popkin and Stroll (1986: 51–52) clarified the differences between accidental, necessary and sufficient conditions by asking what components are necessary for an individual to fit into the category of 'brother'. They explain someone who is a brother might have blond hair, but this is not a necessary, rather an accidental condition, since many people or even things have blond hair and are not brothers, such as women or dolls. A necessary condition for being a brother is that a brother must be male. But, of course, that is not sufficient, since a male may have no siblings. A second necessary condition of being a brother is to have at least one sibling, but being a sibling is not sufficient, since women have siblings. Thus the necessary and sufficient conditions for being a brother are that the person must be male and have at least one sibling. The *sine qua non* of being a brother, therefore, can be said to include two separate necessary conditions, which, when taken together constitute the sufficient conditions for being a brother.

The *sine qua non* of religion, in like manner, can include more than one necessary condition. When the necessary conditions have been identified, the sufficient conditions for religion to be said to exist have been satisfied. Other factors can be present for religion to be said to exist, but if they do not comprise part of what qualifies as necessary, they equate to accidental conditions. For example, a definition that I initially analysed in *Expressing the Sacred* (Cox, 1992) was suggested by the American scholars Hall, Pilgrim and Cavanagh (1985: 11), who maintained that 'religion is a varied, symbolic expression of, and appropriate response to, that which people deliberately affirm as being of unrestricted value for them'. This definition contains an overly extensive list of attributes of religion, many of which may be classified as 'accidental', similar to a brother having blond hair. The excessively broad nature of this definition is demonstrated by the authors' requirement that religions express themselves symbolically. Of course, this is true, but so do all human activities, including the use of language itself. The presence of symbols might be called a necessary condition for any human activity to occur and as such, when described as indispensable for religion, is so obvious as to be meaningless, or even tautological. Some religions emphasize 'deliberate affirmations', but certainly not all do. Deliberate affirmations in this sense are accidental characteristics of religion, since they belong only to some religions.

These distinctions suggest that by calling for a reductive analysis of religion under the banner of the *sine qua non* of religion, Capps was urging scholars to isolate the most essential characteristic or characteristics of religion without which religion could not be said to exist, and in the process, isolate both the necessary and sufficient conditions constituting a satisfactory definition of religion. For example, if we consider E.B. Tylor's (1913: 424) famous 'minimum' definition of religion as 'the belief in Spiritual Beings', we can see immediately that this is not sufficient, since it does not include in it identifiable communities. I might believe personally in supernatural agents, but I am not a religion. Belief in gods, spirits and deities arguably may constitute a necessary condition on some but certainly not all accounts (Cox, 2010: 12–13). Definitions of religion, in other words, may be expansive including far more than is implied by the *sine qua non* of religion and in the process may overlook the absolutely necessary element or elements in religion, without which religion cannot be said to exist.

Any one version of the *sine qua non* of religion on this interpretation must satisfy a necessary condition for religion to be present, but it is likely that one condition alone, although necessary, will not meet the requirements of a sufficient definition of religion. In other words, this is like identifying one of the necessary conditions, the *sine qua non* for a brother to be a brother, either a male or a sibling, but just one requirement of what constitutes the *sine qua non* of being a brother does not meet the sufficient conditions. A brother must be a male. Without the condition of maleness, a brother cannot be a brother. By isolating the necessary conditions without which religion is not religion, in the Berner *festschrift*, I argued that I was not attempting to identify the sufficient conditions, but merely attempting to isolate at least one necessary condition without which religion cannot be said to exist. I have now changed this position, and am prepared in this chapter to propose conditions that satisfy both the necessary and sufficient conditions for religion to be present in any human activity.

Following my earlier work on Hervieu-Léger, in the contribution to the Berner *festschrift*, I contended that the *sine qua non* of religion, that without which religion is not religion, requires the presence of a tradition that is transmitted within communities with an absolute or overwhelming authority (Cox, 2013a: 313). What I failed to do was to note that this definition comprises not one, but three, necessary conditions: *tradition, authority* and *community*. These conditions require that for anything to be called religion the present generation in an identifiable community must trace its identity and constitute its membership by appeals to a tradition that has been passed on from previous generations with an overwhelming authority. I am now convinced that when taken together, tradition, authority and community, comprise both the necessary and sufficient conditions to constitute what is meant by religion. In the Berner *festschrift*, I illustrated how these conditions operate by referring to two empirical studies I had conducted previously, one of a rain ritual held in Zimbabwe and the other a New-Age shamanic trance dance I attended as a participant-observer in Thetford, Vermont. The Zimbabwe case re-enforced the idea that the absolute authority of ancestors was transmitted through a line of descendants from generation to generation, whereas the trance dance made an appeal to ancient traditions which the organizers of the event claimed to be 40,000 years-old. Following my analysis of these two cases, I reached the following conclusion:

> My case studies of the rain ritual in … Zimbabwe and the trance dance …
> in Thetford, Vermont confirm Danièle Hervieu-Léger's (1999: 88) conclusion that there is no religion without the "invocation" of the authority of
> a tradition, the force of which I have shown for any religious community
> legitimises or authenticates its tradition (Cox, 2013a: 321).

I explained this conclusion in my keynote address to the Irish Society for the Academic Study of Religions at their annual conference held in Belfast in May 2014. This was subsequently published in the on-line journal of the society, *The Journal of the Irish Society for the Academic Study of Religions* (JISASR) under the title, 'Religious Memory as a Conveyor of Authoritative Tradition: The Necessary and Essential Component in a Definition of Religion' (https://tinyurl.com/2015-04-pdf1). In my conclusion to the section in the article, after which I had analysed Danièle Hervieu-Léger's discussion of religion as a chain of memory, I reached the point at which I am now convinced I have achieved a non-theological definition of religion, one that identifies the *sine qua non* of religion in terms of both the necessary and sufficient conditions required by such a definition. In light of my analysis of the necessary and sufficient conditions for religion to be present, I would amend my conclusion that I reached in my contribution to the *JISASR* slightly as noted in the brackets:

> Based on Hervieu-Léger's sociologically inspired definition of religion, I contend that the necessary or indispensable condition (I would now say conditions) for religion to be present in any human activity, *its fundamental defining characteristic* (I would change this to characteristics), requires the existence of an identifiable community, which is constituted by its being bound by and subservient to an overpowering authoritative tradition that is passed on from generation to generation (Cox, 2015: 10).

In my article for the *JISASR*, I added that such a restricted definition is sociological and culturally based rather than theological or quasi-theological, as occurs in most substantive definitions, because it does not depend on belief in supernatural entities nor refer to a postulated transcendental object towards which the community directs its attention. I concluded that this definition is limited entirely to the socially sanctioned authority of a tradition that exercises overwhelming power over members of identifiable communities.

The Sine Qua Non of Indigenous Religions

Just as I have sought to identify that without which religion is not religion, I have also attempted to limit a definition of Indigenous Religions by suggesting the necessary and sufficient conditions without which a religion cannot be called Indigenous (Cox, 2013b: 11). The first characteristic I have identified as a necessary component of Indigenous Religions accentuates the fact that Indigenous beliefs and social structures revolve around systems of lineage, usually focussed on ancestors. Myths of origin often relate in quasi-legendary language tales about how the people were established in the land in the first place, either by autochthonous ancestors who brought the people into being often by miraculous feats or by founding ancestors who led the people to the land they now occupy. Contemporary beliefs, which are derived ultimately from the foundational myths, are centred on how ancestors relate actively to living communities by maintaining a reciprocal relationship with them. The descendants must regularly perform rituals that honour their ancestors and thereby re-enforce the social regulations they originally established. In exchange, the ancestors in various ways protect their descendants from misfortunes and provide the conditions that produce optimal health and well-being. Ancestral traditions stretch back beyond the memory of living communities, but the collective memory is enshrined in rituals, stories and songs that are repeated regularly and passed on from generation to generation.

In this sense, Indigenous societies are restricted by kinship relations. One is born into an extended family or one marries into it. Marriage regulations are carefully controlled to ensure that kinship ties are preserved and that traditional relationships between different kinship groups are observed. The particular social role ancestors occupy in the tradition varies according to the way Indigenous societies are organized, some being hierarchical, others more egalitarian, some patrilineal, others matrilineal, but the one factor they share in common is that they are all defined by and limited to patterns of kinship. If one applies this interpretation of indigenous to the religions of Indigenous peoples, this means that, unlike religions with universal cosmologies, *one can never be converted into an Indigenous society, since ancestors belong only to precise kinship groups* (Platvoet, 1992: 21–22; Cox, 2007a: 61–71).

The second necessary condition I have identified as unique to Indigenous societies stresses that they are restricted not only by kinship ties, but relate exclusively to a particular geographical place or location fixed in the tradition by their quasi-legendary myths. Foundational stories are relayed to the young and passed on to subsequent generations. These local myths form the background on which rituals performed regularly in honour of the ancestors are conducted. When misfortunes occur, explanations are sought to explain why ill-fortune has struck the community. The reasons given usually point to ritual or social infractions committed within the community that have upset the balance or equilibrium whereby the lineage group has been structured. The resulting series of catastrophic events can only be rectified, depending on the organization of the local society, by performing rituals aimed at restoring social equilibrium, which often requires revenge against parties that have broken social norms or by making appropriate compensation to injured parties. The problems encountered by communities, including divining the causes and prescribing proper treatments, occur exclusively within specific geographical regions over which the ancestors are responsible and do not extend beyond the boundaries of their traditional authority.

As such, kinship and locality define what are the necessary and sufficient conditions for a religion to be deemed Indigenous. They delineate that without which an Indigenous Religion does not exist, and thus must constitute the *sine qua non of Indigenous Religions*. Just as I noted in my statement of the *sine non qua* of religion, we find that Indigenous Religions possess characteristics other than kinship and locality, but these are neither necessary nor sufficient conditions for a religion to be called Indigenous. For example, it has often been stressed in scholarly literature that Indigenous peoples do not have a word in their languages corresponding to 'religion' since almost everything in their traditional cultures can be regarded as religious, including such things as work, eating and sexual activity (Baylis, 1988, 3). It has also been pointed out that Indigenous societies transmit their traditions orally through story and ritual, which has consequences for the way their religious beliefs and practices are understood by participants (Schmidt, 1988: 45–48). In addition, the religions of Indigenous peoples have been described as pragmatic rather than dogmatic or doctrinal, meaning that their religious explanations are flexible and can even appear to outsiders as contradictory (Platvoet, 1992: 23–24).

None of these characteristics, although found in most Indigenous Religions, satisfies what would be required by a necessary condition, because any one of them can be applied to religious traditions that are non-Indigenous. For example, it could be argued that all religions, in their pure form, urge their adherents to integrate every activity of life with the central tenets of faith. Or, all religious traditions, even those traditions of the 'book', like Judaism, Christianity and Islam, originally were oral in nature. And certainly, not every religion with a universal cosmology, such as non-dualistic philosophical Hinduism, is dogmatic in nature by insisting that a particular belief is exclusively true and necessary for salvation. None of these characteristics, therefore, could be said to operate as the *sine qua non* of Indigenous Religions, that without which an Indigenous Religion could not be said to exist.

By contrast to previous interpretations in scholarly literature, when I combine my restricted definition of religion, what I am now calling the necessary and sufficient conditions for religion to exist, the *sine qua non* of religion, with the two primary characteristics of what it means to be indigenous, the *sine qua non* of Indigenous Religions, I arrive at a clear, testable and scientific definition both of religion and of Indigenous Religions. For any identifiable community to qualify as religious, it must submit to an authoritative tradition that is transmitted from generation to generation with an overwhelming force or power. For the community that adheres to this authoritative tradition to be indigenous, the tradition must operate within a society that is restricted by kinship ties and it must relate to a specific place or location, and, in each instance, it must apply to no other lineage group or geographical region. If an identifiable community seeks converts, aims at expanding its followers or members beyond a specific geographical location through missionary efforts (as opposed to migrations or warfare) and defines adherents in terms of beliefs and practices that are not limited by kinship ties, it cannot be considered an Indigenous Religion.

Theory and Investigation in Relation to the Theme of this Book

It will be clear from my discussion thus far, in which I relate how my working definition of religion evolved into a strictly delineated and reductive definition, the *sine qua non* of religion as the necessary and sufficient conditions for religion to exist, that my theoretical considerations were motivated by the need to separate Religious Studies from Theology and by rooting a social scientific definition in a sound sociological construction. It also reflected my empirical studies into religious communities, specifically the Indigenous Religions of Alaska, Zimbabwe, Australia and New Zealand and in my research into shamanism and forms of neo-shamanism. The combination of theory and field studies narrowed my definitions, but I still offer them to the wider academic community for critical appraisal, which means that my current reductive definition of religion remains subject to further adjustment as I engage with other scholars in response to their theoretical arguments and empirical findings. As I understand it, this is how knowledge progresses, as part of a heuristic process that always generates new theories that produce fresh empirical investigations.

I have done the same with my narrowing of what I mean by Indigenous Religions. Beginning with my initial studies among the Inupiat and Yupiit peoples of Alaska (Cox, 1991), which I followed with research into the Indigenous Religions of Zimbabwe (Cox, 1998), I became convinced that both societies focus centrally on ancestors, although how ancestors were interpreted in each instance differed markedly and were rooted in fundamentally contrasting social systems. Ancestral traditions also seemed to dominate my research into Māori religions in New Zealand and among the Aboriginal peoples I studied in Australia (Cox, 2014a). Again, the social systems differed greatly and the role of ancestors functioned in distinctive ways in each society. Nonetheless, the focus on traditions that authenticated the structures of the society by appealing to an overwhelming authority situated primarily in kinship and location appeared dominant in each of my areas of investigation. This, accompanied by my reading of studies conducted in other Indigenous societies, caused me to propose a narrow, limited and highly restrictive definition of Indigenous Religions, one that built on the central ideas of kinship and locality, and that incorporated my conclusions about the necessary and sufficient conditions for religion to be present. Recently, I have defended my restricted definition of Indigenous

Religions against the criticism offered by the Norwegian scholar of religion, Bjørn Ola Tafjord, but I have made it clear that his critical review of my limited definition of Indigenous Religions is welcome because the debate it generates advances theory in the field of Indigenous Religions while at the same time holding theoretical considerations accountable to field data (Cox, 2016: 38–57; Tafjord, 2013: 221–43).

It is my restricted definitions of religion and of Indigenous Religions that inform the theoretical framework for the themes I explore in this book. I ask what happens when the 'chain of memory' is broken in identifiable communities, when the tradition no longer is transmitted from generation to generation with an overwhelming authority. Has religion ceased to exist in such circumstances? If so, can it be recovered? Can the chain of memory be restored? I also explore what happens when the tradition of ancestors is forgotten and when the kinship ties and locality associated with Indigenous societies has been disrupted by forces of modernity and globalization. Although they were posed in different ways and in different historical contexts, these are precisely the questions raised by T.G.H. Strehlow's research into the Arrernte communities in Central Australia, which he documented originally in the 1930s and subsequently described in terms of the rapid changes that affected the same communities, which, as we shall see, he contended had resulted in the loss of religious memory among the succeeding generations. In light of my definition of religion and Indigenous Religions, my analysis of the survival and transformations of Arrernte Indigenous Religion hinges on the accuracy of Strehlow's judgements and, on the effectiveness of contemporary efforts by Arrernte Elders to restore Indigenous knowledge based on Strehlow's vast collection of material which he accrued over the 30-plus years he was actively engaged in research in Central Australia. This comprises the primary subject matter of this book, but before beginning to unfold this in a step by step process in the chapters that follow, I need to consider more deeply the theoretical issues raised by referring to religion as contained in the memory of identifiable communities and, which is preserved and transmitted from generation to generation as an authoritative tradition. To do this, I want to return to consider how Hervieu-Léger analyses changing circumstances in contemporary Western societies that are subject to the fragmentation of tradition and to the atomization of beliefs. This will establish the framework in the concluding two chapters where I interpret how similar forces of modernity have resulted in the current movements to revive the Indigenous Religions of Central Australia.

The Demise of Religion in Contemporary Societies

Hervieu-Léger (2000: 124) identifies what she calls 'collective memory' as being critical for any analysis concerning the future of religion in contemporary societies. Collective memory refers to the experience of an identifiable group that sees itself as part of a chain or lineage that depends on memories that are consciously shared and passed on to others. When religions are functioning, they practise '*anamnesis*', which is the act of 'recalling to memory of the past', a practice that normally occurs in rituals (Hervieu-Léger, 2000: 125). In rituals, a 'set pattern of word and gesture exists' in order to re-enact 'the foundational events that enabled the chain to form and/or affirm its power to persist' (Hervieu-Léger, 2000: 125). Hervieu-Léger concludes that 'in all instances it is the recognized ability to expound the true memory of the group that constitutes the core of religious power' (Hervieu-Léger, 2000: 126). By insisting that the persistence of religion depends on communities maintaining their own chains of memory, Hervieu-Léger has established the conditions for her analysis of how, in contemporary Western society, the chain has been broken resulting in the collective loss of memory and with it the demise of religion.

In support of this, she asserts that the primary characteristic of contemporary Western societies is found in the fact that they are no longer societies of memory and with this disintegration of memory comes also the termination of religion as she has defined it. In her Foreword to *Religion as a Chain of Memory*, the British sociologist of religion, Grace Davie, summarized Hervieu-Léger's argument that religion has receded in contemporary times:

> Hervieu-Léger ... argues that modern societies (and especially modern European societies) are less religious not because they are increasingly rational, but because they are less and less capable of maintaining the memory which lies at the heart of their religious existence (Davie, 2000: ix).

Hervieu-Léger, as Davie (2000: ix) points out, refers to the condition of modernity as creating 'amnesic societies', ones in which the memory of traditions is eroded and eventually forgotten. On the definition of religion as a 'chain of memory', this suggests that as societies become 'amnesic', they lose religion; it becomes a thing of the past.

If rationality is not the cause of the demise of religion in the West, what creates the situation that results in the loss of memory? Hervieu-Léger contends that it is rooted in the erosion of community that has accompanied the atomistic individualism of contemporary societies under the hegemonic influence of Western capitalism. The fragmentation of the collective memory that has resulted from the individualism of capitalistic society paradoxically has created a homogeneous common experience shared by individuals whose cultural constructs are dictated by the same capitalistic system (Cox, 2007b: 76–77). Following the work of the French sociologist Maurice Halbwachs, Hervieu-Léger (2000: 128) argues that 'the advent of capitalism and technology ... signified the gradual alignment of all spheres of social life on the sphere of production'. This homogenizing process resulted in 'surface memory, dull memory, whose normative, creative capacity seemed to have dissolved' (Hervieu-Léger, 2000: 128). This loss of the 'normative capacity' or religious memory, rooted as it is in the transmission of tradition, had the effect of producing 'the limitless fragmentation of individual and group memory' (Hervieu-Léger, 2000: 129). Hervieu-Léger concludes that 'the collective memory of modern societies is composed of bits and pieces' (Hervieu-Léger, 2000: 129), which she describes in seemingly contradictory ways as 'the homogenization and fragmentation of collective memory' (Hervieu-Léger, 2000: 129). Memory in modernity, in this sense, can be contrasted with religious memory, which is encapsulated by the phrase, 'the normativity of collective memory', and is 'reinforced by the fact of a group's defining itself, objectively and subjectively, as a *lineage* of belief' (Hervieu-Léger, 2000: 125, emphasis in original).

Hervieu-Léger provides an example of how memory has been eroded in contemporary Western society by drawing from her own culture, that of French Catholicism (Hervieu-Léger, 2000: 130–40). She notes that the majority of French citizens identify as Roman Catholic, but, in contrast to previous generations, they now attend religious services infrequently. She cites statistics that indicate that in the age-bracket of the under 50s less than 10 percent attend church regularly, but in the 18 to 24 year-old age bracket that number falls to 2.5 percent. What this seems to suggest is that the authority of the Catholic Church over people who identify with it has receded dramatically, which in turn has given rise to individual beliefs in such things as astrology, paranormal beliefs and the search for new forms of spirituality. Hervieu-Léger observes that these facts indicate that the decrease in church attendance does not necessarily mean loss of belief, although these beliefs more and more diverge from the official teachings of the Catholic Church (Hervieu-Léger, 2000: 132). The distinctive decline of Catholicism as a religion in this sense is due to its lack of authoritative power over its members rather than the evaporation of belief in response to scientific rationalism. Following the writings of the French philosopher, sociologist and cultural theorist, Jean Baudrillard, Hervieu-Léger (Hervieu-Léger, 2000: 132) refers to the changing conditions in modern France as 'the collapse of the world of tradition', which questions 'any authority that claims to direct conscience and behaviour' and replaces it with 'individual autonomy and the inalienable rights of subjectivity'.

Roman Catholic tradition in France, according to Hervieu-Léger, was established in and maintained by the parish system over which a priest was the authoritative figure. She asserts that 'for centuries the parish represented *the* society of memory' (emphasis in original) that linked every person who lived within the boundaries of the parish 'to a chain stretching from past to future' (Hervieu-Léger, 2000: 132). The church was the centre of the village, and, symbolic of the chain of memory, the cemetery surrounded the church building. The family was at the core of the village and maintained the continuity from generation to generation. Hervieu-Léger contends that it was the 'collapse of the traditional family' due to urbanization and economic changes following the Second World War that caused a rift in the authority of the Church and the continuity of the memory it enshrined (Hervieu-Léger, 2000: 133). In fact, Hervieu-Léger goes so far as to assert that the demise of the traditional family, which was 'wholly dedicated to biological reproduction and the transmission of a biological, material and symbolic inheritance from generation to generation' lies at 'the heart of the modern crisis of religion' (Hervieu-Léger, 2000: 133). The changes in family life became most noticeable beginning in 1965 when the decline in births and marriages became marked, so much so that by 1985 the 'number of marriages fell by one-third' and the number of divorces increased dramatically (Hervieu-Léger, 2000: 133). The fact that these changes occurred in conjunction with the decline in the stability of the rural parish and the corresponding authority of the church is no coincidence. The forces of modernity, although not undermining beliefs in supernormal occurrences, have eroded the transmission of the Church's authoritative tradition and in this sense have signalled the rapid decline of religion in contemporary France.

The Demise of Indigenous Religions

Hervieu-Léger not only describes the conditions leading to the demise of contemporary religions in the West but also applies her analysis to similar factors affecting Indigenous Religions, which she calls 'traditional societies'. She argues that in such societies, which are genuinely homogeneous, or what I have called localized and kinship-orientated, 'religious symbolism is structured entirely by a myth of creation, which accounts for the origin of both the world and the group' (Hervieu-Léger, 2000: 124). As a result, in 'traditional societies ... collective memory is given' (Hervieu-Léger, 2000: 124). By this she means that the collective memory of the group is 'totally contained within the structures, organization, language and everyday observances' (Hervieu-Léger, 2000: 124). There is a parallel in this situation with that of the rural parish in traditional France, which was bound by locality and perpetuated by the family as a source of genealogical continuity. If the memory found in an Indigenous Religion is interrupted by the forces of modernity, it experiences the same situation as is occurring in contemporary Western society in which the collective memory is crumbling and being dissipated by individual autonomy and the search for spirituality, defined as personal self-fulfilment. Hervieu-Léger (2000: 127) explains: 'The affirmation of the autonomous individual, the advance of rationalization breaking up "sacred canopies", and the process of institutional differentiation denote the end of societies based on memory'. She concludes that 'the growth of secularization and the loss of total memory in societies without a history and without a past coincide completely' (Hervieu-Léger, 2000: 127).

When the collective memory within Indigenous societies is forgotten, religion has ceased to function in any meaningful way and only lives on as histories in which records are maintained of stories no longer believed and of ceremonies that are no longer practised. Under these circumstances, the authority of ancestors is eroded and the principal emphasis on locality is dissolved. The decline of Indigenous Religions in this sense, just as Hervieu-Léger argued occurred in rural France, results from the impact created by the forces of globalization, including urbanization, the elevation of individual autonomy over community coherence, mass communication and ease of international travel. In Indigenous societies, these forces are exacerbated by Western economies that replace subsistence ways of securing health and well-being, Western education that is substituted for Indigenous ways of knowing, and, of course, religions with missionary intentions that operate on a global scale.

In both cases, the demise of religion as evidenced in Western societies, such as France, and the decline in Indigenous Religions, the necessary and sufficient conditions for each to be said to exist are under threat and need to be analysed in light of what Hervieu-Léger (2000: 127) calls the 'crumbling memory of modern societies'. This involves an in-depth study, in the case of this book, of what the break in the chain of memory means for the future of the Indigenous Religions of Central Australia. In the final chapter, I return to Hervieu-Léger's analysis of how religion has been transformed in modernity, which I interpret in terms of how these changes directly affect the repatriation of knowledge among the Indigenous groups in Central Australia. It is sufficient at this point to confirm that the theoretical model on which I am proceeding in this book is based on the notion that religion is present only when an authoritative tradition that is lodged in the collective memory of identifiable communities binds such groups together by maintaining a normative power over their social and moral lives and that the Indigenous form of this communally authorized tradition operates exclusively under the two conditions I have identified as kinship and location.

3

ETERNITY: ARRERNTE MYTHS OF CREATION

In contemporary descriptions of Australian Aboriginal Religions, many popular publications identify 'the Dreaming' or 'Dreamtime' with pan-Aboriginal spirituality rooted in ancient myths of creation. For example, in her textbook entitled *Living Religions*, Mary Pat Fisher defines 'Dreamtime (Dreaming)' as 'the timeless time of Creation, according to Australian aboriginal belief' (2014: 69). Another author who has popularized 'Dreaming' is James G. Cowan (1992: 24), who defines the term as expressing Aboriginal 'true reality at the spiritual level'. He explains: 'The Dreaming is, first and foremost, a metaphysical condition denoting the work of divine principles dressed up in the garb of totemic heroes' (1992: 24). Bill Edwards, who was a Presbyterian and later Uniting Church missionary among the Pitjantjatjara people of north-west South Australia, notes that the Dreaming is expressed by local groups in their own languages but that it is a term 'used commonly to describe the Aboriginal creative epoch' through which Aboriginal people experience 'fundamental reality' (Edwards, 1998: 79).

Origin and Critique of 'Dream Time'

The concept 'Dream Time' can be traced to the work of Baldwin Spencer and F.J. Gillen. Spencer, who in 1887 had been appointed Chair of Biology at the University of Melbourne, first came to Central Australia in 1894 as part of the Horn Expedition, which was comprised of eminent scientists from many fields, including zoology, botany, geology, the new field of anthropology, ethnology and geology. The Horn Expedition constituted the first concerted scientific study of the peoples of the remote interior of Australia. Spencer, who was the expedition's zoologist and photographer, edited the expedition's reports and findings (Spencer, 1896). While on the expedition, Spencer met F.J. Gillen, the Alice Springs Postmaster, who had good relations with a number of Aboriginal communities, although his knowledge of the local languages was limited. According to Christine Judith Nicholls of Flinders University, Gillen was the first to translate the Arrernte word *alcheringa* (now commonly spelled *altjira*) as Dream Time, but it was

Spencer who first gave the translation scientific credibility when he used it in his report on the Horn Expedition (Nichols, 2014). Spencer (1896: 111) wrote in volume one of 'The Horn Report' that 'the morality of the black … is governed by rules of conduct which have been recognised amongst his tribe from what they speak of as the "alcheringa", which Mr Gillen has aptly called the "Dream Times"'. Although in their comprehensive book, *The Native Tribes of Central Australia*, Spencer and Gillen did not employ the term 'Dream Times', they defined *alcheringa* as 'a name given to the far past times in which the mythical ancestors of the tribe are supposed to have lived' (Spencer and Gillen, 1899: 395).

Patrick Wolfe (1991: 201) notes that by 1905, when Mrs Langloh Parker wrote *The Euahlayi Tribe*, which contained an introduction by the champion of primitive monotheism, Andrew Lang, Parker was already referring to 'The Dream Time' calling it 'the age of pristine evolution' (Parker, 1905: 2). Wolfe observes that Parker was applying the same concept to the cosmology of the Euahlayi (located on the Australian east coast crossing the boundary of New South Wales and Queensland) as Spencer and Gillen had done to the Arrernte, although there was no connection between the two peoples. Thus, Wolfe (1991: 201) concludes, we see the beginning of the application of a term that ultimately culminated in 'an enormous geographical diffusion … one which was soon to extend to all aborigines'.

The transformation of 'Dream Time' or 'Dream Times' into the now more widely used term 'The Dreaming' or simply 'Dreaming' is largely attributable to the noted Australian anthropologist, W.E.H. Stanner, who began studying the Murinbata people in the far north of the Northern Territory in the 1930s and continued field studies there through frequent visits for the next 30 years. In an essay first published in 1956, Stanner (2009 [1956]: 57) claimed that 'a central meaning of The Dreaming is that of a sacred, heroic time long ago when man and nature came to be as they are'. He differentiated the Indigenous understanding of time as conveyed in the idea of Dreaming from Western concepts of time explaining that he had 'never been able to discover any Aboriginal word for *time* as an abstract concept' (Stanner, 2009 [1956]: 57, emphasis in original). He added, 'the sense of "history" is totally alien here' (Stanner, 2009 [1956]: 57).

Stanner described The Dreaming as referring to 'many things in one' (2009 [1956]: 58). He called it 'a kind of narrative of things that once happened' and yet suggested that it is not restricted to the past because it is a 'charter of things that still happen' (2009 [1956]: 58). In this sense, the Dreaming constitutes a 'principle of order transcending everything significant for the Aboriginal man' (2009 [1956]: 58). Stanner identified three principal elements in stories or myths about 'The Dreaming'. The first he called 'great marvels' which describe:

how all fire and water in the world were stolen and recaptured; how men made a mistake over sorcery and now have to die from it; how the hills, rivers, and waterholes were made; how the sun, moon and stars were set upon their courses; and many other dramas of this kind (2009 [1956]: 61).

The second element explains how social order was instituted for the first time:

How animals and men diverged from a joint stock that was neither one nor the other; how the black nosed kangaroo got his black nose and the porcupine his quills; how such social divisions as tribes, clans, and language groups were set up; how spirit-children were first placed in the waterholes, the winds, and leaves of trees (2009 [1956]: 61).

Stanner's third element demonstrates the close connection between the Dreaming and the present by connecting the Dreaming to the Aboriginal idea of Law. He explains that 'many of the main institutions of present-day life were *already ruling* in The Dreaming, e.g. marriage, exogamy, sister-exchange, and initiation, as well as many of the breaches of custom' (2009 [1956]: 61). He adds that Law does not mean 'legal' or 'legalistic' but the ways of life that describe Aboriginal social structures, rituals and relationships to spiritual or unseen forces. Then, in an often quoted phrase, Stanner described the Dreaming, not as everywhere (spatially) or at all times (temporally), but as both at the same time, the meaning of which he encapsulated in the term 'everywhen' (2009 [1956]: 58).

More recently, but in line with Stanner's notion of 'everywhen', 'Dream Time' has been criticized by Tony Swain as too simplistic and thus prone to misunderstanding. In *A Place for Strangers* (1993: 16) Swain argued that 'The Dream Time' as first introduced by Spencer and Gillen inappropriately imposed Western concepts of time, both linear and cyclical, on Aboriginal world views. In order to overcome the distortions created by Western ideas of time, Swain constructed two fundamental interpretative categories: rhythmed events and abiding events. By rhythmed events, Swain (1993: 19) meant that 'in Aboriginal thought there is nothing beyond events themselves'. Events simply occur. They are observed, are rhythmic and predictable. Examples provided by Swain include: the Milky Way stretched out across the centre of the sky; bandicoots backing into their burrows; light glimmering; the outline of trees and objects as clearly defined; shadows as variegated; the sun sinking (1993: 19). These concrete events occur regularly and demonstrate how time is thought of in pragmatic terms rather than as an abstract category.

The concept of 'abiding events' points to the fact that the true meaning behind the Dreaming is 'not temporal but spatial' (Swain, 1993: 22). An abiding event is secure because it resides in a place. In this sense, abiding events and rhythmic events are coterminous, linked not through time but place. This explains the fundamental importance of the landscape on which sacred places are dotted and about which dreamtime stories are told. For Swain, the Dreaming is made manifest in rhythmic and abiding events, both of which are witnessed in the landscape which embodies the stories of the totemic ancestors crossing the land, making tracks and then by re-entering the land making the particular places where they settled sacred (1993: 23).

The collapse of the distinction between time and space in Aboriginal thought as contained in Stanner's term 'everywhen' and Swain's emphasis on the spatial or locative nature of 'The Dreaming' was anticipated by T.G.H. Strehlow, whose in-depth analyses of Arrernte myths, stories, songs and rituals clarified what was meant by the Arrernte term *altjira* and its linguistic variations. Throughout his writings, Strehlow was always careful not to magnify this local word into a universal Aboriginal cosmology. By contrast, a rather rough initial translation by the Alice Springs postmaster, F.J. Gillen, of complex ideas expressed in the word Spencer spelled 'Alcheringa', has become both in popular and academic writings synonymous with the mythic world of all Aboriginal peoples. This extension of a local concept to a universal application was always disputed by Strehlow. His focus remained on the peoples of Central Australia among whom he grew up and about whom he wrote and collected enormous amounts of information, but even among the various Arrernte groups he studied, he emphasized the significance of local variations. At the beginning of *Aranda Traditions*, Strehlow (1947: 1) wrote: 'Strong stress must be laid upon the essential disunity of every large Central Australian tribe… There is no common system of religion which is embraced by the tribe as a whole'. When discussing Arrernte stories of origin in general, he analysed the word *altjira* and its local equivalents, which rather than defining as Dream Time, he preferred to call 'Eternity'.

I turn now to outline in detail Strehlow's descriptions of Arrernte creation stories, their relation to totemic ancestors and how he interpreted what a host of later writers, following Spencer and Gillen's tentative use of the term, referred to collectively across Australia as Dream Time or The Dreaming. Towards the end of this chapter I draw connections between the myths about the totemic ancestors and the extensive list of genealogies Strehlow compiled during his research among the Arrernte peoples between 1932 and 1970.

In the Beginning: Eternity

In *Central Australian Religion*, about which I write in more detail in the next chapter, Strehlow (1978a: 14) asserts that 'the eternity motif may … be regarded as … the most vital single element of the many that are blended together in any human religious system'. He adds: 'Nowhere were the links between human Time and changeless Eternity stronger in religious thought than in Central Australia' (1978a: 14). In numerous writings, Strehlow outlined the basic structure of Arrernte stories depicting how the world came to be as it now is. One very clear description that emphasizes the eternity theme is found in his long essay entitled 'The Sustaining Ideals of Aboriginal Societies', which was printed first in 1956 by the Aborigines Advancement League of South Australia and re-printed in 1966. In this publication, Strehlow explains that according to Arrernte traditions 'the earth ... was eternal' (1966: 8). Beneath its crust, various 'supernatural beings known as totemic ancestors were believed to have been sleeping from eternity'. At some point in time, these sleeping ancestors were aroused and emerged from beneath the earth's surface at specific locations on the landscape. These became 'sacred sites' that later were located in 'soaks, water holes, clay pans, and so forth' (1966: 8). Each of these supernatural beings was represented by a particular animal or plant. Strehlow explains: 'Thus a native cat ancestor generally moved about in human form, but he could turn into a native cat whenever he chose to do so; and from him the native cats of his original district were believed to have descended, as well as the human beings conceived there' (1966: 8). The same could be applied to numerous other animals or plants, such as honey-ants or kangaroos. The earth, which was 'bare and featureless' when these original totemic ancestors came to the surface from below the crust of the earth, was transformed by their activities: they created 'all the prominent physical features of the present-day landscape – its rocks, plains, hills, ranges, trees and so forth' (1966: 8). In time, these supernatural beings either returned to the earth from which they had first come or they 'changed into sacred rocks or sacred trees or *tjurunga* slabs' [now often called secret-sacred objects] (1966: 8). Although the totemic ancestors are now sleeping as they have done from eternity, Strehlow asserts that 'they still had the power to fill the earth with plants or animals of their own proper totems' (1966: 8).

In *Central Australian Religion*, Strehlow adds more detail to his description of central desert mythological concepts. He explains that the earth, which had existed from eternity, had always been 'covered in eternal darkness, lit only dimly by the distant fires bordering the Milky Way' (1978a: 14). Even the sun, moon and nearby stars were still 'slumbering under the earth's cold crust' (1978a: 14). Although no forms of life could exist in such conditions, on the surface of the earth 'a vague form of human life existed in the shape of semi-embryonic masses of half-developed infants, all joined together in their hundreds' (1978a: 14–15). These strange creatures were connected to one another by 'webs' that joined their hands and toes; even their 'eyes, mouths, and noses were closed' and none could move their arms or legs (1978a: 15). In this state in which they had been enclosed since eternity, these creatures could not develop into human beings, but neither could they experience death. They simply lay inert 'at places which were later revealed as saltlakes or great waterholes' (1978a: 15).

The surface of the earth on which the semi-embryonic creatures were joined was shrouded in darkness and was totally barren. Beneath the crust of the earth, however, 'life already existed in its fullness, in the form of uncreated supernatural beings that had always existed' (1978a: 15). These beings had been sleeping from eternity. Time as we know it began when these supernatural beings woke up and burst through the earth's surface. The places at which they emerged on the earth became 'the first sites on the earth to be impregnated with their life and power' (1978a: 15). At the same time as the supernatural beings appeared on the earth, so too did the sun rise out of the ground flooding the earth with light. Strehlow says that the first life forms on the earth were 'born out of their own eternity', a phrase he translated from the Arrernte *altjiraŋa ŋambakala*, which contains the Arrernte root word, *altjira* (1978a: 15). The beings that were 'born out of their own eternity' varied in appearance. Some looked like animals, such as kangaroos or emus, whereas others appeared as human men or women. There was no sense of superiority or inferiority among the supernatural beings according to their appearances in animal or human guise because, Strehlow explains, 'there was an indivisible linking between elements found in animals (or plants) on the one hand and in humans on the other' (1978a: 15). Those beings that initially appeared as animals 'generally thought and acted like humans', whereas those that had emerged as complete human beings 'could change at will into the particular animal with which they were indivisibly linked' (1978a: 15). Since plants are immobile and inarticulate, those supernatural beings that were linked to plants were always thought of as appearing in a human form.

The supernatural beings became what generally are called 'totemic ancestors' of living communities. They wandered over the surface of the earth creating the Central Australian landscape including mountains, hills, swamps, plains, springs and soakages. Strehlow explains the importance of the wanderings of the totemic ancestors in the acts of creation:

> In the scores of thousands of square miles that constitute the Aranda-speaking area there was not a single striking physical feature which was not associated with an episode in one of the many sacred myths, or with a verse in one of the many sacred songs, in which aboriginal religious beliefs found their expression (1978a: 16).

As a result of the original acts of creation by the totemic ancestors, their descendants, who are linked to them by virtue of the location of their conception sites and thus are regarded as re-incarnations of the original ancestor, are believed to perform the songs in ceremonies precisely as they were recited by the supernatural beings themselves. Because of this inextricable link between the totemic ancestors and their descendants, Strehlow observes, 'the sacred songs sung on ceremonial occasions, the body decorations worn by the actors impersonating the totemic ancestors, and all sacred ritual, were regarded as eternal and unalterable' (1978a: 16).

The missing piece thus far in Strehlow's accounts of Arrernte myths of origin relates to how human beings came into existence. It is at this point that Strehlow re-introduces into the story the semi-embryonic beings that had forever been linked to one another on the surface of the earth before the totemic ancestors emerged from their eternal slumber. These creatures became the original human beings as a result of the work of some totemic ancestors that Strehlow calls 'culture heroes' (1978a: 17). The totemic ancestors who performed the role of culture heroes 'liberated the semi-embryonic masses of humanity into the fullness of life' by separating them into individual persons and then taught them 'the most important things necessary for their survival as mature men and women', such as how to make spears, cook food or make fire (1978a: 17). These original human beings, however, did not carry such importance in later religious life of the Arrernte as did the totemic ancestors. Strehlow refers to the stories about the first humans as 'non-sacred' and likens them to the place occupied by 'the apocryphal writings' in orthodox Christian traditions (1978a: 17).

Strehlow's extended version of the Arrernte stories of creation concludes by noting that when the totemic ancestors had 'accomplished their labours and completed their wanderings, overpowering weariness fell upon them' since 'the tasks they had performed had taxed their strength to the utmost' (1978a: 17). Although all totemic ancestors experienced pain, just like humans, they were immortal and eventually sank back into the earth, usually at the place from which they had originally emerged, or they were transformed into rocks, trees or 'tjurunga objects' (1978a: 18). The places where the totemic ancestors first appeared or where they returned became sacred centres called *pmara kutata*, about which Strehlow discussed in length, and which I analyse in Chapter 4. Strehlow (1971b: 612) explains that 'the sacred centres had to be avoided on pain of death by humans, except on special ceremonial occasions'. The important point in this regard is to note that the most important sacred centres were defined by the location of either the birth of the totemic ancestor or the place where the ancestor returned to the earth, sometimes, of course, these being the same place.

The last act that occurred before the totemic ancestors returned to the earth was to introduce death into human experience. Strehlow explains that 'Death had been brought into the world by the acts of some of these supernatural beings', since stories abound about how rivalry and revenge occurred among the totemic ancestors, resulting in some slaying others as exemplified by the 'slaughter of the grim Eagle Brothers ... by the Mice

Men, and the annihilation of the bloodthirsty and cannibalistic Bat Men'
(Strehlow, 1978a: 17). Although some of the totemic ancestors had been
'killed', they remained immortal and lived on in the form of secret-sacred
objects (*tjurunga*). Strehlow concludes this extended and detailed account
of Arrernte myths of origin in poetic language: 'The sun, the moon, and
rest of the earth-born celestial bodies now rose to the sky; and the world of
labour, pain and death that men and women have known ever since came
into being' (Strehlow, 1978a: 19).

Sky Myths and the Supreme Being

The myths I have related from Strehlow thus far have emphasized the central importance of the earth in the process of creation. It was from under
the crust of the earth that the supernatural beings that made the landscape
emerged and what would eventually become humans existed on the surface of the earth from eternity in the form of semi-embryonic beings inex-
tricably linked by web-like appendages. This stress on earth-bound acts of
creation correctly reflects Arrernte traditions and their connections to ceremonial activities and social structures. Nonetheless, Strehlow notes in several of his important writings that myths were told among various Arrernte
groups and related peoples that referred to the sky and, in particular, to a
Great Father who dwelt in the sky.

Strehlow explains that the Western Arrernte believed that the sky was
inhabited by 'an emu-footed Great Father' who had many 'dog-footed wives'
(1978a: 11). The male children of the Great Father were emu-footed and
the females were dog-footed. These beings lived in an idyllic state 'in an eter-
nally green land' (1978a: 11). The Milky Way flowed like a river through
their abode ensuring that there was an abundance of food. Since there were
no animals living in this sky home, the family ate only fruit and vegetables.
Strehlow notes that 'these sky dwellers were as ageless as the stars themselves, and death could not enter their home' (1978a: 11). Eternal youth
was granted to all those living in the sky so that the Great Father looked as
young as his sons and 'all the women who lived above the stars had the grace
and the full-bosomed beauty of young girls' (1978a: 12). Strehlow notes that
his father, Carl Strehlow, reported similar beliefs among the neighbouring
Luritja peoples and that F.J. Gillen had discovered stories about emu-like
creatures living in the sky around Alice Springs among the Eastern Arrernte.

T.G.H. Strehlow discovered such stories only among the Western
Arrernte, but he found throughout Arrernte speaking areas a consistent
belief that death was limited to the earth and 'that men had to die only
because all connections had been severed between the sky and the earth'
(1978a: 12). Strehlow refers to many stories that speak of 'broken ladders',
which indicate that at some point commerce between the earth and the sky

had been interrupted resulting in a permanent separation of those living on earth from the paradise enjoyed by the sky-dwellers. Strehlow discovered traditions among the Southern Arrernte that referred particularly to large trees that had grown so high they touched the sky and thus provided a link between earth and the sky. The traditions relate how these trees had been chopped down by a horde of 'Blood Avengers' causing 'the bridge to unending life' to have been 'destroyed forever' (1978a: 12).

In *Aranda Traditions,* Strehlow (1947: 78) relates an unusual belief among the Southern Arrernte living about 30 kilometres north-west of Horseshoe Bend. Strehlow indicates that rites performed by the people living on the Finke River in this region were based on the legend that a water-hole contained two venomous snakes that had originated from two well-known ancestor brothers that had at one time belonged to the snake totem. Contrary to customary ways of belief, when they died these snake brothers, rather than returning to the earth, climbed into the sky on a huge spear. Although I will discuss Strehlow's interpretation of this myth in greater detail later in this chapter, in this context it is important to note that Strehlow claims that stories about these two ancestors were unique because they were 'the only totemic ancestors who had ascended into the sky, instead of sinking back into the bosom of the earth as the other legendary chiefs and mythical women had done' (1947: 78). Strehlow explains this anomaly as 'a relic from older legends, a last remnant of half-forgotten traditions which had originated in a society of the older, matrilineal order' (1947: 78). In *Central Australian Religion*, Strehlow suggests that the two totemic brothers, in stark contrast to the normal pattern whereby the totemic ancestors 'remained on the earth' and after growing old, 'returned to the ground and sank back into everlasting sleep', were transformed into 'ageless celestial bodies that knew neither decay nor death' (1978a: 13).

Strehlow's discussion of sky myths might suggest that two traditions, earth-bound and sky-focussed, were operating side by side among the Arrernte with equal importance, but this is not the case. It is clear that the sky myths played no important role in the practical life of the Arrernte nor in their ceremonial functions or social regulations. Only the two brothers who contravened the traditional ways the earth-bound totemic ancestors related to living communities could influence day to day living. This is precisely because they emerged from the earth and not the sky. Strehlow contends that the sky-dwellers he discovered in the myths of the Western Arrernte 'took no interest in anything that happened on the earth beneath them' (1978a: 13). For this reason, they played no role in traditional ceremonies nor had any place in the songs celebrating the wanderings of the earth-bound totemic ancestors.

The Great Father, the emu-footed sky-dweller of Western Arrernte traditions, therefore, cannot be regarded as an Arrernte version of belief in a Supreme Being, according to Strehlow, 'in any sense of this word', precisely because 'neither he nor his family ever exerted any influence beyond the limits of the sky' (1978a: 13). He reiterates this point in *Songs of Central Australia*, in which he asserts that 'to us the term "Supreme Being"' implies 'a personage whose reign affects mankind in some way, no matter how distantly' (1971a: 615). The word 'god' also suggests an 'immortal being that has either created or at least shaped some of its features, and that can influence the lives of men and women' (1971a: 615). This role is reserved among the Arrernte exclusively for the totemic ancestors, whom Strehlow contends 'were as eternal as the earth' (1971a: 615). It is the totemic ancestors who shaped the landscape on which humans live, and it is the totemic ancestors who exercise a 'limited sphere of control over Man and Nature, Animals and plants, winds and rainclouds' (1971a: 615). And it is the totemic ancestors who are honoured at ceremonial sites precisely because 'all human beings owed their very existence to them' (1971a: 615). Strehlow concludes that 'this would seem to leave little enough room for a Supreme Being in the Aranda cosmology' (1971a: 615); that place is occupied solely by the totemic ancestors.

Altjira: Dream Time, God or Eternity?

As we have seen, the Arrernte word *altjira* was translated loosely by F.J. Gillen as 'Dream Times' and now has become so associated with Aboriginal spirituality that its variations as 'Dreamtime', 'The Dreaming' or 'Dreaming' are regarded as the key terms encapsulating the core of Indigenous Religion in Australia. In contrast to Spencer and Gillen, the Lutheran missionaries in the late nineteenth century settled on *altjira* as the Arrernte word for God and still today use *altjira* in Bible translations and in the liturgies of the church as the local equivalent to the Christian God. T.G.H. Strehlow argued that neither Spencer and Gillen nor the Lutheran missionaries correctly interpreted the original meaning of the word *altjira*. In *Songs of Central Australia*, Strehlow wrote that *altjira* 'is a rare word, whose root meaning appears to be "eternal, uncreated, sprung out of itself"; and it occurs only in certain traditional phrases and collections' (1971a: 614).

Strehlow (1971a: 614) contended that Spencer and Gillen's interpretation of *altjira* (spelled by them as *alcheringa* in *The Native Tribes of Central Australia* but changed by Spencer in *The Arunta* to *alchera*) as 'dream time' was 'a vague and inaccurate phrase' that 'has never had any real meaning for the natives, who rarely, if ever, use it when speaking in English'. Strehlow attributed this mistranslation to the poor understanding of the Arrernte language by both Spencer and Gillen. According to Strehlow, Spencer and Gillen had confused the term *altjira rama*, which as we will see shortly is a verb form meaning 'to dream', with *altjiraŋa*, which, Strehlow explains, is best translated as '"out of all eternity", "from all eternity", "ever from the very beginning"' (1971a: 614). Strehlow argued that what he called 'the foolish term' Dreamtime 'implies a division between the time in which the supernatural beings lived and moved and that in which ordinary human beings move nowadays' (1978b: 4). This obviously is not the case because according to Arrernte myths, 'their supernatural beings had always existed (since they were as eternal as the earth) and that they had never died but merely returned into the earth to sleep' (1978b: 4). They lived on through their 'human "reincarnations"', since all humans 'carried in them some of the life of these supernatural beings' (1978b: 4).

We gain further insight into T.G.H. Strehlow's criticisms of Spencer and Gillen by considering the interpretation given to *altjira* by T.G.H. Strehlow's father, the missionary Carl Strehlow, who after arriving in Hermannsburg in 1894 became an expert in the Arrernte languages and compiled extensive word lists of Arrernte terms. In correspondence with the German anthropologist Moritz von Leonhardi in 1901, Carl Strehlow wrote that the word in Arrernte 'to dream is "*altjirerama*"', which to an untrained person would seem to imply that *altjira* translates in English to the noun 'dream' (Cited by J. Strehlow, 2011: 772). This, however, is not how the Arrernte use the word. Carl Strehlow explained: 'They have no word for "dream" as an abstract noun (Cited by J. Strehlow, 2011: 773). Writing in 1947, T.G.H. Strehlow contended that this misunderstanding by Spencer and Gillen demonstrates 'the kind of mistakes which monolingual fieldworkers can make' (cited by Moore 2016: 88).

David Moore, a linguist and translator working in Central Australia, whose BA (Hons) dissertation was written on Strehlow as a linguist (2008: 270–300), sheds light on Carl Strehlow's criticism of Spencer and Gillen's inadequate knowledge of Arrernte grammar. In his contribution to the book Adam Possamai and I edited on 'non-religion' among Australian Aboriginal Peoples, Moore (2016: 87–88) notes that in *The Arunta*, Spencer and Gillen (1927: 306) composed 19 sentences in English that they then asked Indigenous people to translate into Arrernte. Moore contends that Spencer and Gillen misinterpreted the Arrernte speakers in some cases by using the present tense rather than the past tense. This is particularly relevant to the notion of 'Dreamtime', which they mistakenly used as the present tense for sleeping rather than the past tense. Moore argues further that this resulted in the mistaken translation of sentence number 15, which Spencer and Gillen interpreted as 'I lived in the Alchera'. According to Moore, 'this sentence would be a logical impossibility' and would not be used in that way by native speakers of Arrernte (2016: 88). Moore adds that the verbs in sentences 16 to 19 'are translated as "dream"', which is a noun, but this is incorrect because in these sentences *altjira* would always have been connected to the verb *rama*. As *altjira rama*, the entire context of the meaning is changed. Dream, used as a noun in these sentences, misconstrues the actual sense of *altjira*, which as a verb (*rama*), in Moore's words, 'codes a process rather than a thing' (2016: 88). Moore explains that 'the verb "*rama*" cannot be deleted from "*altjira rama*" without producing a change of meaning, or more probably, a complete loss of meaning' (2016: 88). He concludes that 'Dreamtime' was an invention of Spencer and Gillen because it 'was not a functional equivalent' of *altjira* (2016: 89).

An equally problematic alternative translation of *altjira* was introduced by the first Lutheran missionaries working among the Arrernte who adopted *altjira* as the Indigenous word for God. In 1877, the missionaries A.H. Kempe and W.F. Schwarz established the Lutheran Mission along the Finke River approximately 130 kilometres west of Alice Springs. They called the Mission Hermannsburg after the Hermannsburg Mission Institute in Germany, which had commissioned them and trained them. According to Sam Gill (1998: 87), Kempe was the first missionary to settle on *altjira* as the Arrernte equivalent to the biblical God. Gill (1998: 87) quotes from Kempe's diary: 'All of them, the good supernatural beings they call altgiva [*altjira*] as well as the firmament, with the sun, moon, and stars; also the earth, and any things specially remarkable'. In an article he wrote to the Hermannsburg Mission in Germany in 1880, Kempe observed that the Aboriginals believe 'in a good being' they call 'Altjira' to whom they attribute 'the creation of sky and the earth; they say too that he lives in the sky and is well disposed to humanity' (J. Strehlow, 2011: 371). In his extensive study of the early days of the Hermannsburg Mission, John Strehlow (T.G.H. Strehlow's son) concluded that following Kempe's interpretations, *altjira* 'now became the word used for "God" in translations of the scriptures' (J. Strehlow, 2011: 371).

Carl Strehlow had translated the New Testament into the Dieri language during his first mission appointment in South Australia. Although he arrived at Hermannsburg in 1894, he did not begin working on an Arrernte translation of the entire New Testament until 1912. He completed this in 1919, but the manuscript was not published during his lifetime. Even then, according to the Lutheran superintendent, P.A. Scherer, just 'portions of it were typed for use by Hermannsburg missionaries' (Scherer, 1956: 346). In his translation, Carl Strehlow, following Kempe's lead, translated God as *altjira*. In his correspondence with Leonhardi, he explained that 'this god of theirs, Altjira, is eternal' (J. Strehlow, 2011: 773). He clearly identified Altjira (God) with the sky-dwelling Eternal Father that T.G.H. Strehlow described later in *Central Australian Religion* as an emu-footed being, with emu-footed sons and dog-footed wives, who remained entirely uninvolved in human activities. This is evident when Carl Strehlow described *altjira* as 'a tall man' with 'emu feet', which explains 'why he has the nickname "*ili-inka*" = emu-footed' (J. Strehlow, 2011: 773).

While he was the Native Patrol Officer working in Central Australia in the 1930s, T.G.H. Strehlow was persuaded to begin work on a revised translation of the Arrernte New Testament. He commenced work on the project in 1938, completed it in 1950 and saw its publication in 1956. In his translation, Strehlow following the lead of the Lutheran missionaries, including Carl Strehlow, retained the word *altjira* for God. Writing in the *Lutheran Herald* shortly after the publication of his revised Arrernte New Testament, Strehlow explained why he had done so. He admitted that 'the term "Altjira" was originally used only in certain traditional phrases, where it suggested either "eternity" or something that had not been created' (Strehlow, 1957: 4). Nonetheless, he explained, 'the Aranda New Testament undoubtedly brings into the intellectual life of Aranda speakers a new Christian world of ideas which did not exist in the aboriginal way of life in pre-white days' (Strehlow, 1957: 4). In other words, although *altjira* did not originally signify attributes similar to the Christian idea of God, over time and under the gradual influence of Christianity, it had become adopted into the vocabulary of Indigenous speakers (Strehlow, 1957: 4). In a pamphlet printed in 1978 by the Strehlow Research Foundation, Strehlow noted that adopting *altjira* for God 'had been accepted even by many non-Christian Aranda speakers' as early as the 1920s, a fact that can be seen in Spencer and Gillen's *The Arunta*, where they describe 'the exploits of Numbakulla, the mythical being of the Central, Southern and Northern groups of the Arunta tribe' (Strehlow, 1978b: 4). Strehlow calls this 'the most amazing account of syncretism of Aranda and Christian beliefs ever perpetrated by anyone', even though Spencer was oblivious to this fact (Strehlow, 1978b: 4).

Strehlow's decision to produce a revised version of the Arrernte New Testament can be explained by his intimate knowledge of the Arrernte language, including how it is used in everyday speech, and by his careful reading of his father's earlier translation. Nonetheless, it is important to note that he enlisted the assistance for clarification of words and concepts from a select group of Indigenous Christians, particularly the Arrernte evangelist Moses Tjalkabota Uraiakuraia, also known as 'Blind Moses' (See Latz, 2014). After its publication, Strehlow's translation was hailed as a masterpiece by Lutheran leaders (Scherer, 1956: 346) but it must be understood as a project he undertook as a means of making the translation his father completed more up-to-date. Strehlow explained: 'My main object in undertaking the revision of the Aranda New Testament was to transform the language of the existing version so that it should have the genuine ring of a true and original Aranda document' (Strehlow, 1957: 4).

Outside Lutheran circles, Strehlow concentrated on providing descriptions and interpretations of customary Arrernte religious beliefs and practices to preserve for posterity what he regarded as dying traditions. In these contexts, Strehlow related the word *altjira* neither to Dream Time nor to

God, but to the totemic ancestors. He explained that the phrase *altjiraŋa ŋambakala*, as we saw above, literally means 'having originated out of altjira' and 'is used only about the earth-born supernatural beings'. He adds that it can be translated most accurately into English as 'having originated out of his (her, their) own eternity'. This means, according to Strehlow, 'that these supernatural beings have always existed and that no one has created them' (1971a: 614). He explains that when Indigenous people refer in pidgin English to 'dreamin', they mean exclusively 'totem'. This is a translation not of *altjira rama*, but of *kŋanakala*, which means 'someone who has originated'. For example, if an Indigenous person speaks about 'emu dreamin', it would be a translation of the Arrernte phrase *ilia kŋanakala*, which means 'someone who has originated as an emu' (1971a: 614–15).

In an article published in Volume Two of *Historia Religionum*, edited by C.J. Bleeker and G. Widengren, Strehlow, writing for an international audience, repeated his criticism of the term 'Dream Time', which he attributed to Spencer and Gillen and called a 'wrong translation of the Aranda *altjiranga ngambakala*' (1971b: 613–14). The correct translation, he argues, is '"having originated out of eternity", "having originated out of one's own self", "born out of one's own eternity"' (1971b: 614). He adds that 'the root meaning of *altjira* is "eternal", "uncreated"' (1971b: 614). He then returns to the grammatical use of the term explaining that the Arrernte verb *altjira rama*, meaning 'to dream', 'is a transitive verb requiring an object' (1971b: 614). It can be used in two ways: 'either "I see eternal things" (without a stated object) or "I see with eternal vision" (with an added object)' (1971b: 614). For this reason, Spencer and Gillen's translation of *altjira rama* as 'Dream Time', is 'an unfortunate misnomer', whereas his own translation as 'ever from eternity' provides the exact meaning of the word (1971b: 614).

Strehlow concludes that the paramount importance of the totemic ancestors and the quite explicit and concrete stories relevant to current social organization and ceremonial activities associated with them are reinforced by the correct translation of the word *altjira*, rather than as it is widely accepted and promoted 'among white Australians', as Dreamtime, which has become popular due to 'its sentimentality and its suggestion of mysticism' (1971a: 614). We can also understand from his interpretation of *altjira* as 'eternal' or 'uncreated' why Strehlow translated *altjira* as God in his Arrernte New Testament, although he clearly acknowledged that this did not apply prior to contact with Christian missionaries, nor reflect traditional applications of *altjira*. Rather, it made sense in contemporary times due to the changing understanding among Indigenous Christians of the nature of the 'eternal', which in turn reflected the need to contextualize the Christian message within local culture.

The Mythic Activities of the Totemic Ancestors

After they emerged from beneath the surface of the earth's crust, the super-natural totemic ancestors wandered across the country creating mythical trails that resulted in the formation of the geographical features that distinguish the present central desert landscape. The totemic ancestors literally merged into the various landmarks transforming them into sacred sites. They left behind their ancient songs, which their descendants sang during ceremonies and they inhabited secret-sacred objects used in rituals and were present in paintings used in the ceremonies. As we have seen, in various writings, Strehlow indicated that he had traced numerous mythical trails of the totemic ancestors, recorded the stories and songs associated with their wanderings and documented ceremonies in which the songs were performed. He claimed that some of the trails travelled by the totemic ancestors extended over great distances. For example, in an article he contributed to a book edited by R.M. Berndt and Catherine Berndt, he referred to 'the myth of the Dancing Women of Amunurkna' in which the wanderings begin among the Western Arrernte people near Mount Liebig and extend into Eastern Arrernte country as far as Arltunga, over 400 kilometres to the east (Strehlow, 1965: 128). Strehlow cites another example in which he recorded 'many of the mythical episodes, song verses and representations of the honey-ant ancestors' who travelled vast distances from areas in the Gibson Desert to as far as the Sandover River 'in Iliaura [Alyawarre] territory', located approximately 250 kilometres northeast of Alice Springs (Strehlow, 1965: 129). As they travelled, they created the geographical features of the central desert: 'In Central Australia, every landscape feature was associated with some mythical episode or some sacred verse'. As a result, 'mythology was validated by the geography of the *whole* countryside' ... not merely by a few major waters or prominent mountains' (Strehlow, 1969: 11, emphasis in original).

In *Journey to Horseshoe Bend* (2015 [1969]), Strehlow recounts the arduous journey undertaken in 1922 by his critically ill father from Hermannsburg to Horseshoe Bend, a distance of approximately 400 kilometres. At the time, T.G.H. Strehlow (Theo in the book) was 14 years- old. The journey itself can be likened to the ancestral wanderings of the supernatural beings at the beginning of time, since Strehlow, who wrote the book in 1969, describes numerous mythical trails the party crossed between Hermannsburg and Horseshoe Bend, and relates these to the stories that were told about the totemic ancestors in particular places along the route that he had discovered during the many years of research he conducted beginning in 1932. A particularly vivid story, to which I referred earlier in the context of the unique place of sky dwellers, tells how Death came into the world and why all humans have been denied immortality. As Strehlow recounts it in

Journey to Horseshoe Bend, it covers several pages of text, but I will provide the key details to give a flavour of the myths told about the totemic ances-tors. Of course, it is no coincidence that Strehlow goes to such lengths to relate a myth about Death, considering that his own father was days away from dying. It is also worth noting that we will meet references to this myth later when Strehlow claims that all rituals re-enacting this specific myth had been forgotten by the 1950s.

How Death Came into the World (A Summary)

At the beginning of time a shell parrot ancestress came to Ndapakiljara [in south-ern Arrernte territory near the Finke River around four kilometres below Idra-cowra]. After becoming pregnant of her own will by the wind, she gave birth to male twins who later assumed the shape of baby snakes. After giving birth to the snakes, the shell parrot mother flew up into the sky, leaving her babies to fend for themselves. They grew at such a rapid pace that they soon became full adults, wandered around as snakes and at other times changed into young men. The parrot mother returned, changed into the shape of a woman and offered one of her breasts to her sons. The younger brother, who was intensely angry at having been abandoned by his mother, turned back into a snake and bit off her breast. After returning to his human form, he threw the breast away and it immediately turned into a large breast-shaped hill. The mother, in great pain, turned back into a parrot, flew far to the south and gathered a band of avengers to kill her two treacherous sons. She came upon a horde of Tangka warriors in the Lake Eyre region, who had joined forces to avenge several other totemic ancestors who had murdered their nearest kinsfolk. On the trek north to attack the snake twins, the Tangka warriors were attacked by two ancestral eagle brothers. Several hun-dred Tangka warriors were killed but around one hundred of them remained. The slaughter ended when one of the warriors threw a boomerang that broke the left arms of the eagle brothers. The parrot ancestress then took command of the Tangka warriors and led them to the lair of her snake sons. The sons learned of the approach of the Tangka warriors and hid until night had fallen. They turned themselves back into human form, approached the campfire of the war-riors, which they had set up at Uralterinja. The warriors did not know they were actually the snake twins, but mistook them for two local young men. Even their mother failed to recognise them. The brothers woke the Tankga warriors during the night and challenged them to climb on their spears up to the sky. The warriors' spears proved useless for the task but the brothers, whose spears had turned into a snake extending to the sky, effortlessly ascended. The Tangka warriors were amazed and terrified, and thus were too afraid to attempt the ascent on the snake. The brothers withdrew the snake through which the warriors could have climbed to the sky and announced that the route to the sky had been severed forever. The brothers shone like two eternal lights in the heavens from which they pronounced a curse first on the Tangka warriors and then on all humans who would follow: 'You miserable death-doomed wretches, all of you must die now!' (Strehlow, 2015 [1969]: 176–80).

In his comments on this myth, Strehlow observes that Uralterinja 'had come to be regarded as accursed ground' and that the slight elevation from which the snake twins had made their ascent to the sky 'was looked upon fearfully as the very home of Death' (2015 [1969]: 180–81). Only older men who were members of 'local snake totems' were ever allowed to enter this site, and these only on special, secret ceremonial occasions. Such was the power attached to the site that 'all men of other totems, as well as all women and children, were banned on pain of death from entering the several square miles of prohibited country that constituted the private domain of Death' (2015 [1969]:181).

What is significant to note for the theme of this chapter is that the myths telling how the landscape emerged out of the activities of the totemic ancestors often were violent and involved warfare and revenge or what is frequently referred to as 'pay back'. At the same time, the myths served as the foundation for the totemic system that functioned among traditional social groups. The myths also formed the basis on which the ritual life of the Arrernte totemic clans operated and which dictated the strict secrecy with which the names and secret-sacred objects were maintained by the initiated men associated with particular totemic ancestors. The myths, about which the sacred songs were performed, created the structure for the correct protocols that had to be followed and observed in the rituals celebrating the supernatural ancestors from whom members of particular totemic clans obtained their identity. The myths of the Arrernte as outlined by Strehlow illustrate the close connections between the ancestors and their human descendants, including the establishment of the strict social regulations governing traditional Law.

Genealogies

During his research into the religious beliefs and social structures of the Arrernte groups in Central Australia, Strehlow compiled extensive genealogical information which related closely to his accounts of the mythic trails of the wandering totemic ancestors. He argued that the genealogies he constructed represented far more than is apparent to the outside observer who might simply liken them to 'family trees' in Western traditions. In an article published in 1962, he explained that 'the sacred traditions can be fully understood only against the local landscape – a landscape with whose features the incidents attributed to them in the myths harmonize so perfectly' (Strehlow, 1962: 7).

Between 1948 and 1960, Strehlow conducted six research trips to Central Australia in which, he says, 'full genealogies containing many hundreds of names were added to my earlier collections' (Strehlow, 1962a: 7). Because they were closely tied to ancestral traditions as they directly affected current generations in ritual and social contexts, the genealogies did 'not consist merely of meaningless series of names of long-forgotten persons' (Strehlow, 1962a: 7). They included also the totems to which the individuals mentioned belonged, their conception sites and 'the sub-sections of all persons who are mentioned in them' (Strehlow, 1962a: 10). This information was necessary to document important rights relating to land and inheritance as well as confirming the authority of those who passed on traditional knowledge to Strehlow. It also certified the authenticity of the ceremonial acts he witnessed, recorded and filmed.

The genealogical data he so carefully documented also traced marriage patterns among various Arrernte groups, including what Strehlow called 'wrong' (1962a: 10) or 'irregular' inter-tribal marriages (1999: 26). He also recorded in his diaries historical information about what he termed 'accidents and tragedies' that 'had affected a considerable number of persons who figure in these genealogies' (1962a: 10). As such, his genealogical records provide a source of specific information about numerous individuals, their personal totems, kinship groups and collective totemic identities. Although later on his genealogies provided information relevant to Indigenous land claims, at the time Strehlow was collecting the information, these records acted as sources for understanding traditional knowledge, particularly the authority from which such knowledge was derived and how it had been passed on from generation to generation according to ancient traditions. He explained:

> It is possible to learn from these genealogies what were the rights of ownership and inheritance which enabled my informants to relate with authority those of their sacred traditions that they passed on to me, and to perform without impropriety the secret dramatic acts that they showed to me (1962a).

Fifty years before T.G.H. Strehlow compiled his extensive accounts of genealogical information, Carl Strehlow had conducted in-depth research on how kinship classifications operated among the Arrernte and Luritja peoples. Anna Kenny observes that Carl Strehlow's genealogies 'provided a starting point for his son', who 'was in possession of his father's family trees when he produced his own genealogies' (Kenny, 2013: 187). Kenny notes that during T.G.H. Strehlow's research, because he was only able to reproduce information relating to two or three generations into the past, he relied on his father's research, which documented records back to the early 1800s (Kenny, 2013: 187). Kenny explains that T.G.H. Strehlow began with an 'apical ancestor' and traced the genealogies downward from there, in the process outlining the class and sub-class system that followed patrilineal descent patterns (Kenny, 2013: 187). Strehlow used a coding system on his genealogies which, Kenny notes, 'made the notions of descent and blood ties unmistakably clear' (Kenny, 2013: 188). Kenny concludes by drawing attention to the wide application of Strehlow's genealogies for understanding Arrernte society:

> Nearly every person on these family trees has a footnote that is often cross-referenced to his diaries or to other family trees. These footnotes contain an immense variety of historical, cultural, social, geographical (location of sites, sometimes the description is in Aranda) and additional kin information as well as gossip (Kenny, 2013: 188).

Although Strehlow never published the genealogical data he collected for general audiences, according to Tim Rowse (1999: 90), he regarded the information contained in them and the approach they represented as 'a unique basis for recording culture as behaviour and not just as normative statements'. Rowse suggests that this was because Strehlow believed that his genealogies 'would show the actual conduct of marriage and kinship among the Arrernte' (1999: 90). In a paper that remained unpublished until 1999, Strehlow outlined in detail what he meant by 'regular' and 'irregular' marriages among the Arrernte because, he explained, 'no discussion of the social structure of any society is complete unless it embraces a detailed account of the constitution of its most important basic unit – the family' (Strehlow, 1999: 1). He notes that among Australian groups living in the central desert, 'marriages are governed by rules expressed in terms of the classificatory kinship system' (Strehlow, 1999: 1). Although much has been written about how marriage rules work among the Arrernte, the descriptions are so complex, that those who are not experts in anthropology find it extraordinarily difficult to decipher.

I analyse in detail in the next chapter Strehlow's critical discussion of the relationships between personal totems and communal totemic identity, including kinship and marriage rules. My point in this chapter is to indicate that Strehlow believed that his extensive genealogies outlining hundreds of extended families provided an authoritative record not only of traditional protocols relating to marriage and kinship regulations, but also linked these to the myths of the supernatural beings who became the totemic ancestors of the people he was describing in the genealogies he had compiled. The genealogies in turn established the relationships between individual totemic ancestors and the totems of the extended families involved and set the patterns for ceremonial rules governing performances relevant to particular totemic ancestors and the secret-sacred objects (*tjurunga*) associated with them. In this sense, the genealogies that Strehlow documented, and which, as we will see in Chapter 8, are currently being consulted by present-day Elders at the Strehlow Research Centre, do far more than provide evidence for marriage and kinship relations: they form the record on which Arrernte religious beliefs and customs were founded and provide a platform for their revival.

Conclusion

In this chapter, I have traced the key elements in the world view of the Arrernte as Strehlow understood them. I have shown that Strehlow regarded the earth-bound, supernatural and eternal totemic ancestors as the most important figures in stories of creation. Although sky deities featured in the myths, because they played no role in any rituals and are irrelevant to Arrernte social protocols, they were insignificant in practice. This led to Strehlow's conclusion that a Supreme Being in any meaningful sense of the term was absent from Arrernte cosmologies. Likewise, the widespread notion first promulgated by Spencer and Gillen that stories of the totemic ancestors describe a past period called 'Dream Time' or 'Dream Times' is a mistranslation of the Arrernte term *'altjira'*, which Strehlow rendered as 'eternity' or in reference to the totemic ancestors, as being 'born out of their own eternity'. This signifies that in traditional beliefs the totemic ancestors were regarded as eternal; they emerged at a point in time from beneath the earth's surface and have returned to their eternal sleep in the form of the features of the landscape. They continued to exercise a dominant place in Arrernte life by being 'reincarnated' into human beings who carried their totemic identity.

I have also discussed how Strehlow accepted that the missionary interpretation of *altjira* as the word for the Christian God, just like 'Dream Time', was foreign to traditional Arrernte ways of thinking, but, following his own translation of the New Testament, he argued that over time and under the strong influence of the Church, a gradual process of syncretism had occurred so that *altjira* is now widely accepted as an Indigenous word that is equivalent to God. He stressed, however, that this was not the case in the pre-Christian days. Finally, I have shown how Strehlow's extensive work on genealogies preserved records of individual and communal totemic identities for numerous extended families and how these were related directly to myths of origin, tales of the wanderings of the ancestors along mythic trails and to the ceremonial rules that were safeguarded so precisely by members of totemic clans.

My next task is to demonstrate how Strehlow related the myths of origin I have described in this chapter to the critical role the totemic ancestors traditionally played in day to day life among Arrernte groups through a social and ceremonial structure that Strehlow graphically described as 'personal monototemism in a polytotemic community'.

PERSONAL MONOTOTEMISM IN A POLYTOTEMIC COMMUNITY

In 1978, the Australian Association for the Study of Religions published a booklet by T.G.H. Strehlow under the title *Central Australian Religion* that carried the sub-title 'Personal Monototemism in a Polytotemic Community'. This was a reprint of an article Strehlow contributed in 1964 to a Festschrift in honour of the German ethnologist Ad. E. Jensen (Strehlow, 1964). In the Preface to the 1978 reprint, Norman Habel (Strehlow, 1978a: i), then President of the Australian Association of the Study of Religions, observed that Strehlow's original article 'has been acknowledged as a significant contribution to the study of aboriginal Central Australian culture' but that 'it has not been accessible to most students and has not had the impact it deserves'. In this chapter, I analyse in depth what Strehlow meant by 'personal monototemism in a polytemic community'. I contend that this critical phrase defines one of his most significant contributions to understanding the complex social, cultural and religious structures of the Arrernte peoples of Central Australia.

The Genesis of the Concept

In *Aranda Traditions*, Strehlow (1947: 139) noted that 'members of the same family commonly belong to different personal totems'. The notion of a personal totem follows from the Arrernte belief that the conception site establishes the totem of the individual rather than kinship ties. The 'conception site' is the place associated with a totemic ancestor where the future mother first became aware that she was pregnant (Strehlow, 1978a: 21–22). The particular totemic ancestor could be, for example, the honey-ant, the kangaroo or the native cat, each of which in the times of beginnings had left trails as they wandered along the land before going back into the natural environment making the various hills, rocks and geographical formations that define the contemporary landscape. A child is the reincarnation of the particular totemic ancestor at whose sacred site the mother first became aware of her pregnancy.

Based on research he conducted in the 1930s, Strehlow (1947: 87) referred to two main traditions among the Western Arrernte about how a woman becomes aware that she is pregnant and how that determines the personal totem of the child. The first tradition describes how a married woman experiences a sudden pain in her side while she is on her daily search for food. She knows intuitively that this confirms that she is pregnant. She returns home and tells her husband what occurred. He consults with Elders of his own clan, and according to Strehlow, they search 'amongst the legendary records of his group in order to discover the original totemic ancestor who either dwelt in this locality or visited it on one of his wanderings' (1947: 87). Once determined, it is then confirmed that it is this totemic ancestor that has caused the pregnancy and will be reincarnated in the child. The second instance cited by Strehlow refers to a physical object, such as a tree or a rock, that is associated in tradition with a particular ancestor. As the woman passed the object, the ancestor entered the woman's body in order to be re-born in the infant.

In *Central Australian Religion*, Strehlow (1978a: 21) admits that when he conducted research during the 1930s, he was 'not entirely clear' about Arrernte ideas about conception. Subsequently, in contrast to the widespread notion that the Arrernte were ignorant as to how babies were conceived in biological terms, he described the 'doctrine' of the 'two souls'. The Arrernte know that intercourse between a man and a woman produces 'a foetus which has a mortal human "life" (or "soul") of its own' (1978a: 21). This corresponds to what they observe from animal behaviour. Humans, however, are different from animals in that they possess 'an all-important second "life" (or "soul") which is immortal' (1978a: 21). It is this soul that is connected to the eternal supernatural ancestors that 'entered the body of an already pregnant woman at some definite point of the landscape' (1978a: 21). The totemic ancestor chose not just a married woman as the one through whom it would be reincarnated, but a woman who was already pregnant. It is not until the woman first realizes that she is pregnant through, for example, morning sickness or daydreams of having babies, that the ancestor enters her and gives the second 'soul' to the infant she is carrying.

Strehlow explains further that it was necessary that the identity of the supernatural being that constituted the second soul of the child be confirmed beyond doubt. This was because 'it was the second (and immortal) soul which decided the personality of the child after birth' (1978a: 21), and that which established his or her personal totem. This second soul was thus the most important part of the person because not only did the child acquire the 'soul' of the supernatural ancestor but also the personality of the ancestor was transferred to the human being in the reincarnation process. He explains: 'All Aranda men, women, and children were believed to have been completely *recreated* in the images of those totemic ancestors who had become reincarnated in them' (Strehlow, 1978a: 22, emphasis in original). Of course, the totemic being did not restrict itself to the one child who had received the supernatural 'soul'. The ancestor remained attached to the landscape to which it had returned and the ancestor could also be reincarnated into many humans at the same time. This, Strehlow suggests, meant that 'the second soul possessed by each human being was only a *part* of the "life" of the totemic ancestor from which it had come' (Strehlow, 1978a: 22, emphasis in original).

The doctrine of the two souls implied that a human being was the offspring of two forces, one natural and the other supernatural, but both forces were closely intertwined. In physical appearance a person could possess some of the characteristics of his or her totemic ancestor. Strehlow suggests that one could look at the person and see aspects of the supernatural being in the flesh. He notes that even some abnormal physical conditions could be assigned to the supernatural being that had been reincarnated into a person. He cites the example of one man who lived along the Hale River who used to show the bunions on his feet as evidence of his being the reincarnation of the native cat, which, according to the myth, 'had angrily thrust his feet into the campfire of the sons who had left him' (1978a: 23). Or another man from Unmatjera pointed to a light-brown patch of skin on his back as evidence that he was reincarnated from the possum, which often has some copper-coloured fur on its body.

The idea that a person possessed two souls also implied that the second 'life' of the person acted as a kind of guardian spirit of the individual, protecting the person and even assisting in the performance of certain duties. Strehlow cites the example of how a hunter might be seen returning to the camp and from a distance it would appear that two people were walking side by side. The hunter, of course, was being accompanied by his immortal soul (Strehlow, 1978a: 23). In addition, the doctrine of the two souls accounted for the ability of humans to travel in dreams, which were regarded as literal journeys out of the body. These were oftentimes frightening experiences in which the person encountered malevolent forces that were avoided only by returning to the body during sleep. A higher notion of dreaming, according to Strehlow's interpretation, involved the individual seeing 'eternal things' in which it was possible 'to perceive sights and shapes beyond the comprehension of human eyes – sights and shapes which had existed from all eternity' (Strehlow, 1978a: 24).

Personal identity thus for the Arrernte was determined entirely by the totemic ancestor that had re-incarnated itself in the individual at his or her conception site. It is important to stress that the personal totem was established not by kinship or lineage but by the location where the woman first realized she was pregnant, since it was there that the particular ancestor associated with the landscape entered the woman's body and gave the second soul to the child she was carrying. Those men who were reincarnations of the same totemic ancestor were bound together ceremonially by performing rituals aimed at ensuring that their totemic animals or plants remained plentiful and increased. The rituals had to be performed exactly as they had been passed down from generation to generation, in Strehlow's words, 'without any deviations' and the songs sung during the ceremonies had to be performed 'in their unaltered original form' (1978a: 25).

The rituals that were followed so strictly were required to be conducted at the places where they had originally been instituted, and what is most important, 'the human persons who did them had to be – by reason of rein-carnation – of the same substance as the supernatural personages who had first performed this ritual and intoned these verses' (1978a: 25). The rituals dedicated to personal totems occurred in geographical areas where numer-ous other totemic clans functioned and performed ceremonies to their supernatural ancestors. In a response to a paper presented by Father Ernest Worms at a symposium of the Australian Institute of Aboriginal Studies in 1961 and published in 1963, Strehlow labelled this complex system, which connected conception sites and totemic ancestors to localized and rig-idly controlled ceremonies, 'local monototemism' (Strehlow, 1963: 250). He altered this term slightly in his contribution to Jensen's Festschrift in 1964 to 'personal monototemism' that operated in communities that were 'polytotemic'.

Personal Monototemism in Polytotemic Communities Explained

Strehlow clarified what he meant by 'local monototemism' in his response to Father Worms by explaining that no Arrernte groups or sub-groups, whether from Western or Northern or Southern regions, constituted single political units: 'They were split up … into section areas, each of which normally had two subsections which stood in father-son relation to one another' (the extended family or what he called the local *njinaŋa* section) (Strehlow, 1963: 249). He then explained that 'local earth-born supernatu-ral beings were associated with definite local sacred centres' with each centre having its own 'separate cycle of ceremonies which … could be performed nowhere else … but at that particular site' (the *pmara kutata*) (Strehlow, 1963: 249). This had an impact on the religion of the people living in the area: 'Rites belonging to a particular cycle could be performed only at a par-ticular place, by men of a particular subsection', who were bound 'to the supernatural beings whom they honoured in ritual in a form of reincarna-tion relationship, as if they were of the same substance as them' (Strehlow, 1963: 249). As a result of this particular identification with sacred sites and totemic ancestors, 'the human worshippers were divided into a large number of separate groups, each of which normally performed one major ceremonial cycle, honouring only one set of totemic supernatural beings' (Strehlow, 1963: 249). Because monototemism was practised in association with particular ceremonial sites, there were no overall ceremonies 'in which all the local groups could combine on equal terms' (Strehlow, 1963: 250). These various groups collaborated on the basis of 'the principle that religious ritual of the various local groups was of equal importance to the whole tribe' (Strehlow, 1963: 250).

Although the system of 'local' monototemism described accurately the relationships between different groupings within the overall Arrernte social organization, Strehlow came to prefer the term 'personal' monototemism because it emphasized the important role played by the conception site in determining each individual's totemic ancestor. This personal aspect of the identification of an individual with his or her totemic ancestor in turn creates the system Strehlow labelled a 'polytotemic community'. In *Aranda Traditions* (Strehlow, 1947: 139), he asserted that the conception site is 'determined arbitrarily by some whim of the legendary ancestor' and he then argued that this 'cannot be controlled by the leaders of local patrilineal clans', which in turn has an 'inevitable disruptive effect' on local communities. In *Central Australian Religion,* he admitted that his argument thus far had been 'concentrated mainly upon the *individual*' adding that 'for the individual, personal monototemism has been shown to be the basis of all religious thought and ceremonial activity' (Strehlow, 1978a: 39, emphasis in original). At the same time, Strehlow acknowledged, 'religion exercises its strongest hold upon individuals when it possesses the power to knit them together into a large community of men and women' (1978a: 40). This anomaly between the commonly accepted social functions of religion and the apparent individualism of Arrernte religion, prompted his fundamental question about the relationships between kinship and personal totemic identity: '*How could the indispensable feeling of strong religious unity be achieved within a polytotemic community that occupied a geographically well-defined common tract of country?*' (1978a: 40, emphasis in original).

In order to answer this critical question, Strehlow expanded his discussion of the relationship between the *njinaŋa* section, the extended family organized patrilineally (called by Strehlow 'the patrilineal horde') (Strehlow, 1999: 39), and the totemic ceremonial sites linking those that share the same totemic ancestor, called the *pmara kutata* and translated by Strehlow as 'everlasting home' (Strehlow, 1947: 141). In an article he published in 1965 in a book edited by R.M. Berndt and C.H. Berndt, Strehlow defined a *pmara kutata* as 'a ceremonial centre at which mythical ancestral beings were believed to have originated *out of the ground* (emphasis in original) in numbers sufficiently large to populate the surrounding countryside' (Strehlow, 1965: 130). In *Aranda Traditions*, he defined the *njinaŋa* section as including 'all men, women, and children of a given totemic clan who stand to one another in the relation of fathers, sons, brothers, sisters, and daughters' (Strehlow, 1947: 139). Strehlow argued that the disruption caused by the individual identification with a personal conception site is overcome by 'the strong emphasis laid upon the unifying ties represented by the allegiance claims of the *pmara kutata* and by membership obligations to the local *njinaŋa* section' (Strehlow, 1947: 140).

In his contribution to the book edited by R.M. and C.H. Berndt, he explained the relationship between the central ceremonial site dedicated to a totemic ancestor and kinship relations as it operated in the *njinaŋa* section. I have called the *njinaŋa* section the extended family, meaning that the family consists of what in Western terminology would be called father's brothers (uncles) and their wives (aunts) and their children (cousins), including the father's father and his brothers and their wives. Strehlow provides a more detailed account of the organization of extended families than my summary affords; he refers to the *njinaŋa* section as 'the land-based kin-group class system' (Strehlow, 1965: 136). He explains that 'in the pre-white days the men in each of these *njinaŋa section* areas belonged almost exclusively to two classes which stood in a father-son (Aranda *njinaŋa*) relationship to each other' (Strehlow, 1965: 138). The land for each *njinaŋa* section was 'demarcated by episodes in the sacred myths' (Strehlow, 1965: 138). The boundary for each section 'marked the limit beyond which a myth might not be told, a song not sung, nor a series of ceremonies performed by members of a *njinaŋa* section area who shared these traditions with neighbours' (Strehlow, 1965: 138). The barriers separating various *njinaŋa* sections ensured that the land was appropriately and accurately divided: 'No neighbouring groups could quarrel about their borders, since it was believed that these had been set down by their own supernatural beings' (Strehlow, 1965: 138).

Strehlow explains that 'all kin-group classes were based on the numerous *njinaŋa* section areas, each of which was the home of two father-son classes' (Strehlow, 1965: 139), called by Anna Kenny 'exogamous patrimoieties' (Kenny, 2013: 172). Kenny explains that 'in one's own patrimoiety' [us] 'are one's actual and classificatory fathers and their siblings, father's fathers and son's children, and also one's mother's mother's patriline' (Kenny, 2013: 172). She notes that 'in the opposite moiety, … in addition to one's spouse and brothers-in-law there are one's actual and classificatory mothers, mother's brothers and mother's fathers and also one's father's mother' (Kenny, 2013: 172). In order to clarify the complex relationships between the *njinaŋa* section and the *pmara kutata*, I need to insert into this discussion Strehlow's interpretation of the Arrernte kinship and marriage system.

Marriage and Kinship Rules Simplified

In my discussion of Strehlow's genealogies in the previous chapter, I drew attention to an Occasional Paper published in 1999 by the Strehlow Research Centre which Strehlow wrote under the title 'Aranda Regular and

Irregular Marriages'.[1] This article bears directly on the topic of this chapter. Strehlow begins this paper by acknowledging that traditional marriage regulations among the Arrernte were so difficult to understand that to the non-specialist they appear as 'mysteries' and may even suggest an 'apparent chaos' (Strehlow, 1999: 1). Strehlow admits that even he, who had 'known hundreds of married Aranda couples since childhood' frequently had been unable 'to see the wood for all the trees in chapters and papers written on Aranda marriages' (Strehlow, 1999: 1). The entire subject, he explains, 'may be easier to understand if one looks upon it as a living institution' established by men and women 'who are obeying a few simple rules' (Strehlow, 1999: 1).

The two basic marriage rules Strehlow identifies, based on what he had learned from Indigenous people themselves, are exogamy and patrilocal marriage. Exogamy forbids marriage among members belonging to the same extended family. So, members of the 'Nakarakia', translated by Anna Kenny as 'our kindred people', 'cannot marry among themselves' but must marry wives from the 'Maljanuka' or from among a class translated by Kenny as 'my friends' (Kenny, 2013: 172); (Strehlow, 1999: 2). This follows an eight-class (or eight-section) system comprised of two patrimoieties within four sub-classes (or sub-sections) within each 'Nakarakia'. On the eight-class system followed among the Western Arrernte, Strehlow provides the example of one patrimoiety comprising the four sub-classes: Baŋata, Panaŋka, Paltara, and Kŋuarea, who are regarded among themselves as Nakarakia (kindred people) and another patrimoiety consisting of the Purula, Kamara, Ɖala and Mbitjana, which are classed as Maljanuka (friends) (Strehlow, 1999: 3). Following the rules of exogamy those of the same Nakarakia can marry only those from the Maljanuka, and cannot marry among themselves. Thus, Baŋata males marry Mbitjana females; their children are classed as Panaŋka following the patrilineal order. Panaŋka males marry Purula females; their children are classed as Baŋata. Paltara males marry Kamara females; their children are classed as Kŋuarea. Kŋuarea males marry Ɖala females; their children are classed as Paltara. When the system is reversed and the other patrimoiety provides the male partner, the arrangement goes as follows: Puruala males marry Panaŋka females and their children are Kamara; Kamara males marry Paltara females and their children are Purula; Ɖala males marry Kŋuarea females and

1. This previously unpublished work originally appeared as an undated mimeographed article held among Strehlow's papers at the Strehlow Research Centre. It was written after *Aranda Traditions* in 1947, since there are numerous references to this work in it but before *Songs of Central Australia* was published in 1971 as there is no mention of this book in the paper. It was most likely compiled by Strehlow in the 1960s after his series of research trips to Central Australia during the 1950s in which he had added extensive data to his genealogical records.

their children are Mbitjana; Mbitjana males marry Baŋata females and their children are Dala (Strehlow, 1999: 3).

To illustrate this, Strehlow provides a hypothetical case. He asks the reader to imagine that originally a large number of small family groups, later called *njinaŋa* sections, were each assembled around its own ceremonial totemic site (*pmara kutata*). Each *njinaŋa* section consisted of between 40 to 100 members. If these small groups had been permitted to marry among themselves, it would have been impossible over time to have avoided incestuous marriages. Strehlow observes that if such a system had been allowed, the authority of the Elders would have been 'completely wrecked' (Strehlow, 1999: 8) because fathers and sons would have been competing for the same women. This led to the arrangement that came to define Arrernte traditional marriage patterns: members of different *njinaŋa* sections marry one another and not among themselves. At the same time, cross-cousin marriages are banned but 'a scheme facilitating and regularising marriages between the children of cross-cousins' has been devised (Strehlow, 1999: 8–9). This is precisely what occurred in the example provided by Strehlow when he outlined the marriage patterns among the two intermarrying patrimoieties, each one being divided into two sections and each section into two sub-sections.

The system of patrilocal marriage, moreover, meant that children were born and grew up in the district of their fathers. When a daughter was to be married, she moved out of her home area and lived in that of her husband. The sons, by contrast, remained in the district of their fathers, but they obtained their wives from 'the same areas into which their sisters have moved' (Strehlow, 1999: 3). In this way the social structure of differing *njinaŋa* sections remained harmonious (Strehlow, 1999: 9). Strehlow emphasizes that 'the religious needs' of the communities are met by the patrilocal arrangement (Strehlow, 1999: 3). He explains: 'In each area the totemic ceremonies have to be carried out by the males of the resident patrilineal njinaŋa section; and the patrilocal marriage normally ensures that the males born in each district remain in it for the remainder of their lives' (Strehlow, 1999: 3).

Kinship and Totemic Identities among Polytotemic Communities

The marriage rules, kinship relations and patrilocal areas outlined by Strehlow established the social context for the ceremonial functions that occurred within the *njinaŋa* sections. In his contribution to the volume edited by the Berndts, Strehlow explained that the great mythical ancestor totems were made manifest through the dramatic performances at the *pmara kutata*. For this reason, 'every *pmara kutata* possessed its own ceremonial cycle' which consisted of 'a long series of secret dramatic acts in which all the supernatural personages figuring in the local sacred traditions were revealed to the men of that *njinaŋa* section in whose area the *pmara kutata* was situated' (Strehlow, 1965: 140). The importance of the ceremonial site becomes evident when it is understood that 'all these mythical figures, together with their sacred objects, their dramatic performances, their songs, and their traditions, were stated to be resting in eternal sleep at the *pmara kutata*' (Strehlow, 1965: 140). Strehlow emphasized the significance of a specific geographical location for determining the ceremonial cycle for the members of the *njinaŋa* section: 'Aranda religious rites, art, poetry, and drama, were all based on definite geographical centres; and ... complete ceremonial cycles could be performed only at their proper *pmara kutata*' (Strehlow, 1965: 140).

The ceremonial songs, the ritual performances and the sacred objects associated with the ceremonies, Strehlow explains, were 'performed and sung by *all* the men who lived in the *njinaŋa* section in which the *pmara kutata* was situated' (Strehlow, 1965: 140, emphasis in original). The 'totemic clan' is the collective name Strehlow assigned to the entire collection of men who lived in the *njinaŋa* section who called themselves by the name of the principal totemic ancestor of the great ceremonial site at which the cycle of rituals was performed, even if their personal totem was different from that of the totemic ancestor associated with the *pmara kutata*. In fact, Strehlow notes: 'Since the great *pmara kutata* were always places that could not be visited – on pain of death – by the women, there were never many persons living in the *njinaŋa* section area whose personal totem was that of their *pmara kutata* (Strehlow, 1965: 141). Individuals whose personal totem was determined by the conception site 'were believed to have become "reincarnated" from the minor totemic ancestors whose less important sites were not so carefully protected against human visits' (Strehlow, 1965: 141).

In order to make the complex relationship between the totemic ceremonial site, the *pmara kutata*, and the kinship-determined *njinaŋa* section concrete, Strehlow supplied detailed examples derived from his own field studies conducted in the early 1930s. He begins with the case of the kangaroo totem, explaining that the greatest *pmara kutata* of the kangaroo clan is the little soak of Krantji, where according to tradition, the 'kangaroo chief Krantjirinja first came into being' (Strehlow, 1947: 140). Krantjirinja is described by Strehlow as a 'true kangaroo', who during the day looked just like an animal that fed on the plant life surrounding the soak (Strehlow, 1947: 140). At night, he assumed a human shape and decorated his body. At the bottom of the soak, a shield was lying face down beneath which were all Krantjirinja's sacred objects. From beneath this shield all kangaroo ancestors emerged in the form of kangaroos that assumed human bodies and 'peopled the district surrounding the soak for a radius of several miles' (Strehlow, 1947: 140). Today, he explains, 'Krantji is ... the great *pmara kutata* of all members of the Purula-Kamara classes residing in the ancient territory of these kangaroo ancestors' (Strehlow, 1947: 140). Class is determined by the relationship of those living in a region associated with 'the legendary ancestors', what Strehlow calls 'the totemic clan' (Strehlow, 1947: 142). Their sacred objects *(tjurunga)* are all kept safely by the men 'of their own class', traditionally in a cave where they had been stored, 'some of them for centuries' (Strehlow, 1947: 142). They were taken out for use at the great ceremonial centres, the *pmara kutata*, which, in Strehlow's words, 'remained in the protection of men whose class was identical with that of the ancestors who first peopled it' (Strehlow, 1947: 142).[2]

The unifying role of the *pmara kutata* in relation to what Strehlow (1978a: 40) calls the 'membership obligations of the local *njinaŋa* section' is exemplified by members of a *njinaŋa* section Strehlow interviewed who lived at Ellery Creek (approximately 100 kilometres west of Alice Springs). Strehlow explained that those living at Ellery Creek normally belonged to 'the *Baŋata-Panaŋka njinaŋa* section area, whose main ceremonial centre was the honey-ant *pmara kutata* of Roulbmaulbma' (1978a: 40). Strehlow indicates of the 20 persons in the extended family he interviewed, three men and six women belonged to the honey-ant totem. Each of the nine honey-ant persons had their conception sites along the trail that the supernatural honey-ants had covered in mythical times, but, Strehlow emphasizes, 'not one of them had been reincarnated' from the honey-ant ancestors 'that had emerged from the Roulbmaulbma *pmara kutata*' (Strehlow, 1978a: 41). In other words, although nine of the 20 family members from Ellery Creek were honey-ants, their personal totemic ancestors were not derived from the main ceremonial centre of the honey-ant totem in which they lived. The remaining 11 members of the extended family were not of the honey-ant totem, although some, but not all, had their conception sites in the Ellery Creek area.

Strehlow contends that 'the religious obligations imposed by personal monototemism sharply divided these twenty members of an extended family group from one another' (Strehlow, 1978a: 41). What held them together was their common membership in the *Baŋata-Panaŋka njinaŋa* section and 'the allegiance claims' of the honey-ant *pmara kutata* ceremonial centre at Roulbmaulbma (Strehlow, 1978a: 42). How did this work? The Roulbmaulbma *pmara kutata* was the most important ceremonial site in the Ellery Creek area. Strehlow explains that because 'it was the mythical birthplace of hundreds of ancestral honey-ants', the ceremonies performed at Ellery Creek

---

2.   Of course, in the geographical area Strehlow described not all local totemic clans were of the kangaroo totem. Strehlow explains that a large number of local totemic clans occupied smaller areas, the centre of which was the local *pmara kutata*, which is associated with a particular totem that supplies 'a suitable name for the clan' (Strehlow 1947: 143)..

'formed part of the longest and most spectacular ceremonial cycle of the local group area' (Strehlow, 1978a: 42). As such, all males of the *Baŋata-Panaŋka njinaŋa* section were required to be present, even though not all were of the honey-ant totem and the conception sites of those that were honey-ants were not all associated with the *pmara kutata* at Roulbmaulbma.

Some of the rituals at the ceremonial sites were intended to increase the number of totemic animals or plants, but not all can be called 'increase ceremonies'. Strehlow tells us that some of them 'had as their main purpose the reverent commemoration of the supernatural personages who had left their mark behind so prominently in the Central Australian landscape' (Strehlow, 1978a: 29), but in each case 'only men who had been born into the appropriate totem, or who were patrilineally related to the totemites, could participate in the most sacred parts of the ritual' (Strehlow, 1978a: 25). This resulted in a clearly defined hierarchical order for those participating in the rituals. The males who were of the honey-ant totem of Roulbmaulbma 'ranked highest' (Strehlow, 1978a: 42). These were followed by honey-ants whose ceremonial sites were along a track linking Roulbmaulbma with another honey-ant ceremonial site at Ljaba and who were of the *Baŋata-Panaŋka njinaŋa* section. After that came the men who were associated with the *Baŋata-Panaŋka njinaŋa* section, but whose conception sites were not of the honey-ant totem. The reason these men were permitted to participate was because of their inherited honey-ant sacred objects and songs. Strehlow explains:

> All of them had the right to be present only … because of their ownership of the *jiramba* [honey-ant] verses and acts that they had inherited from deceased fathers, fathers' brothers, father's father, father's father's brothers, and older brothers (1978a: 42).

Members of the honey-ant totem at Ljaba, whose conception sites lay along a trail that the ancestral honey-ants travelled linking it to Roulbmaulbma, were permitted to attend the ceremony at Roulbmaulbma, but they were ranked below even the non-honey-ant participants who belonged to the *Baŋata-Panaŋka njinaŋa* section. As such, these outside honey-ants could only act as 'ceremonial assistants' and had to offer gifts of meat to the owners of the ceremonial site at Roulbmaulbma for the right to see the sacred acts performed. They were allowed to perform minor acts from their own honey-ant traditions, in Strehlow's words, 'partly to demonstrate the bonds linking all men in Central Australia who were regarded as reincarnations of honey-ant ancestors, and partly as a sign of their friendship and goodwill' (1978a: 43).

The ceremony concluded with a painting being drawn on the ground covering a hole into which a pole was inserted ceremonially. According to Strehlow, these 'were symbolic objects of the male and female "principles" of Roulbmaulbma itself, and because of their very nature they belonged to *all* living members who formed the [honey-ant] totemic clan of Roulbmaulbma' (Strehlow, 1978a: 42, emphasis in original). Strehlow adds that always those participating in the ceremony who were not of the honey-ant totem but belonged to the *Baŋata-Panaŋka njinaŋa* section also contributed at least one or two acts from their own totemic ancestors, such as the carpet snake, dingo and eagle (Strehlow, 1978a: 42).

The honey-ant ceremony described by Strehlow demonstrates how personal monototemism melded into the polytotemic communities comprised of extended families which included members of other totemic clans. Members of the community whose conception site was determined by the honey-ant ancestors took priority in the ceremonies, but this was maintained within clearly defined relationships to the *njinaŋa* section. This is why members of extended families in the community, even those who were not of the honey-ant totem, took precedence over other honey-ants whose ceremonial site was outside the territory. The extended family members possessed sacred objects and knowledge of songs and verses that played important roles in the acts performed by the non-honey-ant participants who were members of the *Baŋata-Panaŋka njinaŋa* section. Every man who performed during this ceremony had to reveal one of the honey-ant acts, his personal sacred object, that belonged exclusively to him. In *Aranda Traditions*, Strehlow summarized succinctly his interpretation of the relationship between the *njinaŋa* section and the *pmara kutata:*

> The local totemic clan, the patrilineal *njinaŋa* section which is associated with the greatest *pmara kutata* of a given district, is the powerful agent through whose efforts the myths, chants, ceremonies, and general traditions of each subdivision of an Aranda group are preserved carefully and accurately, in their entirety and interdependence, as they have been handed down through untold generations (Strehlow, 1947: 144).

The Complex Nature of Secret-Sacred Objects Called Tjurunga

We gain further clarification as to how members of the *njinaŋa* section were 'owners' of the tradition associated with the central *pmara kutata* by looking in more detail at Strehlow's interpretation of *tjurunga*, secret-sacred objects that played a fundamental role in totemic ceremonies. Traditional *tjurunga* are defined most commonly in anthropological literature as thin, flat items made of stone or wood that are inscribed by markings and are used in ceremonies. Early reports from explorers and ethnologists often describe *tjurunga* as thin, flat stones on which were inscribed markings that were unintelligible to the outside observers. The anthropologist A.P. Elkin (1974 [1938]: 211), writing in 1938, described them as made of 'wood or stone' and indicated that they must be used in all sacred ceremonies. More recently, Christopher

Anderson (1995: 3–4) explained that *tjurunga* are 'wooden or stone objects, often incised, each representing a particular ancestral being and site, and each associated with a particular group of people'. He adds that 'symbols in particular configurations on the objects often depict an aspect of an ancestral being's activities'.

In the opening paragraph of *Aranda Traditions*, T.G.H. Strehlow drew attention to two spellings and hence two meanings of *tjurunga*. When spelled as it commonly is as *tjurunga*, Strehlow, following Elkin and other anthropologists, explains that the word 'refers to the sacred stone or wooden objects' that play a part in the religious life of the Arrernte (Strehlow, 1947: xiii). It can also be spelled phonetically as *tjuruŋa*, which, Strehlow asserts, 'embraces not only the stone or wooden objects ... but also the ceremonies and chants and practically everything intimately associated with the sacred ceremonies' (Strehlow, 1947: xiii). He explained that in *Aranda Traditions* 'I have used the spelling *tjurunga* to denote the sacred stone (*talkara*) or wooden (*ititjaŋarierea*) objects only: the word is well known and generally accepted in scientific circles in this form and in this sense' (Strehlow, 1947: 86). He then added that 'the proper phonetic spelling *tjuruŋa* everywhere implies that the word is being used in its very wide and indeterminate native significance' (Strehlow, 1947: 86). This implies that possession of stone or wooden objects 'brings with it the ownership of the legend, chant, and the ceremonies associated with them' (Strehlow, 1947: 85).

To indicate the varied and complex meanings of the secret-sacred objects, Strehlow outlined 11 separate meanings attached to *tjurunga/tjuruŋa* by the Arrernte, each being determined by the context in which it is used. These different meanings are particularly relevant to understanding how the various uses, applications and subtle meanings associated with the objects help overcome the potentially disruptive social effects of personal totemism in polytotemic communities.

The meanings given to the secret-sacred objects by Strehlow are as follows:

1. Sacred ceremonies
2. Stone sacred objects
3. Wooden sacred objects
4. Large bull-roarer
5. Small bull-roarer
6. Sacred ground-painting
7. Ceremonial pole
8. Ceremonial head-gear commonly used in Northern Arrernte ceremonies
9. Ceremonial head-gear commonly used in Western and Southern Arrernte ceremonies
10. Sacred chants
11. Sacred earth-mound (Strehlow, 1947: 86).

Strehlow concluded the list by emphasizing that the objects are associated with deeper meanings and sacred traditions: they denote 'the sacred stone or wooden objects possessed by private or group-owners together with the legends, chants, and ceremonies associated with them' (Strehlow, 1947: 86). He added by way of explanation that there is no specialized Arrernte word for myth or legend; the word in Arrernte simply means 'to tell a story' (Strehlow, 1947: 86). Nonetheless, we see from Strehlow's detailed account that as material objects, *tjurunga*, particularly when interpreted in light of the phonetic spelling *tjuruŋa*, connected the people to the stories of the times of the beginning, symbolized the power and authority of tradition, and also brought the past into the present through the symbols engraved on them and by their use in ceremonial functions.

With this expanded understanding of the meaning of secret-sacred objects, we are in a position to clarify what Strehlow meant in his discussion of personal monototemism in a polytotemic community. One has to do with the conception site. An explanation as to how a woman became pregnant by the totemic ancestor relates that the ancestor 'hurled a small bull-roarer at her hips and thus caused the acute pains which suddenly came upon her' (Strehlow, 1947: 87). The small bull-roarer literally is a sacred object. Another explanation of how a woman became pregnant is that on its wanderings, the totemic ancestor lost one of his sacred objects, such as a small bull-roarer or what Strehlow calls 'a minor article of personal apparel', such as arm bands worn during ceremonies, or even 'a tuft of down from the ceremonial patterns with which his body was decorated' (Strehlow, 1947: 87–88). These sacred objects disappeared into the ground and are invisible, but they can penetrate the woman with the 'life-giving properties' of the totemic ancestor ((Strehlow, 1947: 88). Strehlow then underscores the significance of the sacred objects and their connection to the eternal supernatural ancestor for the personal identity of the individual:

> The actual birthplace of the child is of no account, and consequently is never remembered in later life; the true home of every man is the site where he once lived and moved without fetters in a more glorious age than the present, at a time when the world had first become awakened out of eternal sleep in the thick, silent darkness that had encompassed the earth ever from the beginning of time (Strehlow, 1947: 91).

A second important use of secret-sacred objects relates to the initiation ceremonies of boys. Strehlow describes in great detail the stages in the initiation, including the enormous pain endured during circumcision and a few months later during the rite of subincision. Strehlow notes that after the second physical operation, the initiate has 'learned to obey the commands of the old men implicitly' (Strehlow, 1947: 99). What follows is the *iŋkura* festival, which takes place on a ground Strehlow describes as 'the real initiation centre of any group' and where 'the novices … are instructed by their elders in the ceremonies and chants and legends of their own clan' (Strehlow, 1947: 100). The relationship between the initiates and the totemic ceremonial centre (the *pmara kutata*) and the collective ownership of secret-sacred objects and the sacred songs and traditions associated with them is complex, but can be shown primarily to relate to kinship as opposed to the conception site of the individual.[3]

To illustrate this, Strehlow cites an interview he had with the Ilbalintja ceremonial chief, in northern Arrernte country. This is the site of what the chief called 'the greatest bandicoot totemic centre' (Strehlow, 1947: 101). He claimed that it attracted men from all over the region. All the sacred objects and their associated meanings in the widest sense of the term, the chief explained, exist 'at the bottom of the soak of Ilbalintja' (Strehlow, 1947: 101). The chief then told Strehlow that 'if we were given six months in which to hold our sacred ceremonies, we should be unable to perform them all in that time' (Strehlow, 1947: 101). Similar totemic sites existed for other ancestors, as we have seen for example, among the honey-ants at Roulbmaulbma. It was believed that the sacred objects, songs and verses 'from all parts of the group territory and from neighbouring sections … have been massed together and hoarded, ever since the mythical times when the ancestors roamed about on this earth' (Strehlow, 1947: 101).

The initiation ceremony involved in the *iŋkura* festival at Ilbalintja, the great bandicoot centre, did not stipulate that every initiate must belong to the bandicoot totem. Many novices would have been associated with 'minor' totemic centres, but the important factor that connects all the young men participating in the festival is determined by kinship relations. Strehlow explains: 'Their fathers or grandfathers or brothers, as the case may be, have belonged to the bandicoot totem of Ilbalintja; and hence all these youths undergo the final initiation rites on the main *iŋkura* ground of their own "totemic clan"' where the greatest 'treasure grove' of the sacred objects belonging to their extended family section is located (Strehlow, 1947: 102). This explains the hierarchical ordering of the ceremonies Strehlow described in his discussion of personal monototemism in a polytotemic community, which gave priority to kinship-related groups who were the collective owners of the sacred objects associated with any great ceremonial site (*pmara kutata*). This also explains why at the conclusion of the ceremony, stone or wooden sacred objects were assembled at the edge of the ceremonial ground symbolizing all the men, living and dead, of the clan who were the traditional owners of the sacred chants, songs and stories.

---

3.   Initiation ceremonies will be described in greater detail in Chapter 5.

The Symbolism Associated with the Transmission
of Tradition through the Generations

In *Central Australian Religion*, Strehlow (1978a) concluded his discussion of personal monototemism in a polytotemic community by graphically describing the links between the present generation to past generations, from whom those currently living received instruction in the songs, chants, stories, ceremonies and meanings attached to the sacred wood and stone objects that they possessed. The present generation of Elders was responsible for passing on the same detailed knowledge to the young men who would carry on the tradition to their sons and so on. The resulting attention to detail in the performance of rituals and in the reciting of the songs and chants served to meld the generations together, in one sense, to erase time altogether. Strehlow (1978a: 43–44) put it in poetic language: 'Every full-scale ceremonial festival was, in fact, regarded as an occasion when Time and Eternity became one, when the border line dividing visible human beings and invisible totemic ancestors became temporarily obliterated'. In this light, the generations that had preceded the current members of living communities, as reincarnations of the original, founding totemic ancestors, came to life again.

The transmission of the authoritative tradition operated fundamentally within the *njinaŋa* section, the kinship determined extended family, and in this way linked, fathers, brothers, father's fathers, father's father's fathers and indeed the entire clan, in a chain secured by the memory of the sacred traditions that had been passed on from generation to generation. This cross-generational chain was symbolized by the sacred objects maintained in the storehouses and which were retrieved and assembled as if the objects themselves were actual participants in the ceremonies performed. Strehlow (1978a: 44) explains that these sacred objects 'represented "the other bodies" not only of all men and women who were still living in the *njinaŋa section* area, but also those who had died'. The participation of those who had died in the present-day ceremonies not only validated that they were being performed correctly but underscored the overwhelming authority with which the tradition had been transmitted. Their participation also encouraged the present generation to repeat exactly the ceremonies, songs, chants and stories they had inherited from those who had died and who were watching the proceedings. This would ensure that knowledge of the traditions would persist into the next generation and on into eternity, as the distinctions between 'Time and Eternity' were collapsed in the ritual present.

According to the ancient stories, what Strehlow (1947: 153) calls the 'wandering hordes of legendary ancestors' covered large tracts of territory creating lines that linked local totemic centres to each other. The myths about the activities of the ancient totemic ancestors and their travels have been passed down through the generations with 'painstaking accuracy' (1947: 159). The owners of specific myths are confirmed by their possession of the sacred objects that are stored in 'local sacred caves'. The actual words of the stories are not memorized, according to Strehlow, but every detail mentioned in the stories 'is based on ceremonies and chants which are rehearsed assiduously year after year under the guidance of the oldest men' (1947: 159). The myth, Strehlow explains, 'is the sum total of the many and varied explanations given by the old leaders of a group to the younger men concerning the traditional chant, the sacred ceremonies, and the physical features of the landscape associated with the life story of any given totemic ancestor who is revered by the group' (1947: 159). The permanence of the myth is reflected in the landscape: 'rocks and hills and mountains do not change, and even trees outlive many generations' (1947: 159)

Those members of a totemic clan who are charged with guarding and caring for the ceremonial site (*pmara kutata*) dedicated to the totemic ancestor are responsible not only for the care of the site but also for the sacred objects that are stored in nearby caves. Strehlow emphasizes once again that 'it is the duty of the ruling elders of the clan to inculcate the chants, ceremonies, and myths firmly and accurately into the memories of younger men' (1947: 159). Authority is vested in the older men who possess the knowledge to settle any disputes that might arise among the younger men 'in regard to religious matters' (1947: 159). Strehlow then reverts back to a discussion of the *njinaŋa* section, which he asserts, maintains its own traditions, chants, songs and sacred objects. There are times, of course, because of shared totemic myths, that the sacred stories, chants and verses of one *njinaŋa* section may cross over with members of another section. In such cases, Strehlow explains, 'both sections become responsible for their safe-keeping' (1947: 160).

Strehlow has gone to such pains to stress the ways in which the myths, legends, stories, chants, inscriptions on sacred objects and their associated meanings are preserved and transmitted from one generation to another to support his argument that 'there is hardly a possibility of local sacred traditions undergoing a change even in respect of minor details during centuries of oral tradition' (1947: 160). He describes the religious life of the Arrernte as intimately connected to 'the closely-meshed network of totemic sites which dot every portion of the landscape' and to 'the elaborate ceremonies associated with all of these centres' (1947: 160). The chants and songs repeated at these centres were composed with intricate detail and contain 'a variety of clever metres' (1947: 160). These religious expressions, Strehlow concludes, reflect 'the amazing heritage of an age-old native culture of no mean order' (1947: 160).

Women in the Ceremonial Tradition

We have seen that, according to Strehlow, women were strictly excluded from participation in the sacred ceremonies, and even the knowledge of the meanings of the sacred objects associated with their conception sites was denied to them. Strehlow's estimate of the role of women in Arrernte religious life gradually changed as he conducted more research in the central desert region between 1932 and 1960, although by the mid-1960s he admitted that 'the full extent of the knowledge that the Central Australian women once possessed of the sacred lore of their community' will never be known (Strehlow, 1978a: 38). Strehlow suggests that what he initially described as almost total ignorance by the women of the sacred traditions may not have been so complete as he originally thought. An examination of Strehlow's rather brief accounts of the place of women in the mythic and ceremonial traditions may serve to balance what appears to be an entirely uneven distribution of sacred privilege.

In *Aranda Traditions*, Strehlow (1947: 93) indicated that 'the women of the Aranda tribe must remain uninitiated and pass their days in comparative ignorance' because 'no sacred myth ever reaches their ears'. In the social structure, he explains, a woman, due to her particular conception site, may be 'entitled to a position of supreme authority in her own community' and she may own 'the most sacred' of the secret-sacred objects, but 'all knowledge of them is carefully hidden away from her' (1947: 93). Strehlow provides an example of precisely how this operated by citing the case of a woman belonging to Ljaba, what he calls 'the greatest honey-ant centre in Aranda territory' (1947: 93). He says that 'in theory' this woman was 'one of the ceremonial chiefs' of this great totemic centre, and the sacred objects that represented her body were 'held in deep and affectionate respect by the guardians of the sacred store-house' (1947: 93). At the honey-ant rituals held at Ljaba, this woman was honoured by 'almost all Aranda groups both near and far' in 'ceremony after ceremony' (1947: 93). Her name is still mentioned with reverence and respect by the most senior of the Elders at Ljaba. The woman herself, however, never knew the stories, songs and ceremonies held in her honour. These secrets were maintained by the men who performed her songs and guarded her sacred objects.

This case illustrates the anomalous relationship between women and men not only in the ceremonial aspects of Arrernte life, but also in the hierarchical ordering of the social structure. Strehlow calls this anomaly a 'curious paradox' whereby a sacred object representing the body of a woman is 'reverently tended by the men of her totemic clan' whereas the woman herself 'is treated without any respect or consideration' (1947: 94). This paradox is made even more evident when one considers that female ancestors are given high regard in the myths about them in which they are depicted as 'awe-inspiring figures, who enjoyed unlimited freedom of decision and action' (1947: 94). In the mythology, these female ancestors were sometimes described as more powerful than male ancestors instilling fear in her male counterparts. These ancient female ancestors helped form the landscape, they established their own sacred objects and they instituted ceremonies in which their songs were embedded. Today, Strehlow observes, the songs associated with the myths about these female ancestors are still sung, but by the men in whose care the sacred objects of the women are entrusted. These men 'are the fathers or brothers of the women whose sex precludes them from sharing in the religious life of the community' (1947: 94). This ceremonial exclusion extends to how women are treated generally in traditional Arrernte society: 'Aranda men look down upon their own women with a certain measure of pitying contempt' (1947: 94). In an interview Strehlow conducted with a male Elder, presumably from Ljaba, Strehlow quotes the Elder as describing women as 'fallen from the estate of our great feminine ancestors', to which he adds the comment: 'Why, we do not know' (1947: 94).

In *Central Australian Religion*, Strehlow (1978a) qualified his description of the rigid divisions between the ceremonial roles of men and women in Arrernte religious life, although he continued to maintain that women were 'less aware' of their own songs and the 'exact nature' of their personal sacred objects. He repeats that they could not sing their own verses; 'only their fathers and brothers could do this service for them' (Strehlow, 1978a: 38). Nonetheless, he admitted in a way he did not do in *Aranda Traditions* (1947) that 'women know their totems and their conception sites' and they even are permitted to see 'from a distance' the decorated men who appear to them at the conclusion of the great ceremonies (Strehlow, 1978a: 38). This fact leads Strehlow to conclude that all the older women at least 'were well aware of many of the sacred totemic patterns' (Strehlow, 1978a: 38). He adds that 'all the older women that I have known obviously had much more knowledge of sacred matters than their husbands and male relatives were prepared to admit' (Strehlow, 1978a: 38). Part of the knowledge women maintained included what Strehlow calls 'secret charms' that they did not share with the men (Strehlow, 1978a: 38). He anticipated this fact in *Aranda Traditions*, when in a footnote he comments, 'certain chant verses … are the exclusive property of native women, and of which men are kept in ignorance', but he did not expand on this assertion (Strehlow, 1947: 93fn). He merely observed that not enough research has been done on the songs of the Arrernte women, which he calls a 'fascinating treasure of native folk-lore' (Strehlow, 1947: 93fn).

Clearly, then, women had a higher position in traditional Arrernte society than Strehlow first realized. The relationship between women and their sons was of particular importance in transmitting sacred knowledge.

Although the sons could not inherit sacred objects, songs, myths and chants from their mothers as they could from their fathers, they were permitted to attend the totemic ceremonies of their mother's totem as 'important ceremonial assistants' (Strehlow, 1978a: 38). We have seen that in the rituals conducted at totemic ceremonial sites, members of the same totem that were not from the *njinaŋa* section were permitted to attend as ceremonial assistants. In this case, this totemic allegiance of the son's mothers also served as a legitimate right of entrance for the sons into the ceremonies of their mother's totem. Further evidence that women held a higher place in society than Strehlow initially acknowledged is found in his description of burial ceremonies. A man was buried usually in an upright sitting position with 'his face turned toward the conception site of his mother', which became, in Strehlow's words, his 'eternal home' (Strehlow, 1978a: 39).

Although he continued to stress the importance of the patrilineal kinship system among Arrernte peoples, we see that Strehlow modified his earlier description of women as being religiously unimportant and ignorant of the sacred traditions. He concludes his section on 'women and the sacred' in *Central Australian Religion* (1978a) by noting that both 'men and women' were represented in 'the work of supernatural beings who had become reincarnated in their own persons'. Whereas, as we have seen in *Aranda Traditions*, he described the status of women as being regarded by the men with 'pitying contempt' (Strehlow, 1947: 94), by the time he had completed his contribution to the Jensen Festschrift in 1964, re-printed in 1978 as *Central Australian Religion*, he had reached a far different conclusion: 'In such a community the life of *every* person was of importance and value' (Strehlow, 1978a: 39, emphasis added).

Conclusion

In this chapter, we have seen how in great detail Strehlow outlined a complex social and cultural arrangement he dubbed 'personal monototemism in a polytotemic community'. This system demonstrates that, although the personal totemic ancestor system is not associated with one lineage group, it is closely woven into a structure that centres on lineage, as all members of the extended family are patrilineally related to the principal ceremonial centre. This relationship includes ownership of the songs, chants, verses and sacred objects that have existed mystically from eternity beneath the earth at the sacred ceremonial site. The preference accorded to the patrilineal totemic clan affirms the structural superiority of localized, kinship relations over extended regional associations and non-kinship identities. This fact is demonstrated in ritual performances in which those who share the same totemic ancestor but who are not of the same locality nor of the extended family fall lowest in the hierarchical ordering at the sacred ceremonies. Even those

who do not share the totemic ancestor for whom the ritual is being conducted but belong to the extended family living in the location of the ceremonial centre rank higher than those of the totemic ancestor living outside
the location and who are not part of the extended family. Moreover, those
who are of the extended family but whose conception sites lie outside the
location of the ceremonial centre but still live within the region of the ceremonial centre occupy a higher place in the rituals than those whose conception sites might be similar but who are not of the extended family. This
demonstrates the priority of kinship over the personal totemic ancestor and
suggests that location, that is, living in a place associated with the ceremonial centre and of the same extended family, is paramount in determining
societal structures. This conclusion was confirmed by Strehlow (1965: 132)
when he declared, 'the kin-group class system constituted the firm foundation for the entire social organization and the whole cultural complex of
religion, poetry, drama, and art in the Aranda speaking area'.

5

Songs of Central Australia

In the previous two chapters, I discussed T.G.H. Strehlow's descriptions of Arrernte myths of creation and how these related to the social organization of localized, kinship groups in Central Australia. We saw the fundamental importance to traditional Arrernte religion of the totemic ancestors and how these formed the basis for the institution supporting the socio-religious order Strehlow termed 'personal monototemism in a polytotemic community'. Although these chapters provided important insights into the traditional life of Arrernte peoples, they remain incomplete without an in-depth study of the rituals that emerged from the myths and that re-enforced the structure of society. In other words, to see religion in practice, as it occurs in lived experience, requires a thorough study of the rituals through which religious beliefs come to life and become real to the participants.

This approach to the study of Arrernte religion is derived from the phenomenological method in the study of religion, which asserts that rituals, as a typological classification, occupy a central place in the religious life of believing communities (Cox, 2010: 90–103). The phenomenological method encourages students of religion, through careful and detailed descriptions of observed rituals, to enter empathetically into the experience of religious adherents (Cox, 2010: 52–55). Through rituals, religious communities approach a space and time that is clearly distinguished from ordinary space and time because it is in ritual space and time that religious communities come into direct contact with the sacred personages that are told about in the myths. In the case of the Arrernte of Central Australia, the totemic ancestors are brought to life as the people re-enact the creative travels of these primordial eternal beings. They repeat the ceremonies as they were originally instituted by the totemic ancestors and they chant the songs and verses that first came from the mouths of these supernatural figures who emerged from beneath the earth's surface at the beginning of time.

It is precisely from the phenomenological contention that students of religion must gain access to the ritual life of believing communities if genuine understanding of their religion is to be achieved that the most critical problem for students of Arrernte religion arises: the most important rituals are shrouded in absolute secrecy and are open only to initiated men. Regulations governing proper ritual performances, including those permitted to attend and the assigned roles of those involved in the ceremonies, were strictly enforced. Violations of the rigid rules that dictated ceremonial behaviour, at the most sacred events, could result in death for those guilty of breaking the codes of ritual conduct. Outsiders, women and uninitiated males were absolutely forbidden from even viewing the ceremonial ground, and they were prohibited from seeing the symbols that adorn the costumes and bodies of the ritual performers.[1] The sacred songs, which were chanted during the rituals, because they were believed to have been uttered originally by the totemic ancestors themselves, were also maintained with utmost secrecy. Writing in 1969, Strehlow acknowledged the problem for scholars caused by the strict rules of secrecy attached to knowledge of Arrernte ceremonies: 'One of the most frustrating characteristics of Aboriginal religion is the veil of deep secrecy behind which the most important parts of the sacred beliefs and ritual have always been hidden to guard them from uninitiated persons and from strangers' (Strehlow, 1969: 11).

Although Strehlow was not initiated formally into any Arrernte group, he was regarded by numerous Arrernte communities as an insider, one who could be entrusted with knowledge of the sacred songs and one who was permitted to view the secret rituals – even to film and record them. He was also charged with the care of some secret-sacred objects, the *tjurunga*, on which secret symbols were engraved or with which sacred chants were associated, and in some cases were even believed to be the totemic ancestor himself. Nonetheless, some of Strehlow's earlier publications contained photographs that could be considered violations of the information that was entrusted to him, and some of his descriptions of Arrernte religious life approached the boundary separating what would be considered by Indigenous informants as acceptable for general dissemination and that which must remain in the possession of initiated males.

Strehlow's book, *Songs of Central Australia*, published in 1971, which A.P. Elkin (1975: 245) called his '*magnum opus*', contains the most sensitive material derived from Strehlow's extensive research in Central Australia. Although there are no photographs in the book, Strehlow transcribes the secret-sacred songs chanted during high totemic festivals in the Arrernte language, beneath which he offers English translations. He also includes

1.   Although we saw in the previous chapter that towards the conclusion of *Central Australian Religion* Strehlow qualified this absolute decree with respect to women, even suggesting that some women were permitted to view the ceremonial ground from a distance, the general description of exclusive rights to knowledge of the most sacred ceremonies as restricted to initiated men under the leadership of senior Elders still applied when Strehlow began his research in 1932.

notes he made in his diaries alongside some of the songs he recorded. In addition, he provides detailed descriptions of rituals he observed and which he recorded on tape, some of which he also filmed. Arguably, by making the sacred songs available to the general public, Strehlow could be accused of transgressing the trust his informants placed in him to preserve solely for later Arrernte generations traditional knowledge that was rapidly disappearing.

In Strehlow's defence, I would argue that his primary aim was to provide general knowledge of Arrernte world views and social organization, which he intended would encourage understanding of Arrernte religion among a wide range of outside audiences, both in Australia and internationally. He also believed that his writings would lead to an informed appreciation of the ways of life as traditionally practised among Indigenous groups in Central Australia, and in the process, promote tolerance and improve relations between Indigenous and non-Indigenous Australians. If I am correct that understanding any religion can only be attained by a close study of the rituals through which the foundational myths are brought to life, Strehlow was providing a fundamental service to Indigenous people by fostering an informed but compassionate understanding among his readers of traditions that had been regarded in earlier literature as evidence of a stone-age mentality that was doomed to die out, along with the people who practised the rituals and the traditions that sustained them.

It is for this reason that I have chosen to discuss in this chapter Strehlow's accounts of Arrernte ceremonial life, including some of the songs associated with the most sacred ceremonies. As I explained in the Preface to this book, I have used only Strehlow's English translations, omitting the actual sacred words in Arrernte, and I have avoided including some potentially offensive references that I consider tangential to the main content of Strehlow's material. In the end, I have carefully selected for analysis only those accounts of Arrernte songs and ceremonies that, true to the phenomenological method, offer detailed, but fair, descriptions of rituals and songs that are necessary for my attempt to provide, through Strehlow's eyes, empathetic interpretations of traditional Arrernte religious beliefs and practices.

Songs of Central Australia: Background

Strehlow began collecting material for *Songs of Central Australia* during his first research trip to Central Australia in 1932. He notes in the Introduction to the book that he continued to compile records of the songs and ceremonies of the region on numerous research journeys until 1955. He adds that some additional important information was acquired in 1958 and 1960. In total, he 'gathered four thousand two hundred and seventy aboriginal song verses' over the period of his research (Strehlow, 1971a: xiv).

The vast majority of the songs he recorded came from Western, Northern and Southern Arrernte regions, but some verses also were collected from Luritja, Unmatjera and Alyawarre peoples (Strehlow, 1971a: xiv). Writing in 1962, nine years before its publication, Strehlow (1962: 7) explained that *Songs of Central Australia* 'was intended to be a reference book for use during my later translation of all the aboriginal songs which I had collected in the various Aranda dialects'.

In the Introduction to *Songs of Central Australia*, Strehlow emphasized the close connection between the songs he recorded and the ceremonial sites in which they were used in rituals. By 'songs', Strehlow was referring to what he called 'the traditional native poems of Central Australia which are intoned according to traditional rhythmic measures' (Strehlow, 1971: xiii). He explained that each poem 'is associated with a definite ceremonial centre and with a mythical supernatural being or mythical group of ancestors' (Strehlow, 1971: xiii). He added that each song denotes 'the complete set of the verses associated with any single mythical being or group of local totemic ancestors' (Strehlow, 1971: xiii). When we examine the songs, therefore, it is important to note that they would not be understood by those who recited the verses simply as poetry or as telling part of a larger story, but would always be chanted at a sacred site dedicated to a particular totemic ancestor and in the context of a specific ceremonial event. Studying the songs as recorded by Strehlow in this way is akin to participating in a ritual.

Songs of Central Australia, which extends to nearly 800 pages, including the Introduction, Index and Glossary, is divided into four parts. The first two parts are devoted to an analysis of the poetic rhythm, musical measures, language and verse structure of the songs. Part three, which focuses on the subject matter and themes of the songs is most relevant to this chapter, since Strehlow discusses songs performed during rituals including increase ceremonies, rituals held to remember and honour the totemic ancestors, songs relating to initiation rites, and songs celebrating the *pmara kutata*, which, as we saw in the last chapter, Strehlow identified as the most important ceremonial site for rituals honouring the totemic ancestors.

Part Four of the book offers Strehlow's final summary in which he includes songs to specific totemic ancestors including the Dingo, Honey Ant and Native Cat, among others.

It is important to note that Strehlow did not intend *Songs of Central Australia* to be evaluated as a major contribution to the field of anthropology. He admitted that Part Three of the book 'may not always give descriptions of ceremonies in all the detail that cultural and social anthropologists may desire' but he contended that they are 'sufficiently detailed to enable all readers to visualize under what conditions and upon what occasions these songs used to be sung' (Strehlow, 1971: xvi–xvii). As a trained classicist and linguist, Strehlow's approach at times reads like a comparative study of Aboriginal poetry and Western folklore. Many pages are devoted to citing from classical Greek or Roman stories and from the literature as it has been preserved from old Norse or Celtic sources. From the perspective of the strict social sciences, these references could be regarded as irrelevant at best, but in the worst light could be seen as creating false and misleading comparisons. He explains in the Introduction that he has attempted to produce a multi-disciplinary study analysing the songs as 'musical compositions, as literary productions, and as traditional, religious, ceremonial and social documents' (Strehlow, 1971: xv). Strehlow defended his frequent references to classical and old European literature by arguing that they foster understanding by creating a 'sympathetic attitude in the mind of the white reader towards aboriginal verse and towards the aboriginal world of ideas' (Strehlow, 1971: xl). He explains that when non-Indigenous readers encounter what they might regard as 'crude' practices or even cruel behaviour embedded in Aboriginal songs, they need to be reminded that their own ancient stories contain quite similar ideas.

In the remainder of this chapter, I consider three primary types of rituals as Strehlow described them in *Songs of Central Australia* and other sources. I illustrate these types of rituals by analysing how the songs Strehlow recorded are used in the ceremonies and cross-reference my interpretation of the rituals with Strehlow's own descriptions, most of which are based on accounts of ceremonies he personally witnessed. The types of rituals I will consider follow Strehlow's own major classifications as he presented them in *Songs of Central Australia*. These include initiation rites, increase ceremonies, and ceremonies to commemorate the totemic ancestors. He described other ritual activities, such as those dealing with what he called magic and sorcery, fertility rites, women's secret rites and love-magic ceremonies, but I consider these less essential for understanding the core of Arrernte religion and thus will not discuss these classifications.

Initiation Rituals

In his contribution to *Historia Religionum*, edited by C.J. Bleeker and Geo Widengren (1971b: 609–28), Strehlow provided a broad overview of Aboriginal rites of initiation. He explained that such rituals were conducted for all males shortly after they reached puberty, usually between the ages of 14 and 16. He noted that in Central Australia, circumcision and subincision were widely practised. The rituals took place at specially designated locations and followed months of preparation and involved intricately planned stages leading to the young men becoming fully initiated males. Strehlow (1971b: 618) asserts that the social function of initiation rituals was to prepare 'youths for admission to full social status as men' and that their religious aim was to introduce them 'into full communion with that spiritual world which was open to them by reason of their reincarnation from the supernatural beings'.

In *Aranda Traditions*, Strehlow (1947: 96–112) provided meticulous accounts of initiation rites as they were practised in Western, Northern and Southern Arrernte regions. His descriptions are precise and provide exhaustive details of the elaborate procedures that needed to be followed exactly as prescribed by tradition. I will provide a summary of Strehlow's account of the Northern Arrernte initiation rituals, which he witnessed and recorded. His own interpretations are based in part on interviews he conducted with leading Elders who were principal actors in the ceremonies. Following my summary of Strehlow's in-depth descriptions of Northern Arrernte initiation rites and based on his accounts recorded in *Songs of Central Australia*, I will discuss the verses performed during the physical operations conducted on the initiates and those chanted during the period when the novices were in a liminal state, neither still boys nor yet men.

Among the Northern Arrernte, the first stages of initiation took place at a special location called the '*pulla*' ground (Strehlow, 1947: 96). It is here that the ordeals of circumcision and sub-incision were endured by the initiates. Prior to being circumcised, the initiate was permitted to witness some ceremonies of his totemic clan, which had been concealed from him during his childhood years. He then was circumcised, following which he was awarded a 'large bull-roarer' and assumed the title of *rukuta*. As a *rukuta*, the young man lived in hiding for several weeks carrying his large bull-roarer with him. He was overseen by his 'class-brother' or 'class-cousin' (Strehlow, 1947: 97). As he moved from place to place, he would swing his bull-roarer at regular intervals to warn any women or children that he was in their vicinity, since he must not be seen by any uninitiated males or by women. During this period, the *rukuta* must commit to memory a series of easily learned chants which are exclusively his own and, Strehlow explains, these 'must not be used by fully initiated men' (Strehlow, 1947: 98). During their period as a *rukuta*, the initiates were taught 'to respect and even to fear the supreme power wielded by the old men of their clan' (Strehlow, 1947: 99).

A few months after becoming a *rukuta*, the initiate underwent the sub-incision operation, following which he was permitted to observe further ceremonies that previously he had been forbidden from witnessing. The physical pain of the circumcision and sub-incision procedures, according to Strehlow, had instructed the novice 'to obey the commands of the old men implicitly' (Strehlow, 1947: 99). He was now ready to proceed to the next stage of initiation by participating in the *iŋkura* festival, which was the primary initiation ritual for which the novice had been preparing by learning special songs and chants. By the time he was ready for the *iŋkura* festival, the young man would have surrendered his large bull-roarer, which Strehlow calls 'the particular *tjurunga* designed for use of *rukuta*' (Strehlow, 1947: 100), and now he entered the next stage in the initiation process by assuming the title of *iliara*.

The *iŋkura* festival took place on the *iŋkura* ground, a place where, Strehlow explains, 'novices who have passed all stages of their physical manhood rites are instructed by their elders in the ceremonies and chants and legends of their own clan' (Strehlow, 1947: 100). The *iŋkura* ground was located near the major totemic ceremonial site, the *pmara kutata*, for the region. Strehlow provides the example of the totemic centre at Ilbalintja among the Northern Arrernte, whose major totemic ancestor is the bandicoot. In an interview with a ceremonial Elder, Strehlow was told that 'Ilbalintja was the greatest bandicoot totemic centre amongst the Aranda people' and that 'all their tjurunga and all their ceremonies have been left behind, at the bottom of the soak of Ilbalintja' (Strehlow, 1947: 101). At the Ilbalintja *iŋkura* ground, the people believed that the *tjurunga* had been stored from the beginning of time when the totemic ancestors moved around on the surface of the earth.

When plans for the *iŋkura* festival at Ilbalintja had been completed, invitations were extended to all other bandicoot centres, which, according to Strehlow, were 'solemnly accepted' (Strehlow, 1947: 102). After a meeting of the 'old ceremonial chiefs of the combined clans', the ground was prepared by scraping away the surface soil creating a shallow depression which was 'carefully levelled and smoothed down' (Strehlow, 1947: 102–103). This depression was called the *rala ŋkura*. During the months that followed, the *rala ŋkura* provided the location where rituals were to be performed and the place where the *iliara* slept. The soil that had been dug out to form the depression was placed in the centre of the *rala ŋkura* creating a 'long narrow mound called the *rala parra*' (Strehlow, 1947: 103). The ashes from the fire that burned during the night to keep the *iliara* warm while they slept, each morning were placed on top of the *rala parra* making the mound grow higher with each addition. Strehlow explains that 'the *rala parra* was regarded as the greatest and most sacred of all the *tjuruŋa* on the *iŋkura* ground' (Strehlow, 1947: 103).

At the beginning of the festival, each initiate had been given a small bull-roarer on which symbols of his own personal totem had been carved. After receiving their bull-roarers, the *iliara* would swing them almost constantly so that 'from morning till evening, and for the greater part of the night, the sound of the bull-roarers shrills out over the *iŋkura* ground' (Strehlow, 1947: 103). A principal ritual followed involving decorating the bodies of initiated male dancers with blood obtained from their arms and white down which was separated by lines of black charcoal. As the bodies of the ritual performers were decorated, sacred songs were intoned. They then assumed their places at the edge of the *rala ŋkura* and to the magnified sound of the small bull-roarers being swung in unison, the leader of the ceremony uttered 'a long, vibrating call known as *raiaŋkintja*', which prompted the *iliara* to rush forward swinging their bull-roarers (Strehlow, 1947: 104). As they did this, they joined in what Strehlow describes as a 'shuffling dance' and then was heard the loud shout '*wa! wa! wa!*' (Strehlow, 1947: 104). In response to this, the dancing performers, whose bodies had been decorated with blood, white down and black charcoal moved their bodies, described by Strehlow as 'a violent quiver', forcing the white down to fly off their bodies 'in all directions' (Strehlow, 1947: 104).

It is at this point that the most important songs were chanted by the old men who were seated around the *iŋkura* ground. Strehlow explains that these old men 'chant the traditional verses relating to the original episode in the life of the ancestor which is being re-enacted in the ceremony' (Strehlow, 1947: 104). After the dancing continued for a short while, the performers concluded their part in the ceremony and a principal Elder then addressed the *iliara*. Strehlow adds that this Elder was 'the owner of the ceremony they have seen' (Strehlow, 1947: 104). During his comments to the initiates, he explained the meaning of the ritual they had just witnessed and also referred to the meaning of the songs that have been chanted. At this point, the young men were told that they must go out hunting for the remainder of the day. While they were away, the Elders began preparations for what Strehlow calls 'a more important ceremony than the earlier one that the *iliara* were allowed to witness' (Strehlow, 1947: 104–105). The Elders were assisted by young newly initiated men who participated in the ritual as performers. They also were told that they would be expected to donate their blood to be used in the ceremony. The old men then carefully instructed the recently initiated men in the songs and sacred verses to be chanted during the ritual. This took several hours during which time the Elders sang continuously to the young men, in Strehlow's words, to 'fix the traditional chanted forms of the sacred verses indelibly in their minds' (Strehlow, 1947: 105).

The *iliara* returned from their hunting much later in the day, exhausted and hungry. The animals they killed during the hunt were offered to the Elders at the appropriate signal from the ceremonial chiefs. The initiates ran forward, placed the game in front of the Elders and then joined in a ceremonial dance. The meat that the initiates had presented to the Elders was then cooked, but the *iliara* were served last. Later, as darkness was falling, further rituals took place, normally featuring a high pole, called a *tnatantja* pole, around which the men walked slowly while keeping their hands on the pole. The ceremonies around the pole resumed early the next morning, but the novices were awakened several times during the night to take part in what Strehlow calls 'a peculiar primitive dance' (Strehlow, 1947: 106).

This involved movements around the mound in the middle of the ceremonial ground, with their hands held behind their backs and their bodies bent low in the direction of the mound. Strehlow describes the scene: 'They utter a series of loud, harsh trills, *hrr / hrr / hrr* interrupted from time to time by a fierce *wa*! which is yelled at the *rala parra*' (Strehlow, 1947: 106–107). While they were doing this, some men watching them joined in 'riotous jesting and boisterous laughing' intended to test the stamina of the initiates and to instruct them in obedience to the Elders (Strehlow, 1947: 107). Following these interludes, the initiates were allowed to rest, but just for brief periods. These ceremonies persisted for many days and nights with the *iliara* continuing their hunting tasks during the day. Strehlow explains that 'the young *iliara*, who are allowed but little rest and have to do all the hunting, naturally get the smallest share of the food supplies' (Strehlow, 1947: 107–108).

During the many months of the initiation rites, the *iliara* learned the songs and chants of their major totemic ancestors. They were required to recite the songs, but without fully understanding their meaning, since the Elders did not explain all at once the stories that were connected to the songs. Of particular importance were the chants related to the sacred *tjurunga*, which the *iliara* were required to commit to memory without error and repeat exactly as they had been transmitted to them by the Elders. Finally, the last day of the long initiation process arrived with the sound of bull-roarers awakening everyone on the *iŋkura* ground just after midnight. Strehlow describes the scene as one of 'expectation and suppressed excitement' (Strehlow, 1947: 111). The fires that were nearly extinguished were brought back to life and a tall *kauaua* pole came into view as daylight increased. It had been placed in the ground near the central, sacred mound, the *rala parra*. The bodies of the *iliara* were decorated with red-ochre and charcoal in patterns representing the great totemic ancestors (Strehlow, 1947: 111). As dawn approached, the final ceremony began with the *iliara* uprooting the *kauaua* pole, which Strehlow describes as symbolic of the '*rala parra*, the greatest of all the sacred *tjuruŋa*' (Strehlow, 1947: 111). The initiates grabbed the pole, carried it on their shoulders, following which they stripped it of its black and white rings, threw it into a gulley and covered it with branches. Strehlow interprets this act as representing the relief the *iliara* experienced after the long months of suffering they had endured. They 'exhaust the strength' of the *kauaua* pole, just as they had been stripped of their strength during their initiatory ordeals (Strehlow, 1947: 111). Following this final act of liberation, they and the Elders left the sacred ground to rejoin the remainder of the community, but they returned no longer as boys, but as fully initiated men who, in Strehlow's words, 'are at liberty to marry and lead their own private lives in the midst of their own community' (Strehlow, 1947: 112).

Songs Associated with Initiation

In *Songs of Central Australia*, Strehlow discusses at length songs that are related to the physical ordeals experienced by the initiates through circumcision and subincision, as well as referring to other ordeals that taken together comprise the entire collection of rites aimed at preparing young men to assume adult roles in society. However, he does not record the songs sung during rituals conducted at the *iŋkura* ground, possibly because of their most sacred, and hence secret, significance. In this section, I will illustrate Strehlow's choice of verses relating to initiation ceremonies by reviewing his relatively brief accounts of circumcision and subincision songs.

For his example of a circumcision song, Strehlow focused on the hawk totemic ancestors of the Alkirapuntja people located in the Eastern MacDonnell range. He selected these verses to draw attention to how the physical acts involved in the circumcision operation are described in the song as being conducted in a ruthless and seemingly cruel manner. Strehlow emphasizes that the song is chanted throughout the ritual as each boy is circumcised. The hawk totemic ancestors are described in the verses as 'swooping down' from the 'vault of the sky' (Strehlow, 1971a: 400). As hawks, they are particularly vicious hunters, who 'decapitate their prey as they fly' and who 'hold their prey in their claws' (Strehlow, 1971a: 400).

As these totemic ancestors approach the ceremonial *pulla* ground, a shield is struck producing a loud clanging sound to announce the arrival of the supernatural hawk ancestors. As they first appear, the ancestors are described as 'furiously sucking their beards' (Strehlow, 1971a: 400). They then begin the actual operation on the initiates as they chant, 'Our stone knives are decorated with fresh bands' (Strehlow, 1971a: 400). Following this, the hawk ancestors begin singing with frantic voices the following verse:

> The skin-covered penis! Sever it!
> The flayed stump! Let it gleam white!
> The flayed stump! Let it be stripped of its skin! (Strehlow, 1971a: 400).

Strehlow points out that these lines reveal the peculiarly brutal nature of the operation, which involves intense pain on the part of the initiates. To make things even more frightening to the boys undergoing the ritual, the operation is undertaken in an unfeeling manner with a callous attitude expressed by those performing the ritual act. This is confirmed by the following verses, which the ritual actors intone repeatedly as they execute the surgery on the young initiates:

> At the very neck! Cut it through!
> In furious anger! Cut it through!
> Filled with angry glee! Cut it through! (Strehlow, 1971a: 400).

Strehlow concludes his account of these rather gruesome verses by observing that 'there used to be no escape from this rite for the young lads of central Australia' (Strehlow, 1971a: 403). As if to emphasize the fear and suffering involved for the initiates, he reminds the reader that the novices would have undergone their first initiation operation at the average age of around 14 (Strehlow, 1971a: 403). He notes that without the circumcision ritual, the initiates would never pass to manhood and assume normal duties in society as husbands and fathers. This conviction was mirrored in how the Arrernte regarded Indigenous peoples living along the coasts who did not practise circumcision. Strehlow says that their males were always treated with a 'strong measure of contempt' (Strehlow, 1971a: 403). Their men remained always 'merely boys (*wora or wia*) ... whatever their age or standing might be in their own communities' (Strehlow, 1971a: 403).

As we discovered above, the initiates underwent a second physical operation, subincision, while they were in the liminal state called *rukuta*, several months after enduring the circumcision ritual. Strehlow describes the subincision chants as much more gentle than he found among songs performed during circumcision rituals. He writes: 'In marked contrast to the savage Circumcision Song, the Subincision Song depicts father and sons living together in a happy family group' (Strehlow, 1971a: 404). The songs Strehlow recounts come from the native cat totem at Ltalaltuma in Western Aranda territory, which relate how the legendary totemic ancestor, Malbaŋka, performed the subincision ritual that turned his sons into full men: 'One is taken, subincised, turned into a full man; then he is released, another one is seized, subincised, and released, And so on' (Strehlow, 1971a: 404). Malbaŋka is described as being filled with sorrow as he performs the operation on his sons.

The verses cited by Strehlow begin by describing Malbaŋka, 'the great sire', as 'hurrying along' (Strehlow, 1971a: 405). He then raises his 'great pole' and is followed by a 'jostling crowd' that separates into 'two opposing groups' (Strehlow, 1971a: 405). These groups join into a circle and force game towards the centre, which are killed with their clubs. Malbaŋka, 'huge of body', is seated around the great pole. Although he is 'sad at heart', he takes his sons and 'slices open the urethra till the penis grows broad' (Strehlow, 1971a: 405). When the operation is completed, the young men are given a pubic tassel, which the verse says 'glistens and gleams' and is 'altogether beautiful' (Strehlow, 1971a: 407). They then enjoy the game that has been killed: 'With thin sticks they are roasting the game ... The fat of the animals is juicy and plentiful' (Strehlow, 1971a: 407). That this scene is fundamentally different from the circumcision song is emphasized by Strehlow who comments that Malbaŋka 'had to subincise his sons with grief in his heart' (Strehlow, 1971a: 406), whereas the circumcision chant seems to express glee on the part of the actors who perform the operation on the young men.

Despite their differences in tone, both initiation rites dramatically rein-
force the authoritative transmission of tradition as it is passed on from
generation to generation, allegedly as it came directly from the legendary
supernatural totemic ancestors. The songs that are sung during the rituals
and the bodily transformations that the initiates underwent taught com-
pliance with the rules of society. The pain and deprivation endured by the
novices imparted in them patience and perseverance, qualities they would
need to develop as they grew older when they themselves would assume the
roles of Elders and ceremonial chiefs. The series of long, complicated initiation rituals, as they are described by Strehlow and recorded in his collection of Songs, has as its principal aims that of instilling in the young
knowledge of the transmitted tradition, respect for the authority of Elders
and obedience to the social regulations that are embedded in the myths of
the totemic ancestors.

Increase Ceremonies

In his contribution to the Bleeker and Widengren volume, Strehlow explained that Arrernte increase ceremonies involved members of one particular totemic clan who performed rituals to replenish and extend the
numbers of animals or plants associated with their own totem. These rituals, he notes, occur 'at sites where it was believed that these creative rites
had been instituted by the local totemic ancestors' (Strehlow, 1971b: 620).
He offers the example of the kangaroo totem located at Krantji, north of
Mount Hay among the Northern Arrernte regions. The kangaroo men
believed that they were reincarnations of the kangaroo totemic ancestors
who at the beginning of time had sprung forth from the Krantji water hole.
The men would gather periodically and sing the special totemic songs to
increase the number of kangaroos. The participants had to be from the
kangaroo totemic clan who, when they performed the rituals and sang the
songs, were required to replicate exactly 'all original actions and words of
the local kangaroo supernatural beings' (Strehlow, 1971b: 621). The performance of these rituals and songs was required if new kangaroos were to
emerge from the ground, in Strehlow's words, 'as they had done at the beginning of time' (Strehlow, 1971b: 621).

Increase ceremonies featured dramatic re-enactments of the stories told
about the original totemic ancestors. These frequently involved drawing
blood from the ritual performers' bodies, either from their arms or from their
urethra that had been cut during the subincision procedure. As reincarnations of the original totemic ancestors, the ritual performers believed
they were soaking the ground with the blood of the totemic animal. This
transformed the blood from being merely human blood into the sacred
blood of the ancestor, which, Strehlow explained, 'as a sacred liquid …

contained the power to create new life' (Strehlow, 1971b: 621). Additional instruments formed part of the ritual apparatus, including 'painted shields, ground paintings, or totem poles' on which were engraved symbols that had the power when used in conjunction with the sacred songs or verses and the blood of the reincarnations of the ancestors to produce new members of the totemic species and thereby replenish the supply of those animals or plants that defined the identities of the members of the clan (Strehlow, 1971b: 621).

In addition to the increase ceremonies themselves, Strehlow notes that the plants and animals of a totemic clan could be renewed by certain mechanical means, such as rubbing stones, hitting branches of special trees with stones or pouring blood derived from the totemites on rocks or boulders believed to be the physical manifestations of the original totemic ancestors.

I call these mechanical because they involved performing particular actions on objects to ensure a successful outcome, but this does not mean that these movements were devoid of mystical content. On the contrary, whenever these actions were performed, they were accompanied by chants or verses from the sacred songs relating to the totemic ancestor. Strehlow explains:

> In all cases it was believed that man could bring about the increases of plants and animals, and also of rain, only through the supernatural beings, by repeating their original creative actions and by intoning their original creative words (Strehlow, 1971b: 622).

In *Songs of Central Australia*, Strehlow (1971a: 277) accentuated the pragmatic nature of the songs associated with increase ceremonies by insisting that without the songs being chanted any mechanical actions 'would have remained absolutely ineffectual and fruitless'.

It was required that increase ceremonies be conducted at the *pmara kutata* associated with the principal totemic ancestor of the region. At these sacred centres were located rocks, trees and the secret-sacred objects (*tjurunga*) belonging to the relevant totemic clan, and which generally, Strehlow (1971a: 279) explains, 'represent the actual bodies of totemic ancestors'. Preparations for the ceremonies occurred when the *tjurunga* were removed from their storage places, sometimes from nearby caves, and covered with red ochre while the participants chanted the songs associated with the objects. Strehlow adds that if stones or boulders were present at the site that represented the actual body of the totemic ancestor, these were soaked with the blood of the reincarnated ancestors or they were rubbed with other stones resulting in a red dust that represented blood (1971a: 279).

In the actual ceremonies, it was normal practice for the ritual performers to put on costumes symbolizing the totemic ancestor. In the case of a plant totem, such as the grass-seed (*ntjira*) totem, headgear was worn symbolizing the fertility of the plant ancestor, called by Strehlow 'two grass-seed totemic ancestresses' representing 'the ntjira grass in its seeding stage' (1971a: 280). Or, as in the case of the kangaroo increase ceremony at Krantji, the performer wore on his head what Strehlow calls 'a ceremonial rara para', which he explains represents a 'kangaroo penis' (1971a: 280). Strehlow says that this particular ritual, which had not been described in earlier literature, either by Carl Strehlow or by Spencer and Gillen, provides proof 'that the men who first instituted them indicated in them symbolically the biological connection between sexual intercourse and fertilization' (1971a: 284). Strehlow emphasizes that each performer in increase rituals must be related directly to the totemic animal or plant for which the ceremony is being conducted, either as an actual reincarnation of the ancestor or as 'brothers, sons, or sons' sons of men whose totem it was or is' (1971a: 280).

Songs of Increase Ceremonies and Associated Rituals

In *Songs of Central Australia*, Strehlow translated numerous increase songs, which were chanted during rituals honouring both plant and animal totemic ancestors. He explains that increase songs 'describe the animals and plants as the natives know their appearance in a good season when water and grass are plentiful everywhere' (1971a: 284). In this way, the songs encourage the animals and plants to emulate the times of plenty as related in the songs by producing bountiful harvests. Strehlow suggests that the chants themselves contain power or what he calls 'magical potency' (1971a: 284) stressing that '*it is the power of the chanted words which alone quickens dead symbolism into life* (1971a: 284, emphasis in original). During the rituals when the songs were intoned, no direct appeals or invocations were made to spirits of the totemic ancestors; the songs themselves, when chanted, performed the necessary operations required for the increase ceremonies to be effective.

The songs accompanying the rituals performed for the increase of the *ntjira* plant are discussed in detail by Strehlow. He explains that *ntjira* is a grass found throughout the sandhill regions of Central Australia and that it produces very small reddish seeds, which provide an essential part of the diet of people living in these dry areas (1971a: 286). In the first part of the song, reference is made to the actions and the costume of the performers. The second part of the song refers to birds 'raising mounds of grain', a phrase that is repeated numerous times in the verses in connection first to a bird called in Arrernte *urula* and to a second bird, an *inintjilapilapa* (1971a: 287). Strehlow explains in a footnote that he could not find English words equivalent to the names of these birds, but they are appropriate to the song because both birds 'live largely on the ntjira seed' (1971a: 288 fn82).

The two totemic ancestresses who performed dances during the singing of the songs were related directly to the myths about the *ntjira* grass ancestors. The myth recounts that the *ntjira* totemic ancestresses originally emerged from the ground as the two birds spoken of in the songs. According to the story, the two ancestresses were able to extract so much red grain from the *ntjira* grass that they created enormous mounds of seeds each day. This is what is referred to in the song lines:

> The urula bird, the urula bird
> Is raising mounds of grain, is raising mounds of grain.

> The inintjilapilapa bird, the inintjilapilapa bird
> Is raising mounds of grain, is raising mounds of grain (1971a: 287).

In preparation for the ritual, a shallow hole was dug in the ground around which white down was laid, held in place with blood. Strehlow explains that the hole symbolized the original opening created by ants over which the two totemic ancestresses husked the grain by stamping their heels on the grass. During the ritual, the two actors representing the ancestresses squatted down beside each other maintaining this position by putting their weight on their toes while being supported by two sticks that had been covered in red ochre. Strehlow says that these two ritual performers 'moved slowly around this hole, side by side, putting their bodies into the customary ceremonial quiver from time to time' (1971a: 288) as the participants repeated the chant: 'Stamping incessantly with their heels, they are producing a heap of gleaming red grain' (1971a: 287). This is followed by the verses: 'Supporting themselves on red-ochred sticks, they have covered [themselves] with [a headgear of] red grain' (1971a: 287) (inserts by Strehlow). This verse refers to the red sticks used by the performers and to the fact that they wore red headgear, each of which was employed in the ritual to symbolize the red seeds of the *ntjira* grass.

The second part of the ritual dramatizes the totemic ancestresses leaving their home. The faces of the actors in this ceremony were covered with red down and they wore red headdresses, both reflecting the huge amount of red seed that had been harvested by the ancestresses. This time, however, the red headgear had been adorned with bird feathers, red from the black cockatoo and hawk feathers that had been covered with white down to represent the *ntjira* grass at the stage before it produced the red seeds for the harvest. Strehlow explains that in this section of the ritual the two performers 'stood one behind the other, each one supporting himself on two red-ochred sticks' (1971a: 288). Between the participants in the ritual, who were chanting the songs, and the two actors, two shields that had been covered in red ochre had been placed. At this point, the performers began stamping their heels again as the chant was repeated: 'Stamping incessantly with their heels, they are producing a heap of gleaming red grain'(1971a:

287). Strehlow notes that the actors lifted their knees high as they stamped 'in time to the stresses of the verse' (1971a: 288). The two ancestresses then sat down, one in front of each shield, but with their backs to the chanting participants.

The different verses sung during the *ntjira* grass ceremony had a different impact on the effectiveness of the increase of the grain. The verses that began with the phrase 'stamping incessantly', Strehlow explains, were 'dramatic verses only', not part of a 'real' increase ceremony (1971a: 289). This is because they were conducted in the absence of the *tjurunga* objects. The verses in which the names of the birds were used, however, were related directly to the names associated with the secret-sacred objects and, as a result, had the effect of increasing the supply of red grains. This is because the *urula* bird and the *inintjilapilapa* bird were given totemic names, and were sung as the *tjurunga* were being rubbed. In this sense, when these verses were sung, they were regarded by the participants, in Strehlow's words, 'as grain increase charms' (1971a: 289).

Like the plant increase ceremonies, rituals to replenish the supply of animals were conducted to ensure that the people had enough food to sustain them during difficult times. Strehlow explains that the animals were depicted in the songs 'as browsing about in large numbers, sleek, fat, and contented' (1971a: 295). The songs that were intoned were believed to influence the animals to replicate the conditions described in the verses, particularly during times of drought and poor supply of meat. The increase chants that were performed during rituals therefore had aims other than multiplying the numbers of the animals. Some chants were intoned specifically to make the animals fat, because, Strehlow notes, 'animal fats were essential for the physical welfare of the natives' (1971a: 296). One particularly important ritual was performed during the chanting of the kangaroo fattening verses, which Strehlow recorded at the kangaroo totemic centre of Rar' Ilba along the Hale River.

Strehlow explains that the kangaroo fattening verses were chanted particularly during drought seasons when the kangaroos would be thin due to lack of vegetation. At Hale River, where he observed this ritual, Strehlow cited the Indigenous belief that the verses were sung originally by the kangaroo ancestors while they were 'gutting the fat kangaroos they had slaughtered' (1971a: 296). Just as it was with the plant increase songs, it was believed that by intoning the verses describing fat and healthy kangaroos, the power contained in the chants would have the effect of fattening the drought-affected kangaroo population. Strehlow cites one verse aimed at increasing the welfare of the starving kangaroos, which emphasizes the state of kangaroos when they were fat and healthy: 'The fat around the intestines is very rich; the fat around the intestines is very plentiful' (1971a: 296).

A related series of verses cited by Strehlow recounts the songs performed at the Northern Arrernte rock wallaby centre at Tailitnama, where Strehlow reports that there exist 'rock-wallaby creative rocks' (1971a: 297). These rocks were endowed with special powers and were rubbed while various songs were sung. One of Strehlow's important informants, Makarinja, who was associated with the rock-wallaby centre at Tailitnama, offered Strehlow interpretations of the songs and their associated rituals. Strehlow reports that Makarinja cited the following four verses as the most important in the rock-wallaby increase ceremonies:

> [Having rushed] out of the thicket of bushes,
> They scatter in all directions (i.e. the wallabies).
>
> [Having rushed] out of the thicket of bushes,
> They are standing still, watching intently.
>
> With echoing hops they are ascending rocks
> In the tjuara thicket, in the tjuara thicket.
>
> He imprints his penis everywhere –
> His penis swelling with liquid (1971a: 297–98) [information in brackets
> inserted by Strehlow].

Strehlow explains in a footnote that the tjuara thicket in the verse refers to 'a common shrub growing among the boulders of the MacDonnells' (1971a: 297 fn105).

Strehlow draws attention in particular to the last verse of the four cited above. He claims that it was used to increase the number of rock wallabies in the region. However, it is quite unusual because it refers to the biological act of procreation, a reference that Strehlow found in no other verses. Although the verse clearly describes the penis full of semen ready to be released in the sexual act, Strehlow notes that it was sung by *rukuta* novices, whom as we have seen were recently initiated young men who had undergone the circumcision and sub-incision operations. According to what Makarinja related to Strehlow, the *rukuta* were deliberately given a false interpretation of these rock wallaby verses. They were told that the four verses taken together refer to the female wallaby, and that the final verse referring to the penis, actually is speaking about the large tail of the female wallaby which leaves deep imprints on the ground as it moves around. This interpretation is plausible because the Arrernte word for penis, *para*, can be translated either as penis or tail. However, the word actually used in the verse, *eramintja*, Strehlow explains, 'is a word in the Northern Aranda secret rukuta language meaning penis only' (1971a: 298). Strehlow adds his own interpretation to the double meaning attached to the fourth verse by suggesting that its ambiguity was meant to 'mystify the rukuta novices' by preventing them 'from associating the magic fertilization of female wallabies carried out in their own day

with the original act of copulation carried out by the wallaby totemic ancestor in animal form' (1971a: 298).

After having discussed the kangaroo fattening verses, followed by his
discussion of the rock-wallaby increase songs used by the *rukuta* novices,
Strehlow then moved to describe in detail the euro or common wallaroo
increase ceremony that he witnessed in 1933 in Makarinja's area. The euro
increase ceremony Strehlow describes was conducted by Makarinja himself. Strehlow explains that Makarinja and his brother Apma were heirs
of the euro *tjuruŋa* of the Kaput' Urbula totem. The increase ceremony
began with Makarinja and Apma decorating themselves with down from a
bird, representing the original ancestors, Ntjikantja and Kwaneraka. In the
ritual Makarinja and Apma assumed the identities of the original totemic
ancestors. Ntjikantja (Makarinja) wore four upright down-covered *tjurunga* on his head, while Kwaneraka (Apma) wore headgear comprised
of wooden *tjurunga* that symbolized 'the backbone and the ribs of a killed
euro' (1971a: 300). When the two performers were ready to begin the ceremony, what Strehlow calls 'the original tjurunga and bull-roarer' were
pulled out of two ground paintings that had been prepared before the ritual
began (1971a: 300). Their places were taken by Makarinja and Apma
themselves, since they had assumed the identities of the original ancestors,
who had been literally embodied in the original *tjurunga* and bull-roarer.
In this way Makarinja and Apma were transformed into the totemic euro
ancestors Ntjikantja and Kwaneraka. At this point, the two actors reclined
on their elbows as if they were asleep. The other participants in the ritual
were then invited to come forward quietly. No ceremonial call was invoked
nor was any dancing performed. Two men then began chanting: 'Out of
the rockplate let them issue forth – Out of the glistening one let them issue
forth!' (1971a: 300).

The ceremony proceeded with the two ancestors rousing from their sleep,
slowly and almost regretfully. The greatest ancestor, Ntjikantja, carried out
his motions associated with waking or coming to life, in Strehlow's words,
'with the greatest deliberation, slowness, and dignity, as befitted the greatest euro totemic ancestor of the Aranda' (1971a: 300). The same scene
then was re-enacted as Kwaneraka woke up. They both sat up on their back
haunches, faced each other and began to 'quiver'. They then returned to
their original positions of slumber. All during this performance, the verses
'Out of the rockplate let them issue forth – Out of the glistening one let
them issue forth!' were chanted in a slow dirge-like fashion (1971a: 300).
When the two ancestor brothers had resumed their sleep, this part of the
ritual was ended. The chanting stopped and the decorative headgear was
removed from Makarinja and Apma, signalling that they now had returned
to their original state and were no longer embodiments of the original euro
totemic ancestors.

At this point, two young men were summoned forward; one of them was Makarinja's grandson. The two young men laid down on top of the ground paintings facing downwards. The older men then rubbed their backs with grease after which the down that had been put on the ground paintings was removed and the *tjurunga* that had been used in the ceremony were stripped of their decorations, including the red and white down that had been put on them. While these sacred objects were being dismantled, the following verses were sung:

> Out of the Rockplate let him issue forth –
> Let Ntjikantja issue forth!
>
> Kwaneraka is slowly rising up.
> From plucked fur he is slowly rising up.
>
> "Our heads drenched in blood we are going home;
> Both of us are going home."
>
> "Tied into bundles, we are lifting [the game] up [on our heads]
> Both of us are lifting [the game] up [on our heads]."
>
> Sprung from the Rockplate, let them fight one another playfully;
> Sprung from the glistening [one], let them fight one another playfully!
>
> Out of the Rockplate let them issue forth –
> Out of the glistening [one], let them fight one another playfully (1971a: 301–302, inserts by Strehlow).

The two young men, whose backs had just been rubbed with grease, were painted on their backs with the design of the Kaput' Urbula totem. Strehlow explains that 'this design represented Ntjikantja and Kwaneraka at work, disembowelling a killed euro' (1971a: 301). The scattering of the down as the verses were chanted was intended to produce new euros, and after one year had passed, in Strehlow's words, 'there would be an abundance of game for every one' (1971a: 301). Although Strehlow interprets the purpose of the verses as intending 'to create animals which will yield ample meat and fat to the hunters' (1971a: 303), it is equally clear from the ceremony itself, which featured the two brothers as incarnations of the original ancestors, and from the role played by the two young men, that the ritual re-enactment served to perpetuate the inter-generational transmission of knowledge of the songs and the associated ceremonies while at the same time re-enforcing the age-old authority of the traditions among the younger generation. The fact that Makarinja and Apma represented the living face of the ancestors by replacing the *tjurunga* with their own bodies not only made the totemic ancestors come to life, but their actions directly connected the current generations in a chain stretching back to the beginning of time.

Commemoration Songs and Rituals

The final type of songs that I will consider in this chapter is arguably the most important. I am referring to songs and rituals that honoured or commemorated the original totemic ancestors. I call this the most important type because this category of performance re-enacted the myths of origin of particular totemic ancestors by literally bringing the ancient stories to life. In his contribution to the Bleeker and Widengren volume, Strehlow (1971b: 619) explained that commemorative ceremonies were organized into cycles and that each cycle, which took place at the sacred centres, the *pmara kutata*, was tied to particular myths related to the totemic ancestor being honoured. Strehlow asserted that the ceremonies 'presented the supernatural personages represented in the myths before the eyes of the men who were believed to be reincarnated from them' (1971b: 619). The aim of the rituals was to make the day to day living of members of the community conform in as close a proximity as possible to the patterns and codes of conduct established originally by the founding ancestors. This meant that in every aspect of life, the living communities sought to emulate the activities of the supernatural being that had brought them into existence and to whose totem their most sacred centres and secret objects were associated. The purpose was not to appease angry or slighted ancestors, nor was it to protect against misfortune. This is because the actors in the rituals themselves were regarded as the reincarnations of the original ancestors and, Strehlow contends, 'men do not propitiate themselves or pray to themselves' (1971b: 618).

The commemorative ceremonies were not all of equal importance nor did each convey the same sacred significance. Some rituals re-told the stories of 'minor figures of a myth' or referred to 'the less important episodes in the stories of the major characters' (1971b: 620). In these cases, the strict code of secrecy was not enforced. Strehlow says that these minor ceremonial acts 'were freely shown to all members of the appropriate audience, including young initiates' (1971b: 620). The major episodes featuring the most significant sacred ancestors and the *tjurunga* objects associated with them were witnessed generally only by 'older totemic clansmen' and the most sacred rituals 'were never revealed to more than three or four of the most trusted senior members and leaders of the appropriate totemic clans' (1971b: 620).

In *Songs of Central Australia*, Strehlow described in detail a ritual cycle he observed in 1933 at the Northern Arrernte bandicoot (*gurra*) centre at Ilbalintja. The most important factor in this series of rituals, as I interpret Strehlow's accounts, relates to the appearance of the original totemic ancestor in the dramatic re-enactments of the myth of the founding bandicoot ancestor Karora and his first-born son. According to Strehlow's summary of the myth, the first-born son of Karora was awakened by the *raiaŋkintja* call, which, as we saw in the description of initiation ceremonies, involves a leader in the ritual shouting out a rasping noise intended to summon participants to engage in or witness particular ritual acts. In the myth told by Strehlow, after being awakened in the early morning, Karora's son danced around his father before 'finally clasping his father in his arms' (1971a: 350). After this morning ritual was concluded, the son was sent out to hunt bandicoots and returned home in the evening with his catch tied in bundles and flung over his shoulder. As he approached, his father sounded the *raiaŋkintja* call urging his son to hurry. On his arrival, the son threw the game at his father's feet and, after being covered in ritual down, began a dance that continued for many hours. When the son had become nearly exhausted, he threw himself to the ground. His father plucked the down from his son's body and 'rejoiced' over his son (1971b: 351). Strehlow explains that 'the men of the Ilbalintja clan honoured Karora and his many sons in the same fashion in a series of sacred commemorative ceremonies normally extending over several months' (1971b: 351).

In the cycles during which the ceremonies were performed, Strehlow stresses that many hours were spent preparing for the ritual. Verses that were appropriate to the decorations placed on the actors were always chanted during the preparations. The chanting, which continued throughout the preparations for up to four to six hours, was interrupted occasionally by the *raiaŋkintja* call or by sounds produced by the swinging of bull-roarers. After the actor representing a particular totemic ancestor had been prepared, one of the Elders emerged from the bushes, behind which the secret decorations had been assembled and the verses intoned, and sounded the *raiaŋkintja* call in the direction of an assembly of people that included young men and strangers who had been invited to witness, and, in some cases, play minor parts in the ritual. The chorus then began chanting the appropriate verses while some men performed a shuffling dance around the person who represented the totemic ancestor. The ancestor then 'quivered' so violently that the tufts of down that had been placed on his body flew off in all directions. At this point, it was normal for another member of the chorus to sound again the *raiaŋkintja* call or to swing a small bull-roarer, which was followed by a dramatic 'fierce loud cry' that brought this portion of the ceremony to 'a sudden halt' (1971b: 351). The dancers then placed their hands on the principal actor in the ritual, in Strehlow's words, 'to soothe his emotions' because 'he is supposed to be deeply stirred from playing the part of the totemic ancestor' (1971b: 351).

During the preparations for the ritual, when the actor was being decorated, Strehlow notes that 'two couplets would be heard recurring time and again' (1971b: 356). The first couplet referred directly to the decorations put on the body of the actor:

The whirlwind is encircling his waist;
Stripes fall down his back from his shoulders, and the whirlwind is encircling his waist (1971b: 351).

The second couplet re-enforced the identity of the participant, and in this
way affirmed the authenticity of the ceremony:

"Are you indeed a bandicoot?
Are you one indeed?" (1971b: 351)

If the ritual being conducted featured as the main actor Karora, the original ancestor himself, the verses sung during the ceremony would include
the following:

The great sire Karora
Is gazing about watchfully.

Lo, the great sire, tall and broad-shouldered;
Lo, the great sire, in the pride of his strength!

Lo, the great sire, in the pride of his strength;
Lo, the great sire, with his rippling muscles!

Lo, the great sire, in the pride of his strength;
Lo, the great sire, proudly keeping to his own home! …

Lo, the great sire of the painted ground;
Lo, his limbs, firm, hard, and strong! (1971b: 351).

If the ritual centred on one of the sons of Karora, variations of the verses
were inserted, but, Strehlow explains, those chants describing the strength
and personal appearance of the ancestor 'were applicable also to Karora's
eldest sons' (1971b: 351).

It will have been noted that in the accounts above of the bandicoot ceremony at Ilbalintja Strehlow refers to visitors and strangers who are invited
to observe parts of the ritual. We see in this context precisely what I referred
to in Chapter 4 about the participation of outsiders in major ceremonies.
In *Aranda Traditions*, Strehlow explained that different *pmara kutata* which
share 'interlinking legends' normally invited members of the same totemic
clan, but belonging to different ceremonial centres, to witness and participate in their own local ceremonies and even to exchange, usually temporarily, *tjurunga* objects (1947: 160). Strehlow provided the example of the
links between the Ilbalintja men of the bandicoot totem in the Northern
Arrernte regions and those bandicoot men from Owen Springs in Central
Arrernte areas. He noted that members of the Ilbalintja bandicoot totemic
centre also shared common interests with some members of the euro and
kangaroo totems, which meant they also would normally be invited to witness some of the ceremonies honouring the bandicoot totemic ancestors.
One of Strehlow's informants explained that this 'shows that we are living

at peace with our neighbours' (1947: 161). This must be seen in the light of what Strehlow emphasized in *Songs of Central Australia* that '*each ceremony … was carefully localized*' (1971a: 357, emphasis in original). In the case of the ritual at the Ilbalintja *pmara kutata* featuring the original bandicoot ancestor, Karora, the ancestor was depicted just as he was understood to have been active at the Ilbalintja waterhole, and was not transferable to other ceremonies of the bandicoot ancestor, for example, at Owen Springs. This localized feature of the ceremonies required co-operation among other totemic centres which in turn acted, in Strehlow's words, 'as an effective method of cementing peace between the groups concerned' (1947: 161).

Strehlow's Interpretation of the Ilbalintja Cycle

I have given just a brief sample drawn from Strehlow's elaborate descriptions of the Ilbalintja cycle of ceremonies which took several months to complete and which, in *Songs of Central Australia*, occupy 30 pages of text. Nonetheless, the key themes in the cycle have been described, including the importance of body, ground and *tjurunga* decorations, an example of some of the chants conducted during the preparations for the rituals, the myth on which the cycle of rituals was derived, the central importance of the secret-sacred objects and the social interaction that took place among related totemic groups not associated with the local *pmara kutata*. At the conclusion of his day-by-day accounts of what occurred during the cycle of rituals over the three months he observed them, Strehlow offered his own analysis of the significance and meaning of the commemorative ceremonies he observed.

The first point he stressed was that although the rituals 'celebrate the lives and deeds of the totemic ancestors' (1971a: 375), they are intended to have a practical effect, which Strehlow puts into the category of 'magic concepts' (1971a: 375). For example, he cites the common belief that when the down used to decorate the actors in the ritual falls to the ground during the act of quivering, after the next season of rain, it will be transformed into the actual animal (or plant) of the totemic ancestor being commemorated. In the case of the ceremonial cycle he witnessed in 1933 at the Ilbalintja ceremonial centre, the participants believed that the down would turn into bandicoots. Although Strehlow calls this 'magic', I think it would be better understood as evidence of the pragmatic nature of rituals, which, as we saw above, Strehlow understood and noted. Rituals are performative and dramatic, but they also have causal effects, in this case, from the believers' perspectives, producing the actual increase of the totemic animal being commemorated.

A second point made by Strehlow relates to the sacred ritual centre, the *pmara kutata*. In normal circumstances, the entire ceremonial cycle would be conducted at the *pmara kutata*. In 1933, this was not possible, Strehlow explains, first, because that season had been particularly dry and the Ilbalintja soak had no water in it, but, secondly and more significantly, because the land itself had come under the control of a white cattle farmer who had leased the territory on which the *pmara kutata* was situated. This, of course, provided evidence of variations due to natural causes, but chiefly it suggests that by 1933 changes introduced by the Government had made the perpetuation of traditional ceremonies extremely difficult. Changing locations in a localized community that celebrated age-old myths through traditional ceremonies in a space that had been set apart and near which the most secret-sacred objects were stored created far more than an inconvenience; it contravened the authoritative tradition itself. Strehlow's stark reference to the changing social and historical circumstances that were disrupting the sacred tradition and its ritual re-enactments foreshadowed his later assertion that the in-depth records he had begun recording of the myths, rituals and social customs of Arrernte peoples in the early 1930s would provide an essential resource for later generations who had lost all knowledge of their ancient stories and customs.

Strehlow's third point emphasizes that the complete cycle of ceremonies did not occur annually but only during a time when a sufficient number of young men were ready for the initiation rituals to be conducted. He explained that only the earth mound (*rala parra*), the ground painting and the *kauaua* pole were owned communally by those associated with the *pmara kutata*. The remainder were owned privately and thus individual rituals were conducted frequently, at least once a year, by the immediate family. On occasions when the entire ceremonial cycle was anticipated, the Elders of the totemic clan discussed among themselves the necessity of holding the rituals and then confirmed that there would be enough young men ready to be initiated. They also had to ensure that there was sufficient food to be prepared during the rituals and that there were enough visitors related to the totemic clan that would attend.

If all these conditions were met, the invitations were issued to those qualified to attend and preparations of the ground for the sacred ceremonies were begun. Strehlow reiterated that although the commemorative cycle was always conducted during the same period as the initiation rites were enacted, the ceremonies were not in themselves initiation rituals. He explains: 'They are religious ceremonies performed both in order to introduce the totemic ancestors to their human clansmen, and in order to honour and please these supernatural beings themselves' (1971a: 377).

Finally, Strehlow refers to what we have already discussed in Chapter 4 concerning the difference between individual totems determined by conception sites and the overall totemic clan associated with the *pmara kutata*. This meant, for example, in the Ilbalintja ceremonial cycle, many participants individually possessed *tjurunga* from totems other than the primary totemic animal, the bandicoot. As we saw, this meant that those belonging to the *njinaŋa* section who had varying personal totems were invited during the cycle to perform some of the rituals relevant to their own totemic ancestor. Strehlow explains: 'As a result, the number of ceremonies at a commemorative festival could be very great, and the various acts could relate to a multiplicity of totems' (1971a: 377). Nonetheless, certain very strict regulations applied. For example, it was required that at the *iŋkura* ground the *rala parra* of the totem of the *pmara kutata* at which the ceremonies were being performed must be the same as that of the main totem connected to the *pmara kutata* and could not be appropriated by owners of personal totems.

Conclusion

In this chapter, I have focussed on Strehlow's accounts of sacred Arrernte ceremonies by examining a selection of the types of rituals performed and relating them to their appropriate song chants as he recorded them over several decades of research. Three essential points emerge from these descriptions that are relevant to the concluding chapters of this book. The first accentuates the fundamental importance to the religious life of Arrernte peoples occupied by the totemic ancestors. During the rituals, the original ancestor comes to life, appears to the people and re-enacts the stories that have been told about his primordial activities. As in the case of the bandicoot totemic clan, the ancestor is described as a powerful creature whose home he has established in the location of the people's ceremonial ground and to whom his descendants derive their identity both individually and communally. In the commemorative rituals, the ancestor appears through the elaborate decorations painted on the body of the central actor in the ceremony. The community is linked together by the blood extracted from ritual participants who, as reincarnations of the totemic ancestor, are smearing the ancestor's own blood on the body of the principal actors in the ceremony, on the ground paintings and on the secret-sacred objects. The songs that are intoned tell the story of the totemic ancestor's original acts, and some of the verses were believed to have come directly from the voice of the ancestor himself. Through these detailed and dramatic performances, the participants share in an experience that brings the past into the present and makes the autochthonous ancestor come alive in the ritual re-enactment.

A second point relating to the purpose of the rituals follows directly from the first. As we have seen, commemorative rituals in honour of the ancestors are not performed in order to win their favour and thereby achieve optimal health and well-being for the community because, as Strehlow has emphasized, the participants themselves are literally reincarnated from the totemic ancestors and deities do not pray to themselves nor seek to win their own favour. For that reason, I have stressed that the ritual performances bring to life the *original* stories about founding ancestors and make them come to life in face-to-face encounters with their descendants. In this way, the foundational myths are transformed in each ritual re-enactment into living, experienced realities. In like manner, the songs that are chanted collapse the past into the present by re-vivifying the original ancestor who speaks just as he did at the beginning of time. This is what I have called elsewhere 'presentational art', whereby the viewers and participants are brought face-to-face with the central figures of their religious faith (Cox, 2010: 114–16). In this sense, the 're-incarnation' of the totemic ancestor is a literal 'incarnation' – the founding ancestor is seen in the flesh.

Thirdly, although Arrernte rituals are not intended to propitiate the ancestors, pragmatic ends define one of the principal purposes of the ceremonies. In the cases we have examined, it is clear that the songs that are chanted are intended to increase the number of animals or plants that are being honoured in the ceremonies. This has a direct impact on the food supply of the communities who depend on the animals and plants for survival. We have seen that Strehlow called the idea that chants could affect the supply of game and ensure the growth of vegetation 'magic'. By magic, he meant attributing causal connections to mystical activities, whereas in reality no causality can be established scientifically. For example, when the members of the chorus intone the verses that describe the rock wallaby as being fat and healthy, no causation between the verses sung and the actual conditions producing fat wallabies can be made, apart from what Strehlow termed 'magical' thinking that assigns efficacy to the intonations. This, however, misses the point. The idea that ritual performances can influence conditions conducive to a community's welfare defines one of the fundamental purposes of rituals in general. In other words, from a believer's point of view, the ceremonies and songs Strehlow described and recorded not only have the so-called elevated spiritual purpose of making the stories come to life by bringing the people into face-to-face contact with the primordial ancestor, they also aim to achieve the very practical end of increasing the supply of food for the community. The issue of actual causality cannot be discussed without first understanding the differing pre-suppositions which distinguish the experience of the participants in the ritual from that of an outside observer. It is sufficient at this point to note that the practical aims of ritual performances operate virtually everywhere in all types of religions, whether they are global in intent or primarily local in their outreach.

Finally, we find in Strehlow's accounts of rituals and songs further evidence that the religious life of the people was rooted in an authoritative tradition that must be passed on just as it was received from generation to generation. The elaborate initiation rituals underscore just this point. The tradition is taught to young men through a gradual introduction to the content and meaning of songs, ceremonies and secret-sacred objects. Authority is re-enforced by the long, painstaking trials the boys undergo in their transformation from carefree children into men who must assume their roles as adults in the well-established social structure. By the time they have finished their initiation process, the young men will have become knowledgeable of some of the ancient traditions, they will have learned the necessity of obedience to those same traditions and they will have been prepared to marry and bring up children of their own to whom they will pass on the traditions. As they become older and move to the position of respected Elders, knowledge of the tradition increases and eventually they learn the most secret songs, of which access to and knowledge of is restricted to the most senior leaders in the community.

In this and the previous two chapters, I have attempted to summarize the contribution of T.G.H. Strehlow to promoting the understanding of Arrernte Indigenous Religions as he first encountered them as an adult in the 1930s. I began by recounting the myths whereby the totemic ancestors were described as founding the world and society as it had been experienced by particular Arrernte totemic clans, in Strehlow's words, from 'eternity'. I then examined in detail his descriptions and analyses of the complex social structure found among Arrernte communities, which was based on totems, both personal and communal. I have suggested that the concept conveyed in the phrase 'personal monototemism in a polytotemic community' provides one of Strehlow's most important contributions to fostering an understanding among a wide audience of the interconnections between Arrernte religious life and the social organization that supported it. Finally, in this chapter, I have shown how Strehlow linked the socio-religious structure of totemic communities and their foundational myths to the ceremonies that transport the stories into the present and that re-enforce with absolute authority the social structure that derives its legitimacy from the same primordial myths and their ritual re-enactments.

In the next chapter I analyse the changes that Strehlow observed from the time he first began his research in Central Australia until his death in 1978. We will see that he became convinced that the radical changes experienced by Indigenous people as a result of colonial influences, Christian missions and the advance of modernity meant that the authoritative transmission of traditional knowledge had been so severely disrupted that it could never be restored and was threatened with being forgotten forever.

6

'ONE HOUR BEFORE SUNSET':
THE LOSS OF INDIGENOUS RELIGIOUS KNOWLEDGE

I turn now to consider the judgements of T.G.H. Strehlow about how severely the transmission of the authoritative tradition and with it the collective memory had been disrupted among the Arrernte peoples of Central Australia by 1960. Beginning in the nineteenth century, persistent, calculated and carefully planned projects were inaugurated in Australia by missionaries, colonial agents and eventually the Government with the explicit aim of disrupting, annihilating and replacing Aboriginal cultures with the values and aims of the invading European culture. The stories of those involved in the 'stolen generations' provide explicit and well-known evidence of official Government efforts to assimilate the Indigenous population into mainstream culture by cutting the young off from their families and traditions (Cox and Possamai, 2016b: 185). Mission agencies also co-operated in the aim of replacing traditional Indigenous Religions with Christianity as it was interpreted in terms of the dominant Western European traditions (Loos, 2007: 45).

The concerted effort to replace Indigenous culture with the values and practices of the colonizing culture provided one of Strehlow's chief motivations to preserve records of the rituals, ceremonies, stories, social obligations and genealogies as he found them when he began conducting research among the Arrernte in 1932. He used as many tools as possible that were available to him, including making detailed notes in his own personal diaries that contained interviews with Elders explaining ancestral stories, meanings associated with *tjurunga*, and also in which he recorded detailed descriptions of rituals and ceremonies that he had observed. He took great care to produce sound recordings of interviews and ceremonial functions, including the songs that were sung during the ceremonies. Later, he was given permission to film some of the most important rituals relating to particular totems that were conducted at sacred ceremonial sites. His notes and publications contained maps on which he drew boundaries based on genealogical evidence and on which he traced the mythical wanderings of the primordial ancestors. He used his extensive knowledge of

Indigenous languages to translate stories and songs into English. It is important to remember that from childhood Strehlow had spoken Arrernte and regarded it as one of his native languages. Growing up on the Hermannsburg Mission on which he was the only white child among the many Indigenous children living there provided him with memories of stories relayed to him by his peers, including attitudes towards initiation rites. In addition, he relied in part on his father's own detailed notes and personal correspondence, as well as his father's extensive and published research on Arrernte oral traditions, to confirm his own descriptions and interpretations of traditional Arrernte beliefs and practices (J. Strehlow, 2010: 44–46).

Throughout the 40 years that T.G.H. Strehlow actively conducted research in Central Australia, he was able to document the extensive changes that had resulted from the intervention of outside forces. He concluded that the traditions he first encountered as a child and began recording as a young man had been so extensively disrupted that, apart from the detailed data he had produced, virtually all knowledge of the ancient traditions had been lost. In this chapter, I consider the evidence Strehlow provided for his conclusions about the demise of Indigenous knowledge among the Arrernte in preparation for my discussion in Chapter 8, where I analyse the current repatriation of knowledge project emanating from the Strehlow Research Centre in Alice Springs, which is using Strehlow's vast collection of documented material in precisely the manner he intended, as a means for restoring among members of the present generation links to age-old, traditional ways of life.

The Situation as Strehlow Found It in 1932

By the time T.G.H. Strehlow returned to Central Australia in 1932 at the urging of his academic supervisor, J.A. FitzHerbert, missionaries had been working among Aboriginal peoples in the region since 1877, when the first Lutheran missionaries, Hermann Kempe and Wilhelm Schwarz, established the Mission they called Hermannsburg alongside the Finke River. As we have seen, Strehlow's father, Carl, arrived in 1894 at a time when the Mission was in crisis, and through diligence and hard work, as well as a sympathetic attitude towards the people among whom he was working, was able to make the Mission a centre for Christian activity that produced numerous converts, many of whom lived on the grounds of the Mission. Carl Strehlow was forced to leave the Mission in 1922 due to illness. He died at Horseshoe Bend, some 300 kilometres southwest of Hermannsburg, as he was desperately trying to get to Oodnadatta, a four-week journey from Hermannsburg by horse and buggy, where the nearest railhead was located and which T.G.H. Strehlow (2015 [1969]: 22) explained 'was the nearest place to which a doctor could be asked to come in order to give medical treatment to a patient from Central Australia'. Carl Strehlow was replaced in 1924 by Friedrich Albrecht, who regarded Indigenous religious rituals as pagan and who urged Christian converts to give up their traditional beliefs and practices, including, and perhaps principally, their attachment to the secret-sacred objects, the *tjurunga*.

Writing in 2004, Paul G.E. Albrecht (2004: 112), who was Friedrich Albrecht's son and Field Superintendent of the Finke River Lutheran Mission between 1962 and 1983 before becoming a Bible translator stationed in Alice Springs (Veit, 2004: 214; Austin-Broos, 2009: 80), described Friedrich Albrecht's primary missionary aim as that of replacing the 'traditional Aboriginal corporate life based on the *tjurrunga*' with the Christian interpretation of 'corporate life based on the word of God'. In particular, Friedrich Albrecht saw *tjurunga* ownership 'as being incompatible with the corporate life of the Christian community' (P. Albrecht, 2004: 112). As a result, after 1924, the Hermannsburg Mission adopted as its primary missionary strategy one I have called elsewhere, 'replacement', which I have defined as a 'theology' that 'attempted to provide the benefits of western civilization and western religion to people who were regarded as lower on the scale of social, intellectual and moral development' (Cox, 1992: 31). In order to enforce its interpretation of Christian morality on the Indigenous population, the Lutheran Mission at Hermannsburg resorted to a number of punishments, including excommunication, banishment from the Mission for a set period of time and corporal punishment (P. Albrecht, 2004: 112). These punishments were determined by 'church meetings' with corporal punishment being 'administered by elders and/or the kin person who had responsibility for administering such punishment' (P. Albrecht, 2004: 112).

The efforts to convince Indigenous people living in or near the Hermannsburg Mission to renounce their allegiance to traditional customs and beliefs is demonstrated by an event that took place in 1928. Friedrich Albrecht specifically sought to discredit the people's belief in the power of *tjurunga*, which were intimately associated with Arrernte religious traditions, so much so that A.P. Elkin (1974 [1938]: 210) described them as 'symbols of the eternal dream-time'. In an article outlining the continuing historical significance of *tjurunga*, Philip Batty (2014: 297) of the Humanities Department, Museum Victoria, asserted that Albrecht was concerned that the Indigenous people living around Hermannsburg had not genuinely converted to Christianity, despite the Mission having been in the area for over 50 years. Batty relates that a few kilometres west of the Mission station was a sacred cave called Manangananga that contained numerous *tjurunga*, which according to the authoritative tradition, could be seen and handled exclusively by initiated men. So strict were the regulations surrounding the *tjurunga* that if women or children even came near the cave, they were told that they would experience severe consequences, including death. To demonstrate that the *tjurunga* actually possessed no power at all, Albrecht enlisted the cooperation of a small number of Arrernte Elders who had converted to Christianity and who were active evangelists for the Christian faith. Albrecht and his Aboriginal colleagues organized a Christian worship service at the cave, which included the singing of numerous hymns in Arrernte. At the conclusion of the service, the *tjurunga* were removed from the cave and women and children were invited to come forward to touch the objects. No consequences followed this action, which for Albrecht proved that the traditional reverence for the secret-sacred objects was rooted entirely in 'pagan superstition' (Batty, 2014: 296–97).

This incident, of course, entailed more than an attack on a collection of *tjurunga*; it was a direct challenge to the authority of the tradition and to the religious memory that was enshrined in the tradition. This view is confirmed by the anthropologist Diane Austin-Broos (2009: 71) who observed that 'the Lutheran mission not only acted to expunge indigenous rite but also sought to bring a new hierarchical order to competing social-moral worlds'. The place of the Elders as carriers and preservers of the age-old stories, myths and ceremonies was undermined and, in the eyes of Albrecht at least, totally discredited while the truth of the Christian message had been confirmed convincingly. Austin-Broos (2009: 71) cites an interview she conducted with a Lutheran pastor who claimed that events following the confrontation at Mananganang a Cave demonstrated that '"Our God proved greater than theirs"'.

Despite the apparent success of the Lutheran Mission that occurred at Mananganang a Cave, T.G.H. Strehlow discovered that traditional totemic ceremonies and initiation rites were still being observed when he began his research in Central Australia in 1932. This is confirmed by Paul Albrecht (2004: 112) who suggests that the Indigenous Elders knew what the Lutherans were planning at Mananganang a Cave and removed the most important secret-sacred objects before the event took place. If this is true, the apparent success of the incident, which was intended to destroy Indigenous trust in the power of the *tjurunga*, was foiled by the surreptitious act of the Elders who anticipated the desecration of their most secret-sacred objects under the direction of the Lutheran Mission and simply transferred them to a safe location. This may have confirmed the fears of the missionary Albrecht that conversions to Christianity were superficial and that much work was still required if genuine adherence to Christian teaching was to be achieved among the Aboriginal population at Hermannsburg. Paul Albrecht argues that the aim of the Lutheran Mission to create a Christian community at Hermannsburg based on the teachings of the 'Word of God' produced converts and appeared successful, but it could not be maintained in the long run because the strategy required members of the church to isolate themselves from their traditional culture and to renounce elements within their communal existence that defined their identity (P. Albrecht, 2004: 114). As we have seen, allegiance to the totemic ancestor was paramount and in some cases the ancestor was believed to be identical to the *tjurunga* object itself.

A different version of the incident at Manangananga Cave is related by Peter Latz in his biography of Moses Tjalkabota Uraiakuraia, otherwise known as 'Blind Moses', who was one of the Indigenous Christian leaders that participated in the Lutheran service conducted at the cave. Latz was the son of the Lutheran missionary Arthur Latz, who supervised the construction of the water pipeline from Alice Springs to Kaporilya near Hermannsburg that began in 1934 (Austin-Broos, 2009: 65). In his book on Moses Tjalkabota Uraiakuraia, Latz, who was born in 1941 and grew up on the Mission, describes the circumstances surrounding the desecration of the *tjurunga* at Manangananga Cave and confirms that the apparent victory of Christian teachings over the traditional law was superficial and that belief in the power of the secret cave with its sacred objects remained long after the Manangananga Cave affair concluded. Latz explains that the background to Albrecht's decision to go to the cave was in response to a 'payback' incident that had caused a man from Hermannsburg to be seriously wounded.[1] Latz (2014: 137) says that because he 'was sick of the tribal methods of conducting disputes', Albrecht cancelled the scheduled Sunday worship service, an act that had never been done before. This signalled to the Elders that a serious breach of the Lutheran law had occurred. Under the leadership of Blind Moses, the Elders, in Latz's words, 'decided that the only way to break from their old ways was to go to the sacred Manangananga cave and dispose of the *tjurunga* held therein' (Latz, 2014: 138). Latz adds that although both Pastor Albrecht and the Elder Moses preached during the service held at the cave, 'the exorcism was not particularly successful' (Latz, 2014: 138).

As evidence for this judgement, Latz recounts his own experience as a boy in the early 1950s when, because they believed the sacred cave was now safe to visit, 'several of us white kids decided to spend a Saturday visiting the spot' (Latz, 2014: 139). He explains that the white boys 'bribed'

---

1. 'Payback' is a term used to describe traditional forms of punishment or retribution where a serious infringement of Indigenous Law was deemed to have occurred. It often included spearing, banishment or death. As evidenced in Friedrich Albrecht's judgement, this has frequently been regarded by outside observers as primitive and archaic, but, in an article written for the *Australian Law Reform Commission – Reform Journal*, Geoff Clarke (2002), who at the time of writing was Chair of the Aboriginal and Torres Strait Islander Commission, argued that 'customary law should be seen principally and more positively as the application of cultural values and principles to indigenous community life'. He added, 'It can provide the framework for systems of authority, discipline, administration and conflict resolution'.

two Indigenous boys to join them by promising them a free lunch. When they entered the gorge below the cave, the party of boys 'soon came upon an impressive large erect semi-cylindrical boulder, which we knew was the totemic symbol for the important local Twins Dreaming' (Latz, 2014: 139).[2] They proceeded cautiously but as they neared the cave they heard 'strange sounds' that they interpreted as warnings against going any further. At that point the Indigenous boys fled. The white boys, although afraid, continued and discovered that the sounds were simply made by frogs. They then had a picnic and swam in the nearby waterhole. All seemed well until Latz explains that he got into trouble while swimming and would have drowned had there not been a good swimmer among the boys, who rescued him. Shortly after this incident, the boys were threatened by a large rock python, which would have been associated with stories of the dangerous rainbow serpent.[3] Latz concludes that 'none of us kids ever returned to the attractive Manangananga gorge' (Latz, 2014: 139). He adds that for a period following the Lutheran service at the cave in 1928, the region was a popular tourist destination, but now it is entirely prohibited for outsiders to enter it. This no doubt follows the resacralization of the cave as noted by Austin-Broos (2009: 70) that occurred in 1955 and to which, Latz conjectures, 'it is possible that our experience helped in the process' (Latz, 2014: 139).

The Next 25 Years and the Demise of Traditional Religion

What Strehlow discovered over the 25 years that followed the beginning of his research among the Arrernte, part of which, as we have seen, he served as the Native Patrol Officer for the southern part of the Northern Territory, was the gradual deepening of the commitment of local people to Christian values, accompanied by extensive efforts by the Government to assimilate the Indigenous population into mainstream white culture. He believed that

---

2. In *Aranda Traditions*, T.G.H. Strehlow (1947: 118) describes the Twins of Ntaria at the Manangananga Cave as having been born of 'a woman ancestor' who 'once lived with two small children known as *ratapa*'. The children are reported as traversing 'all the sandhills near Hermannsburg, which accordingly belongs to the *ratapa* totem'. In a footnote, Strehlow (1947: 118fn) explains that *ratapa* is not the normal name for a child in the Arrernte language, which is *katjia*. The use of *ratapa* denotes the totemic significance of the mythical child twins.

3. Unlike the rainbow serpent traditions along the coastal regions of the Northern Territory and Northern Queensland, which associate the serpent with creation and life-giving powers, the serpent among central desert peoples is regarded as dangerous and mysterious, living in deep pools and is potentially life-threatening (see Elkin, 1974 [1938]: 260–61; see also, Cox, 2014a: 104–106). See below, where Strehlow describes the 'dreaded' snake ceremonial centre at Uralterinja.

this dual attack by missionaries and the Government on Aboriginal social and religious customs had resulted by the mid-1950s in the almost total dissolution of knowledge of the traditional stories and ceremonies that he had discovered in 1932. This explains, at least in part, why he published *Aranda Traditions* in 1947 as a scientific record describing the traditional social organization and religious practices of a people whose religion he believed was in a precipitous decline.[4]

In a public lecture delivered at the University of Adelaide on 16 June 1954, just after he had returned from one in the series of research visits to Central Australia, Strehlow voiced his conviction that traditional Indigenous Religions were rapidly being forgotten by younger Arrernte leaders (Lutheran Archives: Strehlow, 1954). Strehlow began the lecture by drawing attention to the changes he had experienced between his recent visits and his first research venture in the region. He referred to a return trip he made in 1952 to the Horseshoe Bend district, which was among the locations where he had first begun studying Arrernte Indigenous Religions 20 years previously. He notes in the lecture that in the interim, his original informants, in this case fully-initiated old men of the Horseshoe Bend area, had all died, and his new informants had lost all knowledge of the sacred secrets that had been disclosed to him originally. Strehlow indicates that on his recent visit, he asked local elders to take him to 'the great ceremonial site near Uralterinja', because he wanted to film in Kodachrome the ritual in honour of the great snake he had witnessed previously, and which, as we noted in Chapter 3, he had described in detail in *Aranda Traditions* (Lutheran Archives: Strehlow, 1954). But the current Elders could not even remember where the site was. He then tells how during his 1932–33 research trip what he calls 'the last tjurunga objects of the Horseshoe Bend area' had been brought down from their storage places and shown to him. He describes the scene:

> This was done so that the few surviving old men could guard them without having to wander too far from the station. Only one of these men, whose name was Wutupia, had any heirs. He had shown all the tjurunga to me proudly and said – "When I die, all these tjurunga will go to my son; and when my son dies, they will go to my grandson: he will own all these treasures one day." But only a few weeks later the grandson died unexpectedly in an influenza epidemic; some years later Wutupia's son died without having had further children; and in January last year Wutupia himself passed on, the last of the men of his group (Lutheran Archives: Strehlow, 1954).

---

4.   In the Preface to *Aranda Traditions*, Strehlow (1947: Preface) explains that many changes had occurred between 1935 when he completed writing the three papers that formed the book and its publication in 1947. He notes that 'all the main informants mentioned in this volume have now passed away, taking the last of their secret knowledge with them'.

The present informants took out the same *tjurunga*, which were discoloured from disuse, but they did not know any of the sacred verses associated with them. Strehlow then produced his own diary in which he had recorded the verses connected with these *tjurunga* as they had been relayed to him by the now deceased Elder Wutupia. The men greased and covered the *tjurunga* objects with red ochre, while Strehlow recited from his diary the sacred chants associated with them. He then recounts how the next day, he and his companions passed by an open flat area near the Finke River where for two months in 1933 he had witnessed Southern Arrernte ceremonies involving, in his words, 'ancestral avengers, serpents, emus, and other myth-ical figures' (Lutheran Archives: Strehlow, 1954). Now he says the area has been overgrown and fallen into disrepair adding, somewhat nostalgi-cally, 'Never again would the totemic ancestors reappear on it' (Lutheran Archives: Strehlow, 1954).

A few days later, the party returned to Uralterinja, and this time discov-ered 'the forgotten snake centre' which they had been searching for earlier in the week. Strehlow describes the site as consisting of 'a cleared circular space, occupied by a large cluster of upright stones'. He explains that 'these represent a mythical assembly of avengers, who had come to kill the two venomous serpent ancestors of this region' (Lutheran Archives: Strehlow, 1954). What is significant about the myth, as we noted in Chapter 3, is that these totemic ancestors escape from their pursuers by climbing into the sky, which is unusual since, Strehlow explains, 'normally the supernat-ural beings worshipped in Central Australia have their homes at the sacred centres which are sprinkled through the landscape' (Lutheran Archives: Strehlow, 1954). Because the myth was so extraordinary, Strehlow claims that it had been known throughout Central Australia, and what he calls 'the forgotten site that we had just rediscovered' had been 'a renowned and dreaded ceremonial centre for men belonging to snake totems' over a very wide geographical area (Lutheran Archives: Strehlow, 1954).

The fact that members of the present generation had forgotten even the most important rituals related to sacred ceremonial sites explains why, in Strehlow's view, many *tjurunga* had been given to him personally and why the most safely-guarded secrets known only to initiated men had been revealed to him. He explains:

> The last old men who still have so much to give us are in their sixties and seventies; and their sons and grandsons, if they have them, are completely ignorant of the traditions of their forefathers. This lack of heirs to whom the old native men could pass on their ancient tribal heritage is in one respect an asset to trusted research workers. One of the reasons why sev-eral Aranda informants, now dead, offered their final secrets to me was the fact that they had no possible heirs of any kind; and they did not wish their greatest treasure to die with them (Lutheran Archives: Strehlow, 1954).

The lecture he delivered at the University of Adelaide confirms that by the time he had completed the series of research trips to Central Australia in 1953, Strehlow had come to the firm conclusion that the Indigenous ceremonies, sacred verses, and important sites on the landscape were being forgotten and would soon be lost altogether to the next generation. In an article published in 1962, he asserted that 'the time will soon arrive when the old traditions of Central Australia will cease being told to the younger generations of natives, and when the old songs will no longer ring out in the vastness of the untamed interior' (1962a: 11). In his 1954 lecture, he claimed that the 'native traditions' were in complete collapse, and predicted that 'what has already happened in the Horseshoe Bend area is about to be repeated everywhere else in Central Australia within the next five to ten years' (Lutheran Archives: Strehlow, 1954). And he reiterated his conviction that his own records provided the only source for preserving the lost tradition represented by the collective Arrernte religious culture: 'Now its memory lived on only in my notebooks and photographs' (Lutheran Archives: Strehlow, 1954). Strehlow concluded his public lecture in a lyrical way, quite appropriate to one trained in Classics, Linguistics and English: 'It is now one hour before sunset. After that will come, not twilight, but the sudden onset of a true Australian night – a night of complete oblivion' (Lutheran Archives: Strehlow, 1954).

In an unpublished paper written in 1977, Strehlow qualified his judgement that Indigenous traditions had totally collapsed with respect to initiation rituals, which he admitted were still being observed but in ways that were radically different from those he observed in 1932–33. He explained:

> When the old sacred Aranda songs fell into oblivion, not only at Hermannsburg but everywhere else too in the Aranda-speaking area (and most adjacent areas as well), the lakabara [circumcision] songs too were forgotten. But circumcision itself survived, though it had now to be carried out in what the Aranda of by-gone days called the "Loritja" fashion (Lutheran Archives: Strehlow, 1977: 5).

The reason circumcision songs had to be performed according to Luritja customs rather than using traditional Arrernte verses was because 'Western Aranda lakabara songs are dead today, just as are all the other Western Aranda songs and ceremonies' (Lutheran Archives: Strehlow, 1977: 6). Circumcision, and to some extent, subincision, retained social significance, but without conveying the religious meanings originally associated with them in the context of Arrernte initiation rituals.

Strehlow then reached a decisive conclusion explaining why the songs, ceremonies, secret-sacred objects and meanings associated with socio-religious customs, such as circumcision, had gone into 'complete oblivion' (a word defined in the *Concise Oxford Dictionary* [Allen, 1990: 818]) as 'the state of having or being forgotten'). He asserted that faith in the Indigenous *religion* of the Arrernte peoples had virtually disappeared over a vast area throughout Central Australia. He voiced this conclusion in stark words: 'The old religious beliefs are either dead, or close to death, over most of the Aranda-speaking area, and also in the adjoining Kukatja, Matuntara, Antekerinja, and Unmatjera areas' (Lutheran Archives: Strehlow, 1977: 6). The religion that Strehlow had described in such a poetic fashion in *Songs of Central Australia*, in anthropological language in *Aranda Traditions* and in socio-cultural terms as 'personal monototemism in a polytotemic community' in *Central Australian Religion* could only be studied as a thing of the past; it was for all practical purposes 'dead' and only 'lived' through the notes, diaries, photographs, recordings and films that he had so carefully compiled.[5]

A Different Take on the Demise of Traditional Religion: Diane Austin-Broos on Pepe or 'God's Law'

The loss of collective memory, as suggested by Strehlow, has been re-interpreted by Diane Austin-Broos in light of what the Western Arrernte came to call *pepe*, the Arrernte word for paper, which they applied to the new law contained in the Bible as it was interpreted by the Lutheran missionaries. Diane Austin-Broos describes the circumstances that led to the situation that caused Strehlow to conclude that knowledge of the old traditions had been lost forever. In the place of the ancient Arrernte 'law', the Lutherans at Hermannsburg had insisted on enforcing the new Christian 'law'. According to Austin-Broos (2009: 86), this 'involved conforming to the ritual-moral order of Lutheran Christian community – the Lutheran view of marriage, individual sin and confession, and withdrawal from the "tjurunga cult"'. The adoption of the Lutheran *pepe* had a widespread effect on traditional ceremonial practices. Austin-Broos asserts that this meant that 'God's law as an orthodoxy grew while *tywerrenge* [*tjurunga*] was in retreat. And as the news of *pepe* spread, the Hermannsburg Mission became a "bigger place"' (2009: 87).

5. Strehlow maintained his position about the demise of Indigenous knowledge until his death. In his testimony to the Australian Law Commission concerning questions about official recognition of customary law, Justice M.D. Kirby cites Strehlow as saying: 'I believe in 1978 no completely untouched aboriginal communities exist anywhere in Australia. All aboriginal Australians, even in the furthest regions of the outback, have by now come into contact with European ideas, with white Australian cultural notions, and with white Australian legal notions. I believe that this is a process that can be neither arrested nor reversed' (cited by Kirby, 1980: 187). Strehlow concluded: 'Few, if any … experts and spokesmen have any deep knowledge of aboriginal customary laws anywhere' (Kirby, 1980: 187).

Despite the magnified cosmology associated with the Lutheran *pepe*, Austin-Broos maintains that adherence to the Christian faith did not result in the total collapse of the traditional Arrernte 'law' precisely because the Lutheran message delivered at Hermannsburg was given a local interpretation by the Indigenous community that resided there. We saw in Chapter 4 that Strehlow had described Arrernte traditions as fundamentally local in nature; each group was associated with a particular *pmara kutata*. Austin-Broos contends that the Lutheran missionaries introduced two fundamental changes that affected the traditional lifestyle of the Western Arrernte, but neither uprooted the local character of Arrernte culture. The first of these was economic, involving a move from a hunter-gatherer type of subsistence economy to a pastoral, sedentary way of life. This change was documented by Sam Gill (1998: 57) who observed that the first missionaries, Kempe and Schwartz, adopted a pastoral way of life at Hermannsburg, initially by sheep herding, but later the Mission changed to cattle rearing. The second change entailed the use of literacy in the Indigenous language, particularly through the Lutheran liturgy and Bible translations.

According to Austin-Broos, the Indigenous population at Hermannsburg substituted the traditional foraging economy with pastoralism, but at the same time maintained 'the tenets of' an emplaced and 'kin-based social life' (Austin-Broos, 2003: 313). This meant that other activities played important parts in the economic and social life of the Mission, such as craft work, gardening, painting and tanning, which 'allowed the Lutherans to shape a personalized social order located in a particular place' resulting in 'an unusual degree of localism' (Austin-Broos, 2003: 313). She explains that 'God's law at Hermannsburg was a localized law for a particular place' (Austin-Broos, 2003: 314). She adds that it 'was a ritual order practiced by familiars and anchored by a domestic moral economy comparable in scale … to the Arrernte's own' (Austin-Broos, 2009: 90). This meant that the Indigenous community at Hermannsburg made the Lutheran interpretation of the Christian 'law' conform to a Christianized pattern, which followed the local, place-orientated way of life that represented age-old Arrernte traditions.

A similar process occurred with the introduction of literacy. Indigenous people substituted the oral traditions associated with the secret-sacred objects, the *tjurunga*, with the written Word of God and the Lutheran liturgy. This substitution, just like the adoption of a pastoral way of life, followed a pattern established previously by the *tjurunga* tradition. As we saw in Chapter 4, Strehlow used two spellings for traditional secret-sacred objects, *tjurunga*, referring to the objects made of stone or wood on which secret totemic symbols were engraved, and the phonetic spelling *tjuruŋa*, which implied the entire totemic tradition, including stories, songs, sacred sites and ceremonies. Austin-Broos (2003: 312) indicates that *pepe* was understood by the Western Arrernte living around Hermannsburg in the same way as *tjuruŋa* was in traditional Arrernte culture as referring not simply to the Bible, 'but also to … all the books, buildings, calls to prayer and services that are part of Lutheran practice'.

The primary substantive change that accompanied the new Christian *pepe* and the introduction of a foreign means of subsistence was the universal element that the missionaries substituted for the restricted and localized ancestral traditions characteristic of the Indigenous Arrernte world view. Although Christian universalism, what Austin-Broos (2009: 101) calls 'a new form of transcendentalism', expanded the scope whereby local institutions were related to a broader world, these were understood by local people in ways that conformed to traditional social structures. Austin-Broos argues that the 'new transcendentalism' 'mirrored' the traditional 'stratified society and centralized authority and power' but at the same time it 'sought to replace the "tjurunga cult," the multiplicity of Dreaming heroes and sites that reflected the Arrernte's previous hunting-and-gathering society' (2009: 101). The combination of the magnified Christian cosmology with traditional social structures introduced a dual system, one that saw Arrernte customary notions of 'law' mediate the Lutheran interpretation of the Christian 'law'.

The allegiance to the Lutheran *pepe* while maintaining traditional social structures at Hermannsburg might be described best in contemporary situations as Indigenous people attempting to contextualize the Christian message within customary ways of living. This process was not without complications and contradictions that even today create tensions among Indigenous Christians. This was demonstrated in interviews Adam Possamai and I conducted in the Utopia region in October 2013. On 8 October 2013, we interviewed a man, who was in his late 60s or early 70s, from the small village of Ampilatwatja, in Alyawarr country approximately 365 kilometres northeast of Alice Springs. He referred repeatedly to two ways, what he called 'the Aboriginal way' and 'the Christian way'. During our interview with him, the man sat on the ground and drew two lines in the dirt, and explained: 'Some people are saying we shouldn't follow two ways. Only one way, that's the Christian way. Old way is a bit not right'. He then pointed to the two lines he had drawn in the dirt and asked us 'which we thought was best, two ways or one' (Cox and Possamai, 2016b: 191). We met the same issue when we interviewed a leading female Catholic lay person from Alice Springs who referred to her Indigenous religious traditions as being 'in us', adding 'our religion is in us' (Cox and Possamai, 2016b: 188). She contrasted this innate religion to 'church religion', which she described as 'the religion of prayers, the religion of holy hymns' (Cox and Possamai, 2016b: 188). This conforms to what Austin-Broos described as the dual identity of the people living at Hermannsburg, who followed the traditional law in the guise of the Lutheran *pepe*, a conclusion that was confirmed by the woman we interviewed when she explained: 'I am an Aboriginal Catholic' (Cox and Possami, 2016b: 188). Austin-Broos (2009: 101) calls this 'two laws for different types of emplaced being'; Lutheran Christianity involved local people accommodating to a law that linked morality to the law of a universal God whereas Indigenous Christianity 'sought to assimilate a new and strange world to a more familiar one' (Austin-Broos, 2003: 315).

The Second Wave of Change: Secular Law, the Decline of Pepe and the Revival of Interest in Aboriginal Traditional Culture

In the early 1950s when T.G.H. Strehlow had announced the almost complete destruction of local knowledge of Arrernte stories, songs and ceremonies, he would not have anticipated the second wave of decline, this time of the Lutheran 'law', which was being displaced by secularism fostered by a new awareness among Indigenous peoples of their rights to land ownership. The wave of secularism, paradoxically, was accompanied by a revival of interest in traditional Indigenous customs, stories and ceremonies by Indigenous peoples themselves. This can be explained by the fact that efforts by Indigenous people to reclaim their land began with protest movements in the 1960s that were linked to cultural revival. It is therefore no coincidence that land claims were accompanied by increased interest among Indigenous groups in reviving their own traditional stories, songs and ceremonies.

A brief explanation of the Land Rights Act is needed at this point. A pivotal moment in the movement to restore Indigenous interest in secret-sacred objects and traditional knowledge occurred in 1967 when the Australian Government authorized a referendum that had resulted from intensive campaigning by Aboriginal activists and their supporters. The referendum, which was supported by 91% of the Australian population, gave the Federal Government the power to enact legislation on Indigenous affairs that took precedence over legislation initiated by the states (Central Land Council, n.d.). This was followed by protests and campaigns by Aboriginal activists lobbying for land rights legislation, as evidenced by the setting up of the 'Aboriginal Embassy' on the grounds of the Federal Parliament in Canberra between January and July 1972 and nationwide strikes and marches held on National Aborigines Day, 14 July 1972 (http://generationone.org.au/blog/2010/01/indigenous-timeline-1970-present-australian-museum). After the Labor Government was elected in December 1972 with Gough Whitlam as Prime Minister, legislation was proposed that would affect the Northern Territory. The Whitlam Government established a Commission headed by Justice Edward Woodward, which was charged with making recommendations for appropriate legislation to establish Land Rights in the Northern Territory. Woodward presented his report in April 1974 in which he asserted that the primary aim of Land Rights legislation was 'the doing of simple justice to a people who have been deprived of their land without their consent and without compensation' (Central Land Council, n.d.). The Aboriginal Land Rights Act (Northern Territory) 1976 was passed in both chambers of the Federal Government in Canberra with strong bi-partisan support in December 1976 and became law in January 1977. The Northern Territory was granted self-government the following year (Central Land Council, n.d.).

Although the Law has been amended over the years, the primary effect of the legislation was to make it impossible for Aboriginal land to be traded or given away and to ensure that the traditional owners of the land could control how the land was used, including making decisions about mining applications. Traditional landowners were defined by the Act as Aboriginal people who could be shown to have 'primary spiritual responsibility' for sacred sites on a particular piece of land and who are entitled by Aboriginal tradition to hunt and gather on that land (Central Land Council, 2003: 3). In his ethnographic study of Native Title Claims, the anthropologist Peter Sutton (2003: 173) explains that Aboriginal claimants to land 'need to be able to show that they are a part of an organised society which derives at least substantial elements of its organisation and its relevant rules from those which obtained in the same area pre-sovereignty'. Sutton adds that the primary 'organising principle' of what he calls 'distinctively Aboriginal societies' is 'the centrality of kinship' (2003: 173). In this sense, the 'spiritual owners' of the land can be substantiated on one level according to kinship relations that are established through genealogical records.

Under the current provisions of the Native Claims Act, land is given to a Land Trust, which administers the land for a Land Council, but the Land Trust cannot make any decisions without the consent of a Land Council. The Land Council in turn must consult the traditional landowners, which as Sutton (2003: 173) has shown, is at least in part founded on kinship as the basis for a 'shared normative system'. In a document prepared by the Central Land Council explaining the Land Rights Act, the Council summarized the relationships between Land Trusts, Land Councils and Traditional Owners:

> So a Land Trust owns the land and the Land Council checks if traditional owners agree with proposals. The Land Council then directs the Land Trust to carry out the proposals and the Land Trust must follow the directions (Central Land Council, 2003: 5).

When in 1976, the Australian Government passed the Land Rights Act applicable to the Northern Territory, the Lutheran Mission at Hermannsburg was directly affected. In 1979, the land that had been leased to the Mission since the late nineteenth century was transferred to Indigenous ownership under the provisions of the Act (Austin-Broos, 2003: 314). Just over ten years earlier, in 1966, the prospects for the Lutheran Mission looked very different; it could be described as having reached a high point. A new church building was completed to supplement the previous church which had been dedicated under the direction of Carl Strehlow in 1897. Strehlow had achieved the monumental task of turning around the Mission from the time he arrived in 1894, when for all practical purposes the Lutheran Mission founded by Kempe and Schwartz had been abandoned. (The original church, which was a log cabin, collapsed in 1895 after a severe rain storm.) Sam Gill reports that by the end of 1894, Strehlow had attracted around 60 Indigenous people to the Mission station and that three years after the completion of the new, substantial church, average church attendance had reached 100 (Gill, 1998: 89–90). In the early 1960s, the Mission was attracting such numbers to its services that the church built in the Strehlow era was considered too small and inadequate. As a result, plans were made for the construction of a larger church. Its foundation stone was unveiled at a service held on 22 August 1965 led by the then Finke River Mission Superintendent Gary Stoll (Radke, 1965: 299). The opening and dedication of the new church took place on 25 September 1966, nearly 70 years to the day when the foundation stone of the church built during the early years of Carl Strehlow's ministry was laid (Radke, 1966a: 229). D.J. Radke, the Lutheran pastor at Hermannsburg when the new church was completed, writes that the Lutheran Mission had grown from 'seven baptized aboriginal Christians in 1887 to over five hundred in 1966' (Radke, 1966b: 331).

After the Lutheran Church relinquished control of the land in 1979, a Historic District was created to preserve the memory of the Mission for the general public. The old church and the buildings comprising the Hermannsburg Mission station now constitute a National Heritage Place under the jurisdiction of the Department of Environment and Energy of the Australian Government and is a major tourist centre in the region (https://www.environment.gov.au/heritage/places/national/hermannsburg). The new church that was completed in 1966 remains an active congregation and on 25 September 2016 celebrated its 50th anniversary. However, significant changes occurred following the enactment of the 1976 Land Rights law, the last being the closing of the Lutheran school in 1989 in favour of a state-funded, secular educational system. This marked the end of the Hermannsburg Mission, or as Austin-Broos (2003: 315) put it: 'The Lutheran school had been the Mission's last institutional stand'.

The changes that occurred between 1966, when the new church was completed at Hermannsburg and the end of the 1980s when the Lutheran school was transferred to Government control, marked a movement away from the Lutheran tradition of *pepe* to the dominance of secular influences. Austin-Broos argues that the gradual secularization of Arrernte society was accompanied by the 'growth of a cash economy and welfare bureaucracy' (2003: 314), but at the same time there was a revival of interest among Indigenous peoples in their ancient traditions. This was symbolized by the replacement of the Mission name for the area, Hermannsburg, with the original name for the region, Ntaria. Austin-Broos contends that the administration under the new land title law became both Indigenous and secular, a fact marked by the 'burgeoning outstation system' (2003: 314), which she explains 'allowed Arrernte, and other Aboriginal communities to return to their traditional lands in small kin-based groups' (2003: 314, fn 10). These factors led Austin-Broos to conclude that *'pepe* has lost its footing at Ntaria, and Christianity as practised rite is in retreat' (2003: 314).

Evaluations of Strehlow's Assertions

For all practical purposes, T.G.H. Strehlow ceased active field research in the mid-1960s, although he and his wife Kathleen made one final venture to Central Australia in 1974. As we noted in Chapter 1, *Songs of Central Australia* had largely been completed by 1956, after Strehlow had finished recording data on the ceremonial chants that comprised the main material for the book (Strehlow, 1971a: xiv). This means that Strehlow's conclusions made in the late 1940s and 1950s about the loss of memory of Arrernte traditions and the demise of traditional forms of religion among Arrernte speaking groups were made at the height of the spread of the Lutheran *pepe* and when the economic life of the people had been transformed from a hunter-gatherer form of subsistence into a pastoral and sedentary existence. Indeed his conclusions were reached more than 20 years before Land Rights legislation was enacted and with it the rise of a new wave of Indigenous secularism, which was accompanied by renewed interest in recovering knowledge of ancient traditions.

How then are we to evaluate Strehlow's final conclusion voiced in his unpublished article of 1977 that traditional Arrernte religion was 'dead', remembering that this verdict was based on his direct and intimate experience of Arrernte traditions and the changes that had affected Arrernte religious life between his first introduction to Indigenous customs as a boy and the span of his academic research begun in 1932? Insight into Strehlow's judgement about the demise of Indigenous knowledge is offered by the anthropologist John Morton, who has worked closely in recent years among the central desert peoples on native title cases. Initially, Morton agreed that there is some evidence for Strehlow's conclusion. He writes:

> The indigenous system of authority was placed under great strain after the white invasion of traditional lands. Large ceremonies became difficult to stage and provision when the traditional lands were taken over by white settlers, and some young men found escape from the authority of the elders and the rigorous discipline of initiation by working for white bosses (Morton, n.d.).

Despite the powerful forces that contributed to cultural decline, Morton argues that Strehlow's conclusions were far too sweeping and actually minimized the extent of the knowledge that had been passed on through the generations. Morton contends that 'unbeknown to Strehlow, the old men continued to instruct their young men when they could', suggesting that none of the persistent efforts by outside forces to disrupt cross-generational teaching 'completely obliterated the indigenous system of Law and cultural transmission' (Morton, n.d.).

The research Adam Possamai and I conducted in 2013 in the Utopia region of the Northern Territory demonstrates the complexity that is involved in evaluating Morton's criticism of Strehlow. Possamai and I uncovered deeply felt fears among the present Elders that young people were abandoning tradition in light of the rapid changes affecting contemporary society. In a series of interviews, we found repeated references among the Elders, and also among women's leaders, that the traditional ways of life were under enormous strain. An example of this apprehension was voiced by an Elder we interviewed in the village of Ampilatwatja, who by drawing a diagram in the dirt in front of which we were sitting, put it this way: 'My father here, and me, here today, and we all got to follow from this track … And me, here my son. My son can [follow] his people's track' (Cox and Possamai, 2016b: 186). The fear that members of the younger generation were losing knowledge of the ancient traditions was also expressed by the eldest of a group of six women who were seated talking amongst themselves during the regional football gatherings in Utopia in October 2013. The woman told us:

> Some people might forget … the traditional way. Then grandparents will step in and do that, grandparents. So families have responsibility, like there's Elders and relatives, elder relatives gotta keep up. They got continuously teach. Without ceasing, they gotta keep on teaching, teaching, teaching' (Cox and Possamai, 2016b: 192).

Such widespread apprehensions that were expressed about losing Indigenous knowledge and the determination to preserve it would appear to confirm Strehlow's conclusion that by 1960 'native traditions' were in complete collapse. On closer inspection, they suggest a rather more complex situation created by contemporary events that Strehlow either minimized or could not have anticipated. On the one hand, they show that during the 50-plus years since Strehlow made such claims many Arrernte Elders and leaders had attempted tirelessly to pass on traditional knowledge to the generations that followed. On the other hand, it is extremely difficult to assess how successful the Elders were in actually preserving and transmitting Indigenous knowledge despite their persistent exhortations about the importance of educating the young in traditional ways. It is highly likely that the determination of Indigenous leaders to preserve knowledge of traditional customs is related to the increased pressure for land rights that began in the 1960s and the cultural revival that accompanied it, a movement that reached its pinnacle after Strehlow died. What Adam Possamai and I discovered on our research in 2013, therefore, can only be evaluated in the light of the powerful influences exerted on traditional ways of life by the forces of secularization that since 1976 have been progressively affecting Aboriginal societies in rural contexts, particularly among the younger generations.

John Morton argues that land claims hearings in Central Australia provide firm evidence that knowledge of traditions had persisted and had never been totally forgotten by generations of Elders. The first land claim hearing in Central Australia was considered by the court in 1978 during which, in Morton's words, Aboriginal witnesses gave 'strong and convincing evidence of ceremonial involvement and ties to land – in the process actively denying any claims about their cultural demise' (Morton, n.d.: 7). The connection of land claims to the revitalization of traditional secret-sacred objects and ceremonial sites was also noted by Austin-Broos (2009: 70), who cites the event I referred to above when in 1955, in anticipation of events that would occur in the next decade, Indigenous leaders 'resacralised' the Manangananga Cave, an act that, according to Austin-Broos, 'helped revalue objects and sites', although, she admits, 'in altered ways'.

We noted that under the Land Claims legislation of 1976, in order to be recognized as traditional owners, a group of Elders must be able to demonstrate 'primary spiritual responsibility' for sacred sites on a particular piece of land. Problems with this definition have been discussed at length by Philip Batty (2014: 303), who argues that 'the land rights laws enacted in 1976 made it clear that Aboriginal people would only succeed in claiming land if they were able to prove their credentials as "traditional owners"'. But, Batty asks, how would 'traditional owners' be identified and confirmed? He suggests that it was only on the basis of 'anthropological investigation' that the courts could base their judgements on this matter (2014: 303). Batty notes that in the Palm Valley land claim hearing held in 1994 at the Palm Valley national park, which borders Hermannsburg/Ntaria, frequent references were made to the publications of the seminal ethnologists among the Arrernte, Baldwin Spencer and F.J. Gillen, but also and more particularly, to the work of T.G.H. Strehlow (see also, Austin-Broos, 2009: 23, 105–108). Batty (2014: 303) concludes: 'It was at this point that the Aboriginal subject of Australian anthropology, constituted over more than a century of anthropological investigation, was recruited, reshaped and remade – not without difficulty, as a somewhat misaligned subject of the Australian legal system'.

Of particular importance in establishing traditional ownership in the Palm Valley case was the possession by the claimants of *tjurunga*. Batty (2014: 304) reports that Justice Gray, the judge in charge of the Palm Valley adjudication, likened *tjurunga* to 'title deeds' making the possession of genuine *tjurunga* equivalent to 'written evidence' of land tenure. It is important to underscore, however, as Strehlow convincingly demonstrated, that *possession* of *tjurunga* does not equate to understanding the *meaning* of the secret-sacred objects, nor does it demonstrate that those who produced them at the hearing had knowledge of their ceremonial use. Rather, according to Batty, it demonstrated a different point: 'Australian law and Aboriginal law are simply incommensurate' (2014: 304). The association of secret-sacred objects with Aboriginal land claims did not demonstrate the persistence of Indigenous knowledge, but in Batty's words, 'it was essentially about the moral reformation of the nation's relationship with its indigenous minority' (2014: 304). This discontinuity between Australian and Aboriginal law, and the fundamentally different aims in the production of the *tjurunga* as evidence of 'land rights' as opposed to the transmission of tradition, casts doubt on John Morton's conclusion that the land claim hearings in Central Australia provided evidence contradicting Strehlow's assertions about Arrernte 'cultural demise'.

Diane Austin-Broos adds some further insight on the extent of traditional knowledge at the time of the Land Claims legislation. As we have seen, the interest in *tjurunga* traditions was revived as Australian law sought to return Indigenous land to its original owners. Austin-Broos (2009: 191) calls this the 'milieu' in which cultural revival took place. She refers in particular to the Superintendent's Report compiled in the last quarter of 1975 by the Lutheran missionary, Gary Stoll, as evidence of such a cultural revival. Stoll's report, as cited by Austin-Broos, describes the performance of 'two complete ceremonies involving many days and quite a few nights of singing and re-enacting the travels and exploits of various "ancestors"' (cited by Austin Broos, 2009: 192). In his report, Stoll indicates that the participants in the ceremony ranged in age from 'their late twenties to mid-seventies' and notes that many had grown up on the Mission (cited by Austin Broos, 2009: 192). He expresses surprise at 'the extent and intactness of knowledge and skills retained' by the men (cited by Austin Broos, 2009: 192). He also applauds the 'efficiency of the organisation' of the ceremonies calling it 'impressive' because it was conducted in 'complete independence of any European assistance'(cited by Austin Broos, 2009: 192). This account would seem to suggest that in 1975, when Stoll compiled his Superintendent's Report, knowledge of ceremonies performed for totemic ancestors was 'intact' and widespread.

This conclusion hides the fact that Stoll's description in numerous ways contradicts what might have been expected in traditional ceremonies as Strehlow recorded them in the early 1930s. The participants in this 're-enactment' came from a wide area and are not described by Stoll as belonging to one totemic tradition and thus would not have been associated, even loosely, with one *pmara kutata*. As we have seen, according to Strehlow, those invited to attend major totemic ceremonies were determined by strictly regulated protocols. Austin-Broos (2009: 192) admits that this 'rite involved an intense interaction between Western Arrernte men and others from the south and west', suggesting that the participants were from different totemic clans. In his report, although representatives of the Lutheran Church were invited to observe the ceremonies, Stoll does not indicate if any prohibitions were imposed (although he calls them 'secret') (cited by Austin-Broos, 2009: 192). Under restrictions imposed by the old 'law', participants and observers would have been carefully controlled, with those who violated traditional practices threatened with death. The major problem, therefore, with Stoll's conclusion that this ceremonial re-enactment provides evidence that the ancient traditions had been maintained results from his failure to situate the ritual in any particular, localized tradition.

A critical factor motivating the performance of this eclectic ceremony was what Austin-Broos (2009: 192) calls a 'political dimension'. This explains why representatives of the Lutheran Mission were invited to attend the rituals. Stoll confirms this when he explains that the church leaders were welcomed at the ceremonial re-enactment because the Indigenous Elders needed their help 'by "talking to Government"' (cited by Austin-Broos, 2009: 192). He explains that by observing the rituals, Lutheran leaders would be prepared to 'explain to the outside world what they're on about particularly as regards to land' (cited by Austin-Broos, 2009: 192). This conclusion was based on the assumption that many of the Lutheran Church representatives, like Stoll, were able to communicate in the language and ethos of Australian law and thus could mediate between the Aboriginal community and the courts in land claims hearings.

It is clear from these above accounts by Morton, Batty and Austin-Broos that the cultural revival that accompanied Indigenous lobbying for Land Rights did not translate into a restoration of the memory of traditional religious knowledge associated with the secret-sacred objects, songs, stories and ceremonies, nor did it contradict Strehlow's findings. In one sense, the revived interest in tradition imposed a new law onto the original law, and at the same time superseded the Lutheran law. This new law was determined by the judicial system of the secular state through Land Rights legislation, which, as we have seen, relied primarily on possession of Indigenous secret-sacred objects as evidence of entitlement to land.

So, was Strehlow right after all? There can be no doubt that the concerted efforts by outside forces to disrupt traditional culture by dispossessing Indigenous people of the knowledge of their beliefs and ceremonies had a strong and lasting effect. Among the Arrernte, the Lutheran Mission in particular contributed to the loss of memory when the content of traditional law, including its ceremonies, stories, songs and secret-sacred objects, was replaced by the Christian *pepe*, which included the Lutheran liturgy, prayers, hymns, organization and Bible teachings. T.G.H. Strehlow did not live to see the closure of the Mission at Hermannsburg and with it the increasing power of secularization among contemporary Arrernte peoples. These latter events led to a double loss of memory: the original totemic stories, songs and ceremonies were forgotten while during the second wave of change through secularism, the authority of the Lutheran *pepe* entered a stage of terminal decline.

Conclusion

It is worth reiterating at this point that the descriptions I have documented of Arrernte religious and social practices represented Strehlow's unparalleled contribution to preserving knowledge of ancient Arrernte traditions, a fact that is only recently coming to light in the repatriation project emanating from the Strehlow Research Centre in Alice Springs. It is for this reason that I take a brief detour in the next chapter to discuss Strehlow as a phenomenologist of religion, the aim of which is to establish his credentials as a scholar in his own right in the academic study of religions both within Australia and internationally. I then return to the theme of the loss of Indigenous memory in Chapter 8 where I analyse how and in what ways Strehlow's work is being used by contemporary Arrernte Elders to recover and restore the knowledge that Strehlow contended had fallen into oblivion.

7

Strehlow the 'Insider' as a Phenomenologist of Religion

I have now completed my review of Strehlow's own writings about Arrernte myths, social organization and ceremonies and I have outlined the basis for his claim that knowledge of Indigenous religious practices as he discovered them when he began his research in Central Australia in 1932 has largely been lost or forgotten by the current generation. I am now in a position to draw some conclusions about the theoretical method Strehlow employed when gathering his research data and interpreting his findings for outside audiences. I contend in this chapter that Strehlow's approach fits into the broad methodological scheme I have outlined as the phenomenology of religion (Cox, 2006; Cox, 2010).

That my analysis of Strehlow as a phenomenologist has a direct bearing on current academic methodologies in the emerging field of Indigenous Studies is confirmed in an article written by Marcia Langton of Melbourne University, herself an Indigenous Australian, who claims that Indigenous societies traditionally have been reified, or turned into objects, by academic researchers. Langton argues that the most important innovation introduced by current approaches in Indigenous Studies is 'its restitution of the agency of Indigenous people' through which the scholar brings 'the voice of the Indigenous protagonists into their own history' and explains 'events by reference to the perspectives and theories that they themselves exerted on their affairs' (Langton, 2012: 173). Langton suggests that the important book by Stuart Kirsch, entitled *Reverse Anthropology* (2006), which deals with issues of environment and society from the perspective of the Indigenous peoples of New Guinea, 'admitted and explained the agency of people who had largely been regarded as mere subjects trapped in a world not of their own making' (Langton, 2012: 173). This leads to Langton's conclusion that the 'greatest contribution of Indigenous studies as a field of scholarly endeavour has been to reinstate those people who were once simple subjects as people with agency' (Langton, 2012: 173).

Langton overlooks a widely shared assumption maintained by scholars working in the field of the academic study of religions that the aim of their

research is to achieve an understanding of the communities they are studying. Understanding in this sense is used very much in line with the German
word, *Verstehen*, which carries the connotation, not always evident in English, of 'understanding in depth' (Waardenburg, 1978: 224; see also Swain,
1985). In particular, scholars working throughout the twentieth century
developed a method they called the Phenomenology of Religion which had
three fundamental aims: 1) to enable researchers to gain understanding of
the religions they are studying by overcoming the subject-object dichotomy,
sometimes called the 'insider-outsider predicament'; 2) to provide interpretations of religions that can be affirmed by the practitioners of the religions
being researched; 3) to make the scholarly study of religious communities
a joint effort or partnership between the academics who are conducting
the research and adherents within the religion under study. It will be clear
that these aims are consistent with Langton's call to acknowledge that the
adherents who form the subject matter of Religious Studies themselves possess 'agency'; they are active participants in research projects rather than
passive 'objects' that can be studied as if they were impersonal and non-
organic 'things'.

In this chapter, after outlining the 'insider-outsider' problem in the study
of religion, I discuss the phenomenology of religion as a principal method
in the academic study of religions. I present phenomenology first by summarizing the thought of key twentieth-century phenomenologists of religion,
which I follow by outlining the definitive stages in the phenomenological
method as I have presented it in previous writings. This discussion provides
the background for the main theme of this chapter in which I consider first
T.G.H. Strehlow, as an 'insider' to Arrernte religion and culture, and then
as a phenomenologist of religion who, although he never referred to himself
technically in such terms, employed the main principles contained in the
phenomenological method.

The Insider-Outsider Problem in the Study of Religion

If *Verstehen* defines one of the primary goals of the academic study of religions, the problem immediately arises as to how researchers, who are not
members of the religious communities they are studying, can attain a level
of understanding 'in depth'. This problem is exacerbated when researchers
are studying cultures entirely different from their own, often requiring them
to learn new languages. Cross-cultural study carries the risk that scholars,
even after devoting many years to language study and living in an unfamiliar society, may think they have attained a deep level of understanding of the religious beliefs and practices of the alien culture, but in fact the
understanding reached may remain at a superficial level and be prone to
misinterpretation.

Only someone who has been born into and grown up in a culture can fully comprehend what it means to participate in a religion unique to members of that particular community. For example, in his book, *African Religions and Philosophy*, the Kenyan-born theologian, John S. Mbiti, claimed that, although traditional African views of the world have not been written down, let alone systematized, he possessed an intuitive insight into what African philosophy entails, since, he writes, 'I am by birth an African' (Mbiti, 1969: 2). This would imply that only an 'insider' can attain 'understanding in depth' because only believers know what the experience of participating in their own religious culture 'feels like'.

Yet, 'understanding in depth' is not guaranteed simply because someone is born into a community, is a member of a group or even knows what it is like to be a believer in a religious organization. Academic 'understanding in depth' is based on the systematic formulation of scholarly theories, testing and subsequent interpretations. Such understanding is hampered, however, if the scholar doing the research has a confessional commitment to the community being studied. The insider-as-researcher predicament results when academic believers are unable to separate themselves from the communities of which they are members or in which they grew up. This does not necessarily imply prejudice, but it points to the critical problem that scholars who are also believers may find it impossible to formulate scientific hypotheses and reach objective conclusions about their own religion, since to do so requires detaching themselves from a belief-system to which they are fully committed. The issue I am pointing towards and which Marcia Langton raised from a different perspective is frequently referred to as the 'insider-outsider' problem in the study of religion. On the one hand, an outsider can never see with the eyes of faith, which only an insider is able to achieve, but on the other hand, an insider may find it impossible to step back by providing an objective, distanced interpretation of his or her own tradition. We will consider T.G.H. Strehlow as an insider and an outsider to Arrernte religion and culture shortly, but first I outline how this issue has been addressed within the branch of the academic study of religions called the Phenomenology of Religion.

Key Figures in the Phenomenology of Religion

A formative figure in developing current expressions of the Phenomenology of Religion was W. Brede Kristensen, a Norwegian-born scholar, who in 1901 was appointed Chair of Comparative Religion at the University of Leiden in the Netherlands. Kristensen famously declared 'there is no religious reality other than the faith of believers' leading to his frequently quoted conclusion: 'the believers were completely right' (Kristensen, 1960: 13–14). By this, Kristensen meant that we must call into question any interpretation of religion that is potentially offensive to believers since believers understand their own religion better than anyone from the outside ever could. To gain an insider's perspective, the scholar needs to suspend widely accepted presuppositions about the origin and meaning of religion. Kristensen believed, for example, that evolutionary theories predisposed the scholar to evaluate religions from the outside and thus, in the words of Eric Sharpe (1986: 228), 'to have been responsible for inducing scholars to pass premature judgment on material they had learned to understand only in part'.

The suspension of prior assumptions, both academic and personal, became one of the key elements in the phenomenological method in the study of religion. It was developed by Kristensen's student, Gerardus van der Leeuw, in his seminal publication, *Religion in Essence and Manifestation* (first published in English in 1938), in which he applied the philosophical concept, *epoché*, derived from the German philosopher Edmund Husserl, to the study of religion. The term *epoché* was used by Husserl to suspend all judgements associated with what he called the natural attitude (which naively assumes that what is observed tells us all there is to know about the world) such as material things, science, other humans, and the sequence and order of events. All the things we take for granted about what we perceive as real, to use a term Husserl borrowed from mathematics, must be 'put into brackets'. In solving algebraic equations, for example, the mathematician places the various components of the formula into brackets and works on solving each problem placed in brackets one at a time in order that at the conclusion each limited solution can be applied to resolving the problem of the entire equation (Husserl, 1931: 111; Cox, 2006: 16–30). In the phenomenology of religion, van der Leeuw used *epoché* as a tool aimed at eliminating potentially distorting biases, thereby enabling the observer of religious communities to attain understanding of the subjective nature of religion (its internal structure) and its objective meaning (its broader connections), or to put it in terms of this chapter, to overcome the insider-outsider problem in the study of religion.

Another key idea employed by phenomenologists of religion is the practice of empathy, or cultivating a 'feeling for' religious groups of which the scholar is not a part in order to attain understanding of beliefs, practices and cultural norms that may be entirely alien to those of the one conducting the study. Van der Leeuw (1938: 675) called this method 'sympathetic interpolation', which he defined as 'the 'primitively human art of the actor which is indispensable to all arts, but to the sciences of the mind also' adding that 'only the persistent and strenuous application of intense sympathy ... qualifies the phenomenologist to interpret appearances'. The British phenomenologist of religion, Ninian Smart (1973: 54), preferred the term empathy to sympathy, which he explained, enabled the observer to recognize 'a framework of intentions' among the believers. For Smart, this not only required the active involvement of the researcher, but also included the acts of a believing community (what it intends by its myths, rituals and symbols), which must be apprehended by the observer if genuine understanding is to be achieved. The twin processes of using empathy and interpolating what is experienced into terms the researcher can comprehend defined for Smart the key elements in the phenomenology of religion: first, by enabling the scholar to access the meaning of the religious life and practices of adherents and then by making sense of them intentionally in terms of the researcher's own culture.

The Canadian scholar of comparative religions, Wilfred Cantwell Smith, argued forcefully for a method that includes the perspectives of believers in any academic descriptions and interpretations of religious communities. Writing in 1959, Smith (1959: 34) maintained that the study of religion was undergoing a fundamental transformation from one that regards religion impersonally as an 'it' to a more personal understanding of the inner faith of believers. Smith explained that the first stage in personalizing the study of religion had already occurred, since scholars had begun describing personal faith in terms of what people, referred to as 'they', say, do or believe. This even now is advancing to a deeper level whereby scholars are becoming aware of their own involvement with those they are studying, so that 'we' are now talking about what 'they' say, do or believe. Smith then urged scholars to advance to the next phase in the personalization process by adopting a dialogical approach so that the 'they' is changed to a 'you' and the study becomes one of 'we' talking to 'you'. If this is accomplished, a scholar will finally understand that the study of human faith requires breaking down the old subject-object dichotomy so that the one doing the studying and the one being studied merge into a common enterprise consisting of '"we all" … talking with each other about "us"' (1959: 34). The culmination of the dialogical approach, Smith concluded, results in the recognition that 'in comparative religion man is studying himself' (1959: 55).

In a book entitled *Towards a World Theology*, published 22 years after he wrote these words, Smith re-named and revised the dialogical method, calling it 'corporate critical self-consciousness' (1981: 59–60). By this he was referring to a form of reflexivity whereby the scholar adopts a 'critical, rational and inductive' self-conscious approach to the study of a community of persons, a community that is comprised of at least two people, the one doing the studying and the one being studied (1981: 60). The community, what Smith called earlier the 'we' talking to 'us', becomes aware of 'any given particular human condition, or action as a condition or action of itself as a community' (1981: 60). In other words, when scholars engage in a study of religion, they include themselves as humans in their investigations as well as the participants in the communities they are studying. This implies that the scholar experiences and understands the conditions

or actions he or she is studying simultaneously, both subjectively as participant and objectively as observer. In this way, the subjective experience of
the scholar, comprising a personal and existential involvement much like
faith, is united with objective knowledge, which adopts an external, critical,
analytical and scientific perspective (1981: 60).

The results of scholarship are verified in this way both subjectively and
objectively, experientially and empirically. Smith called this 'the verificationist principle' of 'humane knowledge' (1981: 97). The principle is
applied in three stages. The first requires that an outside observer's statement be acceptable to the faith of the community being studied. He writes:

> No statement about Islamic faith is true that Muslims cannot accept. No
> personalist statement about Hindu religious life is legitimate in which
> Hindus cannot recognize themselves. No interpretation of Buddhist doc-
> trine is valid unless Buddhists can respond, "Yes! That is what we hold"
> (1981: 97).

The second part of the principle applies to the outside observer, so that
what is said about faith communities 'must satisfy the non-participant,
and satisfy all the most exacting requirements of rational inquiry and academic rigour' (1981: 97). Finally, the third aspect applies to people of other
faiths, so that no statement about Muslims, for example, can be regarded
as true that non-Muslims cannot accept. No account of Hinduism can
be legitimate if the Hindu's neighbours cannot recognize the Hindu in
the accounts. 'No statement about Buddhist doctrine is valid unless non-
Buddhists can respond, "Yes – now we understand what those Buddhists
hold"' (1981: 97).

Smith offers an example of how the verificationist principle works by
describing an Indian temple at Madurai in south India (1981: 62–63). He
says that if we are to appreciate the temple in its full significance, we must
'get inside the consciousness of those for whom it is a sacred space' and
experience 'how it feels and what it means to be a worshipper within it'
(1981: 66). At the same time, we must investigate the temple objectively,
learning the facts about its history, gaining an understanding of its impact
on the surrounding community, and comprehending its place in the larger
city of Madurai. We even need to learn to know 'how it is perceived ... by
the small iconoclastic Muslim group in the area, for whom temple worship is a sin' (1981: 66). In a secular state such as India, it will also be
important to become aware of the perceptions of the temple held by Marx-
ists, 'whose analysis of its economic role is impertinent in one sense but
not in both' (1981: 66). Corporate critical self-consciousness thus, according to Smith, if applied faithfully and rigorously, provides true and verifi-
able knowledge of the temple as a human institution. Smith calls this an
example of achieving 'humane knowledge', the aim of which is not pure

objectivity, but 'disciplined corporate self-consciousness, critical, comprehensive, global' (1981: 78–79), a form of knowing that collapses once and for all the subject-object dichotomy that for so long has dominated Western approaches to the study of fellow human beings.

Stages in the Phenomenological Method

Following the writings of the key phenomenologists of religion I have identified, I have organized the phenomenological method into a step-by-step system according to three main phases: 1) the attitudinal phase; 2) the descriptive phase; 3) the interpretative phase. The first step in the attitudinal phase involves performing the technique of *epoché* through which scholars bring to their awareness and attempt to limit the impact of their most powerful and potentially distorting pre-judgements, both academic and personal, which may determine the outcome of their research before any empirical investigation has taken place. The second stage in the attitudinal phase encourages scholars to see as believers see by fostering an empathetic attitude that interpolates from one's own experience into the experience of the religious believer in order to make comprehensible to outsiders what otherwise might seem bizarre or even offensive in the religion the phenomenologist is seeking to understand. The process of getting inside a believer's mind requires a deep empathy through which researchers cultivate a feeling for the religious communities they are describing and interpreting (Cox, 2010: 52). This is followed by the third stage in the attitudinal phase which I have called 'maintaining *epoché*'. By this I mean that in the process of cultivating empathy, scholars must take particular care to separate academic conclusions from confessional statements concerning the beliefs of the communities they are studying. In other words, students of religion do not actually become believers in the religion they are studying, even though they seek to include the believers' perspectives in their eventual interpretations. To avoid what has been called 'going native' (see for example O'Reilly, 2009: 89–92), researchers must suspend judgements not only about their own potentially distorting academic or personal opinions (performing the *epoché*) but they must continue to hold in abeyance any judgements about the truth or value of the beliefs and practices of the religion they are studying (maintaining *epoché*).

After the steps in the attitudinal phase of the phenomenological method have been employed, scholars then are ready to enter the descriptive phase in which they describe the data observed as accurately as possible. This means that 'words, actions, gestures, songs, symbols, explanations by adherents and stories must be recorded in detail' (Cox, 2010: 57). This is followed by the next step in the descriptive phase, 'naming the phenomena', or put in other terms, the creation of classifications or typologies into which the observed and recorded data can be sorted and organized. Phenomenological categories include, among others: myths, rituals, beliefs, religious practitioners, art, ethics and morality. These classifications can be sub-divided into further types, such as: cosmogonic, socio-moral and quasi-legendary myths; life-cycle, calendrical and crisis rituals; shamanistic, priestly or holy person types of religious practitioners. Such classifications and sub-categories are created by the scholar not only for organizational purposes, but also for comparative reasons. This makes it possible to compare and contrast diverse societies in varying temporal contexts with different types of source material. Of course, it is important not to make naïve or superficial comparisons, but by creating typologies and sub-categories, the salient factors that comprise the classifications can be compared according to the criterion on which the classification has been constructed.

This leads to the stages in the third phase where scholars interpret the data that have been inserted into typological categories and compared. It is important to underscore that comparisons are done primarily for empirical reasons and thus they must be rooted in specific and local contexts. The aim of comparisons, however, is interpretative, to elucidate the meaning of particular religious practices which in turn helps academics make generalizations about the classifications themselves. This was done, for example, by the anthropologist Victor Turner, who analysed life-cycle rituals, such as male initiation ceremonies, among the Ndembu of Zambia. Turner, following the outline of the classical anthropologist, Arnold van Gennep (1908), divided male initiation rituals into three main stages beginning with the first stage, separation from the community, followed by a liminal stage, betwixt and between, where the males are neither children nor yet adults and then finally the incorporation stage, when they return to the community as adults (Turner, 1985: 205–10). The stages, which mark significant changes in the social status of young males, are punctuated throughout with rituals that mark different phases in their passage from children to men. Turner's model operated as a paradigm or structure for initiation ceremonies everywhere, but the specific content, context, rituals, and symbols varied according to local situations. It is possible using Turner's formal structure of initiation rituals to make comparisons that help to promote understanding of the religious significance of life-cycle rituals in general while at the same time insisting that the model must be filled with specific content. In this sense, the interpretative stage in the phenomenological method is shown to be based largely on the ability to generalize beyond specific contexts and thus to create informed comparisons that help elucidate the larger meaning of the categories of religious phenomena according to formal structures or what I have called paradigmatic models (Cox, 1998: 8–9).

Traditionally, phenomenologists of religion have sought to offer interpretations not only of the meaning of specific classifications and sub-categories of the phenomena of religion; they have also identified general patterns that can be applied to religious life everywhere. This final step in the interpretative phase is called 'the eidetic intuition', whereby the scholar constructs a general paradigm for religion in general. Examples of influential academics who have formed models for religion in general include Mircea Eliade (1958, 1959), who found 'patterns in comparative religion' by constructing themes around the sacred and the profane, Gerardus van der Leeuw (1938: 23–28), who described the key concept in religion as 'power' and W. Cantwell Smith, whose model of religion focussed on 'personal faith' in a 'transcendent power' that was embodied in a 'cumulative tradition' (1964: 141). These formal structures of religion provided a framework on which religious phenomena could be placed for the purposes of interpreting their meaning and as a means for promoting an overall understanding of the place of religion in human history.

In brief, as a method for the study of religious communities, the aim of the phenomenology of religion as I have described it is to promote understanding of religions in particular and of religion in general. Its techniques attempt to bridge the gap between the subject and the object of religion, the observer and those that are observed, by drawing on common human ways of thinking which can be translated into multiple cultural contexts and individual inter-subjective experiences. Because all phenomenological interpretations follow from the attitudinal and descriptive phases in the research process, testing the interpretations is two-fold: they must be supported by the most careful attention to empirical descriptions and they must be capable of being affirmed by believing communities themselves. This final point means that phenomenologists of religion, as Marcia Langton has suggested, acknowledge and respect the agency of the so-called objects of study by involving them in the research process and by making their voices heard in the final interpretations presented by scholars to the wider academic community and more broadly to the general public.

T.G.H. Strehlow as an 'Insider' to Arrernte Religion and Culture

It is in the light of the defining characteristics of the phenomenology of religion that we can evaluate the role of T.G.H. Strehlow as an interpreter of Aboriginal religions in Australia, first as an 'insider' to Arrernte culture and then as one who employed the principles of the phenomenology of religion to foster understanding of Arrernte religion among absolute outsiders and, as we saw in the last chapter, among the Arrernte themselves who, according to Strehlow, had become virtual outsiders because they had completely forgotten their ancient traditions.

Strehlow's claim to be an insider to Arrernte religion derives, in the first instance, from his childhood experiences of growing up on the Hermannsburg

Mission among Indigenous children, through which he gained mastery of the Arrernte language. He wrote: 'Born at Hermannsburg, I had grown up on a mission station till the age of fourteen with aboriginal playmates only, and Western Aranda had always been one of my "mother tongues"' (Strehlow, 1962a: 4). Being a native speaker of a language, he argued, gave him an intimate understanding of Arrernte culture that was not available to non-native speakers. He explained:

> In my own childhood years I had had the characteristic qualities of meaningful distinctions between the various Aranda sounds brought home to me in the hard manner in which children learn the sounds of their mother tongue – by the merciless ridicule of my dark playmates, who would repeat for days any phonetic errors made by me, the sole white child living on the station. Hence in the transcription that I finally adopted I was careful to lay stress, not merely on those characteristics of aboriginal speech that might have interested a European phonetician, but on those differences between closely related speech sounds whose neglect in enunciation would have led to misunderstandings and to subsequent ridicule in any conversations carried out between two aboriginal speakers (Strehlow, 1962a: 6).

His childhood experiences were not enough to substantiate his claim to possess special knowledge of Arrernte culture. As we have seen, in 1932, he returned to Central Australia for the first time since leaving at the age of 14 years-old when his father died. He had studied literature and languages at Adelaide University and had intended to pursue an academic career in English literature. He explains:

> When I returned to Central Australia at the beginning of April, 1932, as a young University graduate, I was completely unaware that I was entering upon a lifetime of research in the languages, the literature, the religion, and the social organization of the native tribes of the interior. I had accepted a one-year linguistic research grant from the Australian National Research Council largely because the economic depression of the early nineteen-thirties had temporarily closed all avenues of University employment to me; and I looked upon my task purely as an interlude – a temporary field research assignment upon whose termination I would resume my serious work in English language and literature (Strehlow, 1962a: 4).

We have also seen how he had been persuaded by his mentor Professor J.A. FitzHerbert to use his knowledge of linguistics to study and write about the Arrernte language. After he arrived in Central Australia, he immediately began to conduct field studies to substantiate his work on an Arrernte grammar, but soon discovered that language is intimately connected to culture, including how religious ideas are conveyed in myths and ceremonies. This meant as he studied Arrernte grammar, he also immersed himself in the study of Arrernte culture. Relying on his linguistic knowledge and on the basis of his childhood awareness of the Arrernte customs, he soon won the trust of Elders, who became his chief informants. He provides details of this in *Songs of Central Australia* (1971a: xlv):

> I was only a very young newly-fledged University graduate when I returned to Central Australia in 1932. I was watched for twelve months before Gura, the ceremonial chief of Ilbalintja, finally decided to reveal to me his bandicoot ceremonies and to entrust his sacred myth and his song verses to my keeping. Immediately afterwards Makarinja followed suit. From that point onwards I was sure of the confidence of the remaining Aranda and Loritja totemic clan elders. Many of them were, in fact, almost pathetically eager to pass on their totemic secrets to someone whom they trusted, and in whom they placed their confidence that he would do his best to preserve these secrets from oblivion.

He admits that 'before I could start to do any work on the aboriginal languages, I had to become intimately acquainted with the interior and its people'. To accomplish this he travelled vast distances, which he calculated exactly at 2,689 miles [4327.5 kilometres] (Strehlow, 1962a: 4). During these travels, he explains,

> I had noted down the old tribal boundaries and the location of scores of important totemic sites mentioned in the sacred myths and songs, I had won the confidence of some northern Aranda men sufficiently for them to take me to their sacred centres and tjurunga storehouses, and to reveal to me the complete myths, songs, and ceremonial cycles of their own totems (Strehlow, 1962a: 5).

In this way, he confirmed his 'insider' status: he had grown up among the Arrernte, knew their language intimately and later gained such trust from the Elders that they shared with him knowledge that was never revealed to an 'outsider', nor to Arrernte women or uninitiated boys.

As we saw in Chapter 1, Strehlow's first academic book, entitled *Aranda Phonetics and Grammar*, was published in 1944, and, in a natural conclusion to the original funding for his research, was supported by the Australian National Research Council. This book was a reprint of a series of articles that had appeared in the journal *Oceania* in 1942–43 and was based on his Master's thesis submitted to the University of Adelaide in 1937 (Strehlow 1962a: 6). Again, we have seen that his first in-depth discussion of the overall Arrernte society, based on the research he conducted between 1932 and 1934, was published in 1947 as *Aranda Traditions*. We saw how in this publication Strehlow outlined in great detail the structure of the society, how totems operate both socially and religiously, the myths associated with the totemic ancestors and their related ceremonies. *Aranda Traditions* clearly serves as an academic book aimed at informing a scholarly audience, and other interested outsiders, about the intricate and complex beliefs and practices of Arrernte peoples.

Strehlow returned to Central Australia on three occasions between 1947 and 1953 to conduct further research in support of an ambitious book he was writing that contained details of totemic ceremonial rituals, songs and verses, which he was translating from Arrernte to English. He followed these with three further research projects in 1955, 1958 and 1960. He explains the extent of the research he conducted on these six visits between 1947 and 1960 in a published article in 1962:

> During these six journeys extensive tape recordings of myths and songs, thousands of feet of colour films of aboriginal sacred ceremonies, and full genealogies containing many hundreds of names, were added to my earlier collections. My notebooks now contain more than four thousand song couplets and over a hundred myths – all of them written down in native dialects and languages. I have photographs of more than seven hundred and fifty secret totem acts, and several miles of colour films of the ceremonial cycles witnessed in recent years. In addition, there are almost fifty hours of tape recordings of aboriginal myths and songs (Strehlow, 1962a: 7–8).

As noted in Chapter 5, this long series of research visits to Central Australia finally produced *Songs of Central Australia* in 1971. Although it was 25 years in the making, in an address delivered to the Anthropological Society of South Australia in 1978, shortly before his death, he explained that *Songs of Central Australia* 'was published in 1971 but largely written between 1946–49' (Strehlow Research Centre, Articles by Title, Box A). In the first instance, it was intended, in Strehlow's words, 'to be a reference book for use during my later translation of all the aboriginal songs which I had collected in the various Aranda dialects' (Strehlow, 1962a: 7). It became far more than that; it was his chief contribution to scholarly research, one might say published for 'outsiders', largely in the scholarly community. At the same time, in his view at least, he had obtained such a depth of understanding precisely because he had gained the trust of his informants and made one with them as an 'insider', as it were, from birth. And it is clear that he intended it to serve as a resource for absolute 'insiders', the Arrernte themselves, who had become increasingly 'outsiders' through the disruption of the knowledge of traditions that occurred from the dual impact of colonialism and the Lutheran Mission.

Strehlow's Use of 'The Epoché' and Empathetic Interpolation

I now turn to analyse T.G.H. Strehlow as a phenomenologist of religion. In the first instance, it is important to note that he made no claim in any of his writings that he was using a phenomenological method, but clues to how his basic approach to the study of religions is consistent with this method can be found in a number of his important writings. As we have seen, I have referred to the first stage in the attitudinal phase of the phenomenological method as 'performing the *epoché*'. Strehlow's use of this method is demonstrated in his highly critical assessment of the pre-suppositions that determined dominant so-called scientific theories about Aboriginal Australian communities. In the Introduction to *Aranda Traditions*, Strehlow refers to the Report of the Horn Expedition, which, funded by the wealthy businessman William Horn, constituted the first scientific investigation into the remote regions of Central Australia. The Expedition was conducted over a three-month period in 1894 and was comprised of a multi-disciplinary research team under the auspices of the Universities of Sydney, Melbourne and Adelaide. The participants on the Expedition included experts in the fields of botany, geology, anthropology, ethnology and zoology. Baldwin Spencer, who in 1887 had been appointed Professor of Biology at the University of Melbourne, was the Expedition's zoologist and photographer, as well as the author of the Expedition's official report. Strehlow cites a lengthy quotation from the Report, which refers to the 'Central Australian aborigine' as 'a living representative of a stone age' and graphically describes the Aboriginal person as 'a naked, hirsute savage'. As to the religion of the Aboriginal of Central Australia, the Report states: 'he has none', nor does he have any 'traditions'. Rather, the Aboriginal 'continues to practise with scrupulous exactness a number of hideous customs and ceremonies which have been handed from his fathers, and of the origin or reason of which he knows nothing' (cited by Strehlow, 1947: xvi–xvii). Strehlow argues that this section from the Horn Report clearly exposed the assumptions that prejudiced its conclusions:

> Such an observation suggests that the Australian aboriginal was then regarded merely as a highly specialized offshoot of the human species – primitive and incapable of further development, and therefore inevitably and naturally doomed to total extinction from the day when the superior white man entered upon his domains (Strehlow, 1947: xvii).

The Horn Expedition stimulated Spencer's interest in studying further the Aboriginal peoples of the central desert region. He returned to Central Australia in 1896, and in close cooperation with the Alice Springs postmaster, F.J. Gillen, whom Spencer had met during the Horn Expedition, began a study of Indigenous societies in the region. Despite not being a trained ethnologist and whose knowledge of Indigenous languages was poor, Gillen was useful to Spencer because he had forged good relationships with Aboriginal people. As a result, Gillen was able to organize a series of initiation ceremonies and other rituals for Spencer's benefit that formed a major part of Spencer and Gillen's book published in 1899 under the title *The Native Tribes of Central Australia*. In 1927, 15 years after Gillen's death, Spencer published a new and enlarged edition of the original book in two volumes under the title *The Arunta: A Study of a Stone Age People*, to which he attributed Gillen as co-author.

Strehlow repeatedly condemned the assumptions that informed the writings of Spencer and Gillen claiming they had influenced a generation of scholarly opinion about the Indigenous Religions of Central Australia. Spencer and Gillen persistently referred to Arrernte peoples as living representatives of a 'Stone Age' culture that was quickly being superseded by an advanced European civilization. This fundamental presupposition prompted Spencer and Gillen, following an evolutionary model, to conclude that Arrernte culture would inevitably be replaced by the beliefs and values of the higher, more scientific and rational world-view, just as other Stone Age peoples around the world had succumbed to the superior forces of Western civilization. This pre-judgement was voiced by Spencer in the opening words of the Preface to *The Arunta* (Spencer et al., 1927: vii) in a well-known statement that reveals in quite bold language the assumptions that underpinned his research.

> Australia is the present home and refuge of creatures, often crude and quaint, that have elsewhere passed away and given place to higher forms. This applies equally to the aboriginal as to the platypus and kangaroo. Just as the platypus, laying its eggs, and feebly suckling its young, reveals a mammal in the making, so does the Aboriginal show us, at least in broad outline, what early man must have been like before he learned to read and write, domesticate animals, cultivate crops and use a metal tool. It has been possible to study in Australia human beings that still remain on the culture level of men of the Stone Age.

Strehlow regarded the attitude Spencer voiced in the Preface to *The Arunta* as just one example of many 'nauseating insults' that Spencer 'heaped upon his aboriginal informants' (Strehlow, 1978a: 3). That the presuppositions of Spencer and Gillen influenced the reliability of subsequent anthropological findings was confirmed, according to Strehlow, by the 'silence' of later anthropologists, who uncritically accepted Spencer and Gillen's evaluation of the 'primitive' state of Aboriginal peoples. In *Central Australian Religion*, Strehlow argued that work on the religion of Central Australian people had suffered from the failure of scholars to recognize and acknowledge the prejudicial impact of the distorting preconceptions voiced in the works of Spencer and Gillen. He singled out in particular Spencer's biases, which caused his studies of the Arrernte to be dotted with errors and misinformation. Strehlow's criticism of Spencer on just this point is severe, as expressed in *Songs of Central Australia*:

> It is hard to believe that Spencer, a highly-trained man about whose accuracy Sir James Frazer wrote such a glowing eulogy, could ever have stooped to set down his own personal views about the Western Aranda beliefs when he had never bothered to ascertain the relevant information from the Western Aranda natives themselves (Strehlow, 1971a: xxxi).

Strehlow provides an example of how Spencer had influenced the work of J.G. Frazer by citing a section extracted from Frazer's seminal multi-volume work *The Golden Bough*. Strehlow criticizes Frazer for describing the Indigenous peoples of Australia as 'the rudest savages as to whom we possess accurate information' and for ascribing to them the universal practice of magic, whereas 'religion in the sense of propitiation or conciliation of the higher powers seems to be nearly unknown' (cited by Strehlow, 1978b: 8–9). Strehlow credits Spencer and Gillen as the primary source for Frazer's negative judgement of Australian Aboriginal peoples claiming that based on their writings Frazer ranked them lowest on the evolutionary scale (Strehlow, 1978b: 8). Strehlow also criticized Lucien Lévy Bruhl, the French anthropologist well-known for his theory of 'primitive mentality', whom Strehlow claimed had been influenced significantly by Spencer and Gillen. Strehlow asserted that Lévy Bruhl was guilty of making 'attacks upon the "pre-logical mentality" found in "primitive societies"' and 'sneered at the crude nature of "primitive languages"' (Strehlow, 1978b: 9).

As we have seen, the phenomenological stage I have called performing *epoché* was developed in part as a reaction against pre-conceived theories that ranked cultures according to their stage of evolutionary development. This clearly applies to Strehlow's criticisms of academic theories that were rooted in the writings of Spencer and Gillen. Strehlow also criticized the practice of finding explanations for the meaning of Arrernte myths and rituals by reference to a single causative factor. Strehlow voiced strong objections to singular interpretations of religion in *Songs of Central Australia* when he observed: 'I do not for a moment believe that all our present-day psychological or sociological explanations about the aboriginal Australians and their institutions are sufficiently well-attested or statistically validated to survive the criticism of later generations' (1971a: xvi). In particular, he criticized the theories of Géza Rohéim, the Hungarian-American Freudian psychoanalytical ethnologist, who studied the peoples of Western Central Australia in 1928, which resulted in his book *The Riddle of the Sphere* in 1934. Strehlow (1971a: xvii) claims that Rohéim 'nowhere gives us full and unabridged versions either of the sacred myths or of the songs of this area'. Rather, 'he has selected from them only those portions which he could use as illustrations from his preconceived theories' (1971a: xvii). So predetermined were Rohéim's methods of collecting data that Strehlow suggests 'before placing these carefully selected and cooked chunks before his readers, Rohéim has masticated the tougher lumps for the benefit of his readers and saturated them with the saliva of Freudian suggestions so as to make his characteristically Freudian stew easier to swallow' (1971a: xvii).

The *epoché* was used by phenomenologists of religion to filter out biases, such as those based on theories of cultural evolution as expressed by Spencer in the Horn Report and in his later books, the pre-determined notion of 'pre-logical mentality' as articulated by Lévy-Bruhl or psychoanalytical reductionism as exemplified by Géza Rohéim's selection of research data to prove his own Freudian theories. According to Strehlow, the failure to bracket out such distorting preconceptions made producing accurate descriptions and fair interpretations of religious communities impossible. So severe were prior errors in judgement, description and analysis that 'a complete restatement of the aboriginal religious concepts which underlie Australian mythology and ritual' was required (Strehlow, 1978a: 10). To do this Strehlow called for close attention to detail in collecting data which would enable the scholar to note the 'connection between religion, ritual, social organization, and certain purely geographic aspects of the environment'. Although he did not use the term *epoché*, Strehlow clearly conducted his research in a way that attempted to limit the impact of scholars' prejudgements on their research conclusions.

A hallmark of the phenomenological approach relates to step two in the attitudinal phase whereby researchers attempt to get 'inside' the communities they are studying through empathetic interpolation and in the process reflect the perspectives of believers in their detailed descriptions at phase two and in their scholarly interpretations at phase three. Strehlow explained that one of his principal aims in *Songs of Central Australia* was 'to draw attention to the mental attitudes, common human emotions, and uninhibited subconscious drives which seem to find a safe and convenient outlet for their expression through the medium of these songs' (Strehlow, 1971a: xvi). To fairly describe the attitude, emotions and drives of his research subjects required Strehlow to develop an appreciation of what he called 'the language of ordinary conversation'. This involved fostering a sympathetic feeling for the groups about whom he was writing, part of which was deepened by his knowledge of the Arrernte language, but was also enhanced because he had earned the trust of those who shared knowledge of their traditions with him. He explains: 'I have been able to speak Western Aranda since my childhood, and … I have known intimately many Northern, Southern, and Eastern Aranda informants' (Strehlow, 1971a: xvi).

Communicating to outsiders a sense of what it is to think like an Arrernte person required Strehlow to interpolate symbols and meanings gained from studying an Arrernte cultural context into terms familiar to a European audience. Strehlow applied this method repeatedly throughout *Songs of Central Australia* by drawing parallels between Arrernte beliefs and practices, which to the Western reader may appear bizarre or even offensive, and themes commonly found in European, and particularly Old Norse, literature and poetry. On the surface, this might seem to reflect an entirely unempirical method by constructing comparisons between cultures which have no historical, linguistic or geographical relations. But Strehlow's aim was to cultivate a feeling for Arrernte traditions among his European readers by encouraging them to interpolate from their own traditions beliefs and practices that might equally appear bizarre or offensive if placed into an Arrernte context. In this way, the seemingly 'strange' aspects of the foreign religion became more familiar to the European mind and hence comprehensible. Strehlow makes this method clear in the Introduction to *Songs of Central Australia*:

> The European parallels are designed to achieve a more sympathetic attitude in the mind of the white reader towards aboriginal verse and towards the aboriginal world of ideas. For once it can be shown that some of these apparently crude, cruel, strange, or disgusting ideas were once to be found also in ancient pagan Europe, then more thoughtful readers may hesitate to reject them as utterly valueless (Strehlow, 1971a: xl).

Strehlow and Phases Two and Three in the Phenomenological Method: Description and Interpretation

Having established that Strehlow called for prior assumptions to be questioned and the resulting judgements from them suspended and that he encouraged an empathetic attitude through the process of interpolation, we are now ready to consider how he approached the descriptive stages in the phenomenological method. Strehlow indicates that the 'main material' contained in *Songs of Central Australia* was obtained on numerous research trips he made to Central Australia between 1932 and 1960 (Strehlow, 1971a: xiv). He recorded many of the songs that are presented in the book in the Arrernte language, since, he explains 'I often found it easier to set down the explanation of a new word just as it was given to me in Aranda rather than translate it into English' (Strehlow, 1971a: xiv). He adds that during his research trips he 'gathered four thousand two hundred and seventy aboriginal song verses', most of which were from various Arrernte groups living across the region (Strehlow, 1971a: xiv). Strehlow notes that in *Songs of Central Australia* he had described in detail 'the traditional sacred texts used at the various religious rites, initiation ceremonies, and festive occasions' (Strehlow, 1971a: xv). In the process, he claims to have provided 'a cross-section of every type of native song once found in the Central Australia area' (Strehlow, 1971a: xv)

The term 'songs' is Strehlow's attempt to create a general overarching category according to which the verses he collected could be named or classified. He explains that by 'songs' he means 'the traditional native poems of Central Australia which are intoned according to traditional rhythmic measures' (Strehlow, 1971a: xiii). Each song, he adds, 'is associated with a definite ceremonial centre and with a mythical supernatural being or mythical group of totemic ancestors' (Strehlow, 1971a: xiii). He admits that he had considered terms other than 'songs' as a general category under which he could organize his data, principally 'poems' or 'chants'. Both words would have been appropriate, but he preferred 'songs' as the most comprehensive term and one that best fitted what he was trying to convey to the reader. In line with a second step in the descriptive phase of the phenomenological method, Strehlow then sub-divided the general classification 'Songs' into more specific categories for purposes of distinguishing their content and use. He explained that the 'songs' he collected and documented could be classified as 'musical compositions, as literary productions, and as traditional, religious, ceremonial, and social documents' (Strehlow, 1971a: xv).

In the final phase of the phenomenological method, the scholar offers interpretations that clarify the meaning of the material that has been described, and because the attitudinal phase has been followed, lead to understanding-in-depth of the religious communities being studied. In this sense, Strehlow has followed a phenomenological method, by summarizing the essential elements within the classifications and sub-categories he has identified and then suggesting a composite term that encapsulates the overall structure through which Arrernte religion can be portrayed and through which understanding of the traditional Arrernte way of life can be enhanced. As we saw in Chapter 4, the essential social structure within Arrernte traditional religion, according to Strehlow, is found in his pregnant phrase, 'personal monototemism in a polytotemic community'. Studying this concept in detail based on Strehlow's intensive empirical research provides the reader with the key to understanding Arrernte Indigenous Religion. This concept builds on the principal classifications or typologies Strehlow identified: Arrernte myths of creation, Arrernte songs and ceremonies, and Arrernte customary morality. It is important to underscore the fact that Strehlow's phrase 'personal monototemism in a polytotemic community' was derived entirely from empirical studies, and hence was testable and open to modification as circumstances changed and as new research was conducted. In other words, the phenomenological essence, as I am interpreting it in Strehlow's case, is far removed from a Platonic notion of 'essence', unchanging, non-material and ideal. Rather, this strategic phrase indicating the structure of Arrernte Indigenous Religion is meant as an interpretative tool useful for promoting understanding of how the authority of the inherited Arrernte tradition translates into specific and local contexts.

Concluding Remarks

Towards the conclusion of *Central Australian Religion* Strehlow made generalizations about the essential nature of religion, and in this sense, contributed to the broad understanding of religion in the wider phenomenological tradition, as we saw in the examples of Eliade, van der Leeuw and Cantwell

Smith. He summarized the core of religion as showing 'a way of linking …
Time-limited existence with the riches and truths of Eternity by means of
a faith formulated in terms that harmonized with a scientifically-validated
view of the universe' (1978a: 52). Strehlow, however, did not intend his
comments on religion in human life to be prescriptive; he offered them at
the conclusion of his detailed discussion of Arrernte myths, ceremonies,
songs and social organization primarily to demonstrate to his readers that
Arrernte traditional religion was consistent with the religious longings of
humans everywhere. He argued that 'civilized man could improve his prospects of a more secure future by adopting some of the concepts of toleration
and cooperation on which the aboriginal Australians based their social and
political systems' (1978a: 52). This comment formed part of his resistance
against ranking religions from higher to lower and also was consistent with
his attempt to foster empathetic attitudes towards Arrernte religious beliefs
and practices.

In the end, we see that by conducting research on Arrernte culture,
Strehlow's primary aim was not to produce a general theory of the structure of religion. His principal focus was on the Arrernte peoples themselves,
which made his generalizations very close to testable data and one in which
he stressed the local character of the Indigenous Religions he wrote about.
He could be said to have been ahead of his time in this regard, since contemporary studies of religion are notoriously hesitant to make broad statements about religion, precisely because they are difficult to test and because
they foster the tendency to find in the data material that confirms the pre-
determined theory of religion the scholar has formulated (see for example
Segal, 1999: 139–63; Tremlett, 2008; Flood, 1999). Hence, we come back
to the beginning: in Strehlow we find a scholar who, following principles
consistent with the phenomenology of religion, was wary of theories that
pre-determined the results of research and as an interpreter of Arrernte religion made his conclusions amenable to empirical testing and verification.

T.G.H. Strehlow and the Repatriation of Knowledge

Repatriation commonly is associated with returning objects, artefacts or skeletal remains that were regarded as sacred or of important cultural value to their original Indigenous owners. During colonial times, such sacred objects or remains had been taken from Indigenous peoples and transported to museums or other sites, often located in major cities around the world. The return of sacred objects, however, does not imply that knowledge of their original meanings and uses is understood by Indigenous communities. This is because the objects have been separated from their original cultural contexts for generations. T.G.H. Strehlow contended that Indigenous knowledge among Arrernte groups in Central Australia was preserved only in his personal research collection, which was comprised of notes about secret-sacred objects, interviews with Indigenous Elders, films of ceremonies, recordings and transcripts of songs, maps and genealogies. Most of this material is now stored in the Strehlow Research Centre in Alice Springs. In this chapter, I analyse the role of Strehlow's Collection in the current repatriation project being developed at the Strehlow Research Centre in light of Strehlow's assertion, which I discussed in Chapter 6, that the collective memory of the Arrernte Elders had been so severely disrupted by the mid-1960s that virtually all knowledge of traditional ceremonies, songs, symbols and stories associated with secret-sacred objects (*tjurunga*), and even the location of sacred sites, had been forgotten.

The Repatriation of Objects, Artefacts and Skeletal Remains in Australia

On 15 May 2012, the Department of Communications and the Arts of the Australian Government announced membership of the newly established Advisory Committee for Indigenous Repatriation. On its website, the Department explained that the Advisory Committee 'provides guidance on issues relating to Aboriginal and Torres Strait Islander repatriation from the collections of Australian and overseas cultural institutions' (http://arts.gov.au/indigenous/repatriation). The backdrop for establishing a programme of Indigenous Repatriation is explained by the Department:

For more than 150 years Aboriginal and Torres Strait Islander ancestral remains and secret sacred objects were removed from communities and placed in museums, universities and private collections in Australia and overseas. During the 19th and 20th centuries, ancestral remains were collected by medical officers, anatomists, ethnologists, anthropologists, and pastoralists, in some cases for the purposes of scientific research linked to explaining human biological differences (http://arts.gov.au/indigenous/repatriation).

The aim of repatriating ancestral remains and secret-sacred objects to the communities from which they were taken, the Department notes, 'helps promote healing and reconciliation for Aboriginal and Torres Strait Islander peoples' (http://arts.gov.au/indigenous/repatriation).

The Advisory Committee for Indigenous Repatriation was established as a continuation of the Return of Indigenous Cultural Property (RICP) programme that the Australian Government initiated in 1999 with funding of $1.5 million, which in turn was matched by the states and territories. In the 2007–2008 budget for Indigenous Affairs, the Australian Government provided another $4.5 million for four years explaining that 'the return of Indigenous cultural property to the traditional custodians and places of rest is extremely important to the Indigenous communities and to the Australian Government' (https://tinyurl.com/dss-gov-au-budget-2007-08).

The Return of Indigenous Cultural Property programme aimed at returning all Indigenous ancestral remains and secret-sacred objects 'where possible', keeping in mind that 'repatriation can only occur where remains and objects have been adequately provenanced and where the communities are prepared to receive their ancestral remains and secret-sacred objects' (https://tinyurl.com/budget-2007-2008-gov-au). The programme acknowledged that in some cases Indigenous communities preferred museums to retain their ancestral remains and secret-sacred objects under the proviso that ownership was transferred from the museums to the community. The RICP programme involved eight major museums within Australia, which the Government estimated collectively held '7,070 ancestral remains and 11,448 secret-sacred objects' (https://tinyurl.com/budget-2007-2008-gov-au.[1]

Under its current Indigenous Repatriation project, the Australian Government has expanded its efforts to return cultural property beyond Australian museums to include international holdings, most of which are retained in museums in 'the United Kingdom, Germany, France, Poland and the United

---

1. The eight museums are: The Australian Museum, the Museum and Art Gallery of the Northern Territory, Museum Victoria, the National Museum of Australia, Queensland Museum, South Australian Museum, Tasmanian Museum and Art Gallery and the Western Australian Museum.

States of America' (http://arts.gov.au/sites/default/files/pdfs/rics_principles.
pdf). On its web page outlining the aims of the Indigenous Repatriation
project, the Ministry for the Arts explained that 'the Australian Government seeks the unconditional return of Aboriginal and Torres Strait ancestral remains' (http://arts.gov.au/indigeneous/repatriation). In pursuit of this
objective, the Ministry noted that it has established relationships with the
countries holding the majority of the remains and secret-sacred objects and,
in addition, 'is developing relationships with a number of other countries in
order to progress the repatriation of indigenous ancestral remains' (http://
arts.gov.au/indigeneous/repatriation). It will be clear from these descriptions
of cultural property that repatriation is interpreted by the Australian Government in material terms: ancestral remains and secret-sacred objects. The
connection between material and intellectual cultural property is not discussed in any detail in these documents.

This connection was emphasized in a paper written by Kenan Malik for
the *Index on Censorship* in 2007 under the title, 'Who Owns Knowledge?',
which carries the sub-title, 'In a battle over bones, scientists and museums are
losing out to the guardians of indigenous culture'. Malik, who is an independent researcher, writer and broadcaster, begins his article by noting that 'in
May this year [2007], London's Natural History Museum returned the skeletons of 17 Aboriginal islanders to representatives of the Tasmanian Aboriginal Centre' (Malik, 2007: 156). Malik adds that 'the skeletons were part of
the enormous collection of bones, skulls, and other human remains that are
housed in the vaults below the museum' (Malik, 2007: 156). Malik argues
that 'the remains were taken from native countries in acts little short of grave-
robbing' (Malik, 2007: 158). Malik then observes that such tangible objects
must be related more broadly to an intangible cultural heritage, in support
of which he cites the UNESCO International Convention of the Intangible Cultural Heritage which defines heritage as 'all of those things which
international law regards as the creative production of human thought and
craftsmanship, such as songs, scientific knowledge and artworks' (UNESCO;
Malik, 2007: 166).

In this way, Malik has drawn attention to the fact that repatriation has
more to do with a broad interpretation of cultural heritage than is implied
strictly by references to material objects. Repatriation includes the meaning of the remains and secret-sacred objects associated with them, much
of which is contained in the memory of communities through oral traditions, songs and ritual performances. But what happens when the memory
of communities has been disrupted by forces of modernity, including colonial oppression, missionary activities, Western education, global economic
structures, rapidly advancing communication systems and urbanization? If
contemporary events have obscured the meaning contained within the traditional cultural heritage of the tangible objects being returned, this would

appear to render repatriation projects largely symbolic, and arguably, in service of an Indigenous political agenda (Krmpotich, 2012: 163).

The Current Repatriation of Knowledge
Project at the Strehlow Research Centre

As we saw in Chapter 1, the last ten years of T.G.H. Strehlow's life were
consumed by controversy over how he and his wife Kathleen dealt with the
vast material he collected over his years of working among the Arrernte
people, including the *tjurunga* that were entrusted to him for safekeeping
by Aboriginal Elders. After his death in 1978, negotiations between Mrs
Strehlow and the Government of the Northern Territory resulted in the
opening of the Strehlow Research Centre in 1991 in Alice Springs under
terms of the Northern Territory's Strehlow Research Centre Act of 1988.
John Morton reports that Mrs Strehlow 'was employed by the Centre as part
of the agreement', which resulted in 'constant dispute, something which
came to public prominence in 1992 when an Adelaide auction room offered
for sale some 260 Aboriginal artefacts including secret-sacred material allegedly belonging to Carl Strehlow (Ted and Kathy's son)' (Morton, n.d.). The
material never became part of the public domain, since, as Morton notes, it
'was impounded under South Australian heritage legislation', which, after
several years, saw most of Strehlow's Collection deposited at the Strehlow
Research Centre (Morton, n.d.). According to Morton, the material collected by Strehlow included '700 objects (largely secret-sacred), 15 kilometres of movie film, 7,000 slides, thousands of pages of genealogical records,
myths, sound recordings, 42 of Strehlow's diaries outlining his ethnographic
work, as well as paintings, letters, maps and a 1000 volume library' (Morton,
n.d.: 2; see also Hawley, 1987: 28).

Strehlow's far-reaching Collection is now being used increasingly by
Indigenous leaders to return not just secret-sacred objects to their legitimate owners in accordance with recognized genealogical data collected by
Strehlow, but as a source for restoring knowledge of Indigenous cultural traditions, ceremonies, stories and social customs that have been lost or forgotten by members of the contemporary generation. In an interview in 2010
with the then Deputy Director of the Strehlow Research Centre, Michael
Cawthorn, Penelope Bergen cites Cawthorn as stating 'the bulk of the audio
and film recordings are ceremonial acts', most of which 'aren't performed
anymore and we try to be very active in digitally repatriating that material
where we can' (Bergen, 2010).

A project that documented the developing use of the Strehlow Collection began in 2010 under the direction of Hart Cohen and Juan Salazar of
Western Sydney University, in conjunction with Michael Cawthorn, and
later in collaboration with Wendy Cowan, a teacher at the Ntaria School

in Hermannsburg/Ntaria. Initially, Cohen, Salazar and Cawthorn received funding from the Australia Research Council for a project entitled 'Digital Archives and Discoverability: Conceptualising the Strehlow Collection as a New Knowledge Resource for Remote Indigenous Communities'. In a seminar held at Western Sydney University, Parramatta Campus, in August 2015, Cohen, Salazar and Cowan presented a paper that outlined the project's aims and raised important questions about digital repatriation of cultural knowledge. Cohen, Salazar and Cowan referred to how knowledge contained in the Strehlow Collection and the interest of local Indigenous communities cross, particularly how digital technology is being used 'in the re-mediating of image collections' and informing, particularly young Indigenous people, of the stories connected to their traditions. This innovative project is engaging Elders in Hermannsburg/Ntaria and young people by using T.G.H. Strehlow's vast Collection, combined with modern technology, to restore knowledge that has been lost to the current generation of Elders and assisting them in passing it on to the next generation (https://tinyurl.com/ics-events-seminars-2015). Indigenous repatriation in this sense is consistent with the aims of UNESCO's International Convention of Intangible Cultural Heritage that seeks to repatriate knowledge in the form of stories, ceremonies and art that were replaced, at least in part, by Christian religious symbols or Western cultural expressions as a result of missionary and colonial interventions (http://www.unesco.org/culture/ich/en/convention).

In Penelope Bergen's interview, Cawthorn referred to the connection between the Strehlow Collection and the Return of Indigenous Cultural Property programme of the Australian Government. He is quoted as saying that the RICP programme 'provides us with the opportunity to be pro-active in terms of actually contacting people and making them aware that they have material housed in the centre' (Bergen, 2010). In 2009, Adam Macfie was appointed as the Repatriation Anthropologist managing the Indigenous Repatriation Program for the Museum and Art Gallery of the Northern Territory (MAGNT). Based at the Strehlow Research Centre, Macfie has consulted extensively with the Arrernte community in researching the sacred objects and genealogical records held in the Strehlow Collection. In 2013, MAGNT employed two Arrernte researchers, Mark Inkamala and Shaun Angeles, to assist in the development of the Repatriation Project at the Strehlow Research Centre. The purpose of the Indigenous Repatriation Programme in Macfie's words 'is to reconnect Indigenous communities of the Northern Territory with their ancestral remains and their secret sacred objects held in the collections under the care of MAGNT' (http://www.strehlow.co.uk/conference_2014.html, see Abstracts of papers).

In 2014, Macfie, Inkamala and Angeles presented a paper at a conference held in Alice Springs, organized by John Strehlow, the son of T.G.H.

Strehlow, in which they outlined the current work of the Repatriation Project. They explained how central T.G.H. Strehlow's research diaries had become in the efforts to repatriate knowledge among the Arrernte peoples:

> Over the past few years our attention has been drawn more and more to the maps found in the archive which Strehlow … annotated on published government survey map sheets for the region…. The origin of all of these maps can be found in his forty or so handwritten field diaries produced between 1935 and 1971…. Our cultural mapping project is based on archival research and participatory engagement with the traditional owners and has become an invaluable practice for the Strehlow Research Centre and its repatriation programme (http://www.strehlow.co.uk/conference_2014.html, see Abstracts of papers).

Indigenous Agency

On 28 September 2016, an event was held at the Strehlow Research Centre to commemorate the 25th anniversary of the opening of the Centre in 1991. The ceremony honouring this important anniversary contained a welcome speech by the Chairman of the Board, Ken Lechleitner, and an address by Shaun Angeles, who as we noted above, is one of the Indigenous researchers involved in the repatriation project at the Strehlow Research Centre. In his opening remarks, Lechleitner highlighted an important concept that has often been overlooked in repatriation discussions, that of Indigenous agency, which in the case of the Strehlow material, acknowledges that T.G.H. Strehlow was not in total control of his own data collection. Rather, Indigenous Elders decided what to share with him, which *tjurunga* to entrust to him and which ceremonies he was allowed to film and record. Lechleitner suggested the Strehlow Collection was formed in a partnership between 'the real visionaries in this story – the elders who entrusted Theodore [TGH] Strehlow with their cultural knowledge and Theodore himself who dedicated his life to collecting and preserving this knowledge' (*Alice Springs News*, 30 September 2016).

In his address to the assembly, Shaun Angeles (*Alice Springs News*, 30 September 2016), pursued the theme of Indigenous agency. He explained first that he is 'a Penangke man from Ayampe country' (around 70 kilometres northeast of Alice Springs), who began working at the Strehlow Research Centre in September 2013 as an 'Indigenous Repatriation Researcher'. He added that he had

> worked intimately with the collection for three years – analysing field diaries, editing the ceremonial film footage, working with individuals and families with the genealogies, digitising the ceremonial song catalogue and travelling to museums within Australia searching for artefacts that left this landscape in some instances over a hundred years ago.

Throughout this process, Angeles observed, he had begun to feel as if he knew 'these old men, in sometimes tracking their lives through four decades of work with TGH'. After paying respect to Strehlow and the work he completed during his life, Angeles then made a telling remark: 'I want to ... elevate the story of the Akngerrapte (senior cultural leaders) who ... possessed the greatest agency in this story'. By agency, he explained, he was referring to the fact that 'they chose what to show Strehlow'. Certainly, Strehlow had gained their trust, but the Elders freely chose to share their secret knowledge with him; they also selected which information to withhold from him. Angeles argued that it was just this choice which has preserved 'the deepest aspects of Aboriginal men's culture in Central Australia for the benefit of their future generations'.

Indigenous agency is illustrated by the complex circumstances surrounding Strehlow's descriptions of a series of important kangaroo increase ceremonies, called *utnitjia*, that he witnessed at Alice Springs in 1933 as public performances lasting 16 days. In *Aranda Traditions*, he calls the *utnitjia* cycle 'the most secret of all the multitudinous rites performed near the Northern kangaroo centre, rites which in past times might be witnessed only by members of the inner kangaroo clan of Krantji' (Strehlow, 1947: 29). According to tradition, the kangaroo increase ceremonies Strehlow observed should not have occurred in Alice Springs but at the *pmara kutata* at Krantji, which lies approximately 80 miles (130 kilometres) west of Alice Springs. Strehlow notes that it was at Krantji that 'the kangaroo chief Krantjirinja first came into being' (1947: 140). As we saw in Chapter 3, Strehlow described the myth of Krantjirinja as it was told to him by the Elders who referred to Krantjirinja as a 'true kangaroo', who during the day 'was shaped like an animal', but at night 'assumed human shape'. At the bottom of the soak at Krantji 'was the home of the ancestor' beneath which 'lay all his tjurunga' (1947: 140). Strehlow adds that this location literally is the source of 'all kangaroo ancestors' who 'emerged in the form of kangaroos, and then assumed human bodies' (1947: 140).

The fact that the sacred kangaroo increase ceremonies in 1933 were public and performed at a place other than the Krantji *pmara kutata* severely altered their significance and would have made the rituals ineffective in producing a plentiful supply of kangaroos. In his contribution to a book edited by W.E.H. Stanner and Helen Sheils, Strehlow (1963: 249) underscored just this point when he asserted that 'local earth-born supernatural beings were associated with definite local sacred centres, as were all ceremonies, sacred songs and magical practices'. The seriousness of failing to conduct the rituals at the appropriate ceremonial centre had severe consequences: 'Each centre had its own separate cycle of ceremonies which in the old days could be performed nowhere else – on pain of death – but at that particular site' (1963: 249).

In *Songs of Central Australia*, Strehlow explains that because the series of rituals was not held at the sacred ceremonial site at Krantji, two important changes were made by the Elder Ekuntjarinja, who was in charge of the event. First, due to its being held at Alice Springs, 'outsiders', men who were not members of the kangaroo totem and young men, who normally would have been excluded, were permitted to observe the kangaroo increase ceremonies. This condition also applied to Strehlow, who was the only white man at the event and, he assumes, the first white man allowed to view these particular kangaroo rituals (Strehlow, 1971a: 307). The presence of outsiders led to a second important change: Ekuntjarinja omitted important elements in the ceremonies including, according to Strehlow, 'the nightly utnitjia spear-singing; the night acts with their rhythmically different verses; and above all, the final magic fertilization of the ilbantera by means of the ceremonial phallus' (Strehlow, 1971a: 307). Ekuntjarinja made these changes because, on Strehlow's interpretation, he 'wanted to preserve the secrecy of the particular features which were believed to give this utnitjia series its special potency' (Strehlow, 1971a: 307).

At the beginning of the cycle, Strehlow notes, the spectators 'were called to ... a hollow scratched out by kangaroos', which represented the bottom of the waterhole at Krantji where the original kangaroo ancestor was believed to have emerged (Strehlow, 1971a: 308). For ceremonial purposes, the hollow had been hardened with blood taken from the 'veins of the kangaroo totemites at Krantji' and it had been covered with white down, which, Strehlow explains, 'was said to represent the ... kangaroo fat from which all the remaining kangaroo ancestors had sprung into life' (Strehlow, 1971a: 308). At Krantji the hollow measured around 30 inches (76 centimetres) across with a deep hole in the middle of it, but at Alice Springs, the hole was much smaller due to the rocky terrain on which the ritual was performed. At Krantji the hole would have been as deep as a person could have dug by hand, meaning that a man could have extended his arm all the way to the bottom of the hole. At Alice Springs, it was only six inches deep (15 centimetres). These geological differences affecting the size of the holes were significant because the ceremonial 'para' or headgear, which represented the phallus, was meant to fit into the hole, in an obvious reference to fertility. This could only have been accomplished at Alice Springs symbolically because the para was two feet long (61 centimetres), and clearly would not fit into the hole.

The fundamental and critical variations in performing the ritual, however, cannot be explained primarily by the differing geological features present at Alice Springs in comparison to Krantji because, as we have seen, the actual hollow located at Krantji represented the genuine origin of the kangaroo ancestor, whereas at Alice Springs it was merely a representation of the event where the original kangaroo ancestor was believed to have emerged from the earth at the beginning of time. As a result, Ekuntjarinja altered what Strehlow calls 'the vital final scene' by refusing to reveal the most sacred part of the ritual to outsiders and by performing it at a profane location. Strehlow says that Ekuntjarinja felt 'too much shame at the idea of displaying the last mysteries to the vulgar gaze' of non-totemites (Strehlow, 1971a: 312). As a result, Strehlow did not witness the most crucial concluding act in the series of rituals. Instead, he claims, the younger men 'gave me a detailed account of what would have been the correct procedure' (Strehlow, 1971a: 312). He explains that the younger men told him that had the ceremony been held at Krantji and had it been restricted solely to members of those kangaroo totemites from Krantji, in the central concluding act of the ritual, the para or head covering would have been placed between the legs of the men. They would then approach on their knees the arm-length hole that had been dug and, in Strehlow's words, would have performed acts involving 'twisting and turning the para from side to side, and finally thrusting it towards the central hole' (Strehlow, 1971a: 312). This act, simulating copulation, was intended to ensure the increase of kangaroos, and without this act, the ritual would have been rendered ineffective. Strehlow adds in a footnote that to change any part of the sacred ceremony or to omit any section, particularly in the case of the most important element, was 'a very serious offence' (Strehlow, 1971a: 312: fn 142). The Elder Ekuntjarinja, however, faced an insurmountable dilemma at Alice Springs: either he left out the most sacred part of the ritual or he profaned it by revealing it to those who were strictly prohibited by tradition from witnessing it and by performing it at a site far removed from the traditional ceremonial centre.

Two different interpretaticons of this same situation are presented by Strehlow, the first in *Aranda Traditions* and the second the one I just recounted from *Songs of Central Australia*. In *Aranda Traditions*, Strehlow notes that if any changes 'in the slightest' were inserted into the traditional kangaroo increase ceremonies at Krantji, or if they were 'irreverently' shown to uninitiated men, 'some terrible evil is certain to fall upon the offender as a punishment' (1947: 29). Strehlow notes that this infraction of strict rules caused Ekuntjarinja to experience 'acute pains in the neck' (1947: 29), which he and other Elders attributed 'to the anger of the offended Krantjirinja himself, who had struck Ekuntjarinja because the latter had frivolously exhibited the sacred ceremonies to people to whom he had been strictly forbidden to show them by his elders when they first instructed him' (1947: 30). Strehlow comments that the belief that Ekuntjarinja's illness resulted from the anger of the original kangaroo ancestor remained 'unshaken', despite the fact that Krantji is over eighty miles (130 kilometres) west of Alice Springs (1947: 30). By contrast, in *Songs of Central Australia*, Strehlow presents Ekuntjarinja as prohibiting the most secret of the traditional rites from being performed for quite honourable reasons.

According to tradition, such scenes must not be witnessed by 'outsiders' and the complete performance of the ceremonies should only have occurred at Krantji. On this interpretation, Strehlow pits Ekuntjarinja against the younger men who considered omitting sections of the ceremonies 'sacrilegious' (Strehlow, 1971a: 307).

Both accounts and their interpretations provided by Strehlow confirm Shaun Angeles's contention that the Elders were in control of what they chose to reveal to Strehlow and what they deliberately omitted. Strehlow was not permitted to witness key elements within the Krantji kangaroo increase ceremonies held in 1933 following the decision of the Elder Ekuntjarinja, but he was informed of the content of the key stages in the ritual by the younger men who objected to Ekuntjarinja's decision. By 1950, after Ekuntjarinja had died and the younger men had themselves become Elders, the then current Elders agreed to perform the entire *utnitjia* cycle so that Strehlow could film the ceremonies in colour and, as Strehlow explains, 'record them by means of a wire recorder' (1971a: 316).

The kangaroo increase ceremonies Strehlow filmed in 1950 were not performed publicly as had occurred in 1933 in Alice Springs, but they were staged at Strehlow's request as part of research he was conducting under a grant from the Australian National University. The *utnitjia* cycle was performed for Strehlow near Jay Creek, where Strehlow had lived when he was serving as the Northern Territory Patrol Officer in the 1930s. In his critical biography of Strehlow, Barry Hill (2003: 432) reports that Strehlow set up three 'stages' on clearings in the rocky hills located around three miles north of Jay Creek. Hill calls them 'the sets for the shooting', which he likens to 'an open-air theatre' (2003: 433). This meant that the location where the ceremonies were enacted and the context in which they were performed clearly violated the rigid rule that, according to tradition, they should be conducted only at the sacred ceremonial site where the kangaroo ancestor first emerged from beneath the surface of the earth. By 1950, Strehlow strongly believed that these traditional protocols were rapidly being forgotten or ignored, and thus justified filming the cycle of secret rituals as a means of preserving for future Arrernte leaders, and for academic researchers, knowledge of how they were performed and the songs that accompanied them.

In both cases that Strehlow documents, that of 1933 in Alice Springs and the contrasting circumstances of 1950 near Jay Creek, it is clear that the Elders decided what Strehlow was allowed to observe, describe, photograph, film and record. That the Elders deliberately selected what they revealed to Strehlow is confirmed by what Strehlow calls 'a strong veil of secrecy' that 'shrouds the most sacred ritual mysteries' (Strehlow, 1971a: 313). For this reason, it was quite common for 'false versions of ceremonial explanations' to be provided to outsiders by the Elders (Strehlow, 1971a:

313). This fact leads Strehlow to observe in *Songs of Central Australia* 'that it was little wonder' that the most secret act involving the symbolic fertilization of the water soak out of which the original kangaroo ancestors emerged 'was omitted from public performance at the Alice Springs festival in 1933' (Strehlow, 1971a: 313). Because it was a public performance, Strehlow suggests that 'it could have been intended only as a symbolical and reverent representation of the original union between male and female fertility, from which all life was supposed to have originated at Krantji' (Strehlow, 1971a: 313). Strehlow admits that to have questioned his informants further about the meaning of the closing ritual that was omitted at Alice Springs 'would have been worse than useless', not because the Elders lacked an understanding of its meaning nor because 'they were incapable of abstract thinking', but precisely because the 'religious reverence of their descendants has silenced both logical questionings and loquacious explanations' (Strehlow, 1971a: 313).

That Strehlow acknowledged Indigenous agency is evidenced further by the agreement he made with the Elders before they consented to allow him to film and record the kangaroo increase ceremonies in 1950. In his report to the Australian National University on his research in Central Australia, which the ANU had funded, Strehlow admitted: 'I had to give my personal word of honour to the ceremonial leaders that these films would not be shown publicly' (cited by Hill, 2003: 433). The complex negotiations and the contrasting contexts of the *utnitjia* kangaroo increase ceremonies held at Alice Springs and Jay Creek nearly 20 years apart, which I have discussed in detail, confirm in equal measure Angeles's concluding remark made at the event commemorating the 25th anniversary of the Strehlow Research Centre. Angeles had attested that senior Arrernte Elders demonstrated agency by choosing what and what not to disclose to Strehlow, and it was the same Elders who did this for the intentional purpose of preserving 'the deepest aspects of Aboriginal men's culture in Central Australia for the benefit of their future generations' (*Alice Springs News*, 30 September 2016).

The Active Role of Elders as Agents in the Repatriation Programme

Indigenous agency not only applies to the activities and decisions of the Elders with whom Strehlow worked over a period of 30 years, but it also defines how contemporary Arrernte Elders are using material that Strehlow collected which is now housed in the Strehlow Research Centre. In this sense, agency, as Angeles argued in his address during the 25th anniversary commemoration, suggests that the material comprising the Strehlow Collection cannot by itself restore the memory of traditional Arrernte ways of life, but requires consultation 'with our present Elders to realise the collection's true potential'. Angeles, who himself forms part of the younger generation, contended that the Elders are 'the only ones ... who understand its content and are able to enrich it and enrich the lives of our young men who are coming through the ranks'. He added that the Collection, which 'for the past 25 years ... has been like a sleeping giant' can achieve its true potential only by identifying 'innovative cultural ways' whereby it can achieve its 'power throughout Central Australia'. Angeles concluded his speech by underscoring the fundamental importance of involving the current generation of Arrernte people in unlocking the potential of the Strehlow Collection. He referred to the Collection as 'living' and 'breathing' and insisted that as a dynamic source of information about Arrernte culture and religion, it 'needs Aboriginal custodians interacting with it'. The most important 'stakeholders' in T.G.H. Strehlow's Collection, he asserted, 'are the Indigenous people' whom he called 'the custodians and owners of the material' (*Alice Springs News*, 30 September 2016).

By emphasizing the current power of Indigenous agency as Elders interact with the Strehlow Collection, Angeles was arguing that the present Elders must interpret the data contained in the Strehlow Centre in terms of the contemporary situation. This assumes that the Elders possess at least some knowledge of the traditions, particularly with respect to the land, the stories connected to the land and the kinship system that had been taught to them by their Elders. If Strehlow was correct, however, many ceremonies he originally documented in the 1930s will no longer be performed today, or they will have been altered substantially in critical ways either because the traditions have been forgotten or because they were suppressed by outside forces. Strehlow (1971a: xlv) confirmed this judgement when he wrote in the Introduction to *Songs of Central Australia* that 'virtually all the old Aranda pmara kutata are dead and forgotten now' and 'are today only geographical points in the Central Australian landscape'. He claimed that 'it would be unfair to the younger aboriginal generation of Central Australia to accuse them of having lightly discarded the ancient traditions of their forefathers without making any struggle to preserve them' (1971a: xlv). Rather, he laid the blame squarely on 'the white population' which inflicted 'shocking casualties' on Indigenous peoples, through 'the unsympathetic older Mission policies, the many acts of interference by the early white cattle-owners, and, in recent years, a number of repressive administrative acts carried out in the name of the governmental assimilation policy' (1971a: xlv). To regain such knowledge, the present Elders will need to consult Strehlow's vast collection of songs, ceremonies and genealogical records, but it is assumed that they will be able to understand this material because their language, which they have maintained, and their cultural traditions are closely intertwined and because they are able to interpret Strehlow's detailed genealogical records onto which they can place their own lineage and totemic identities.

The active role of the current generation of Elders in using the Strehlow Collection as a source of knowledge for contemporary Arrernte young people is demonstrated in a documentary film entitled 'Ntaria Heroes', which was made in 2015 and released in 2016 by Hart Cohen and Juan Salazar (https://www.youtube.com/watch?v=k-64qnmkvsI).[2] The film features the role of the Strehlow Collection as a teaching tool for contemporary young Arrernte people. It begins by documenting a trip made in October 2014 by a group of young men and senior girls from Ntaria School, who travelled from Hermannsburg/Ntaria to the Strehlow Research Centre in Alice Springs. They were shown genealogical records and old photographs by two key Elders as a means for instructing them in their traditional ways of life, including kinship and marriage rules, conception sites and totemic ancestors. The young men were tutored by Mark Inkamala, one of the Indigenous Researchers at the Strehlow Research Centre, and the senior girls were taught by Mavis Malbunka, a woman Elder and a Traditional Owner in Western Arrernte country. The film also shows interviews with Adam Macfie, Shaun Angeles and Wendy Cowan. In his interview, Macfie observed that during their visit the young people were shown 'evidence that there is a connection between what is recorded in this archive and ... what they are taught about by their Elders'. He added that the 'unifying theme' within the Strehlow Collection, that which 'brings it all together, ... is its tie to country'. This is made evident by the Collection's extensive genealogical records that Strehlow so carefully documented, which Macfie explains, include the family trees showing conception sites. He adds that the 'language itself comes from the landscape'.

In the film, Mavis Malbunka is shown teaching the senior girls about how the family trees indicate kinship relations and thus demonstrate proper marriage regulations according to traditional norms. She tells the girls that the family trees show how the 'old people' got married according to 'the right marriage kinship'. She says in an interview, 'that is what young people should learn', adding that they 'can't marry just whoever' because 'their children will have wrong kinship'. She is shown in the film telling the girls that the family trees trace conception sites and personal totemic ancestors, adding that she is from the 'caterpillar' totem. She says: 'I have seen the caterpillar. We knew what animal dreaming we have, what land we belong to'. She emphasizes in an interview: 'We have to teach the children'. The knowledge of conception sites that Mavis Malbunka displays conforms to the traditional role of women in Arrernte society. In *Songs of Central Australia*, Strehlow (1971a: 648) observed that 'since the personal totem of the child depended on the mother's story of its conception-site, the native women

---

2.   The quotations cited are taken from the full version of the film. The YouTube link allows the viewer to see just the first few minutes of the film.

were inevitably aware of *all* the landscape features associated with the various totems located in their area of residence'.

Mark Inkamala is shown in the film teaching the boys about their family
trees and hence their totemic identities. He discusses their 'skin name' and
tells the boys how they can be traced along a lineage to particular ancestors following Strehlow's genealogical records.[3] He also stresses the importance of language and its relation to culture. Inkamala asserts: 'Without no
language, without no culture, you are nothing'. In his interview on the film,
Shaun Angeles states that for the young people 'looking at genealogies,
looking at old photographs ... has been powerful for them and even also for
us'. Angeles adds that instructing the young people in the traditions of the
people 'needs to be done very soon because we are running out of Elders
quickly'. He concludes: 'We need to do as much with these young people
while these Elders are still alive'.

In a statement read on his behalf before a public lecture I delivered
at Western Sydney University on 9 September 2016, the co-producer of
'Ntaria Heroes', Hart Cohen (private correspondence, Cohen to Cox, 8
September 2016), explained that the intent of the film 'is to foster a relationship between the community and the Strehlow Research Centre where
their collection of cultural materials and relevant cultural information could
be offered as a resource for learning about cultural traditions, genealogical
information and the ancestors to whom the students are related'. Cohen
refers to the process I have called 'the 'repatriation of Indigenous knowledge' as the 'Indigenous reclamation of its valued heritage' and suggests that
the collection of cultural material accumulated by T.G.H. Strehlow 'has the
potential to communicate with, and educate the next generation of Indigenous leaders whose authority will rest on their ability to know their cultural heritage'.

In an interview with Shaun Angeles, uploaded on YouTube on 6 October
2015 by the National Film and Sound Archive of Australia, Angeles confirmed that Arrernte Elders currently are using the Strehlow Collection as
a way of restoring knowledge of ancient traditions that have been forgotten
and fallen into disuse. Angeles observed: 'Arrernte men are able to access
this Collection and revisit the knowledge of our old people and revitalise
all cultural practices that have been lost'. He explained that 'collections
like this are able to fill us up spiritually ... and change people's lives'. Since
he had been working at the Strehlow Research Centre, Angeles confirmed

3. Skin name refers to the kinship system of classes and sub-classes, or sections
or sub-sections, as described by Strehlow in '*Aranda Regular and Irregular Marriages*
(1999), which I outlined in Chapter 4. On its website, the Central Land Council
explained that a child takes the skin name of his or her parents, which in turn indicates to which section or sub-section the child belongs (Central Land Council, n. d.).

that 'men have come in, got a ceremonial film, got the song that goes with it and gone out and taught their young people about it' (https://www.youtube.com/watch?v=eUsv2dISgqs).

That Strehlow's records are being used today by Arrernte Elders was corroborated in an interview I held with a traditional Elder near Alice Springs on 13 October 2015. The Elder asked that his identity not be revealed and thus I will simply refer to him by a pseudonym as Phillip. Phillip appeared to be approximately 65 years-old. The interview took place at his homestead. I was introduced to Phillip by Steve Bevis, an independent researcher living in Alice Springs, who attended the interview. Phillip told me that he had been consulting the Strehlow Research Centre to find out things only about his people, his family, and was not intruding into the business of other families. By family, he explained, he meant extended family – aunts, uncles, cousins – 'a large mob'. He then repeated what Adam Possamai and I discovered during our research in the Utopia region in 2013: 'The younger generation need to know about their traditions. They are forgetting them'. Then he referred to the importance of the Strehlow Research Centre as a source for preserving knowledge of the traditions: 'At the Strehlow Centre there are pictures, stories, songs, genealogies, sacred objects. I am taking pictures of some of these and using them to teach the younger generation of my family'. He added that his 'mob' were using the Strehlow material in ceremonies, particularly initiation and increase ceremonies. About Strehlow himself, Phillip commented: 'A lot of people say he wasn't good, but I think he did good. He preserved the records of people from all over. That was good. He helped us keep our tradition, our knowledge' (Interview: James Cox with 'Phillip', Arrernte Elder, 13 October 2015, Alice Springs). After the interview concluded, Steve Bevis confided in me privately: 'The man was open. He is a good source of knowledge, but his kind are dying out. In ten years, this kind of thing will be gone' (Interview: James Cox with Steve Bevis, 13 October 2015, Alice Springs).

Bevis was underscoring the fact that the present members of the younger generation, as was confirmed graphically in the film *Ntaria Heroes*, lack knowledge of Indigenous ways of life and without the mediation of living Elders are in danger of losing it altogether. The Strehlow Collection becomes critical at just this point precisely because the present Elders, whose own knowledge of songs and ceremonies has been disrupted, are relying on it as a source for their own revival of tradition and thus are using it as a critical tool in maintaining generational continuity. Of course, the Strehlow Collection cannot be regarded naively as a means for restoring the past by returning to the time when Strehlow recorded his data, since the Collection, as Angeles noted, is 'living' and 'breathing'. This means it does not function as a static record of the past, but must be treated as a dynamic source whereby the next generation of Arrernte men and women can respond to the contemporary world with integrity, pride and innovation in accordance with their age-old cultural values. In this sense, repatriation of knowledge does not translate as the resurrection of ancient traditions but suggests a return of traditional knowledge to its rightful owners, who will use such knowledge to engage intentionally and productively with changes confronting traditional society by outside forces, such as Western education, modern forms of communication, laws imposed by the national and territorial governments, commercial interests, ease of travel and the diffusion of family ties through processes of urbanization.

Conclusion

From the above cases describing the current repatriation project developing out of the Strehlow Research Centre, it has become clear that since 2009, when Adam Macfie was appointed Repatriation Anthropologist, and prominently since 2013, when Mark Inkamala and Shaun Angeles were contracted as Indigenous Repatriation Researchers, the involvement of Arrernte Elders in accessing and using the Strehlow Collection has increased. Hart Cohen drew attention to this when he observed that 'for some time, little interest was shown in the potential for repatriating parts of the collection given the sensitivities and complexities relating to provenance and ownership' (private correspondence, Cohen to Cox, 8 September 2016). But, recently, he explains, 'repatriation has been taken on with new earnestness albeit with a changing focus as more material comes to light and more traditional owners express an interest in their materials' (private correspondence, Cohen to Cox, 8 September 2016). The interviews and cases I have highlighted in this chapter demonstrate that Elders are accessing Strehlow's notes and records to confirm their own kinship links and to establish their relationship to the land as traditional owners. We have also seen how this information is being used by current Elders, both men and women, to instruct young people in traditional knowledge, without which they fear it will die out completely. In this sense, Strehlow was correct in his judgement that it was only in his notes, diaries and collected data that knowledge of Arrernte traditions would be preserved and passed on to the next generation. With the active involvement of Arrernte researchers, the importance of transmitting knowledge of the traditions has been made evident to the present generation of Elders with the result that Strehlow's diverse Collection is now serving his original purpose as a means not only of restoring to the current generations knowledge of songs, ceremonies, stories and traditions that had been forgotten and gone into disuse, but also as a living source for interpreting them in new and creative ways that will affect future generations.

9

KNOWLEDGE, TRADITION AND AUTHORITY

After having documented the background to and current efforts to repatriate Indigenous knowledge in Central Australia, we are left with two unresolved theoretical issues still to consider. The first relates to what we mean by the knowledge that is being repatriated. The second explores the thorny problem that results from the implication that repatriating knowledge constructs a dichotomy between tradition and modernity. In this concluding chapter, I analyse how each of these broad areas relates to the themes I have pursued throughout this book, specifically how they elucidate the contribution to knowledge made by Strehlow during his 40 years of research among Indigenous groups in Central Australia, how they apply to the current repatriation of knowledge movement at the Strehlow Research Centre and what light they shed on my own definitions of religion and Indigenous Religions. In the final section of this chapter, I analyse the impact of Strehlow, a man whose life's work was devoted to studying a particular group of people living in a remote locality, on contemporary global studies in Indigenous Religions.

Types of Knowledge

In Chapter 1, I reviewed two academic studies of T.G.H. Strehlow written by Tim Rowse of Western Sydney University. I focussed on Rowse's criticisms of Strehlow as a man whose sense of pride led him into conflicts with academic colleagues and eventually with Indigenous peoples themselves. I deliberately delayed examining Rowse's extremely helpful analysis of types of knowledge as they apply to Strehlow's understanding of his unique Collection as a preserve of ancient Arrernte traditions until this chapter after I had presented Strehlow's writings and described how his Collection is being consulted today by Arrernte Elders and used as a tool to inform young people about their heritage. Following the work of the sociologist J.A. Barnes, Rowse divided knowledge into three types with differing purposes: 1) Knowledge as enlightenment; 2) Knowledge as power; 3) Knowledge as property. I will explain what Barnes meant by these categories before analysing how Rowse applied them to his discussion of Strehlow and how I use them to situate Strehlow in the current academic climate.

Barnes, who died in 2010, before his retirement in 1982 had been Professor of Sociology at the University of Cambridge, UK and previously had held posts at the University of Sydney and at the Australian National University in Canberra. In his book entitled *Who Should Know What?*, he argues that the twentieth century witnessed a shift away from how knowledge had been understood previously as a source of enlightenment to knowledge perceived as power. He explains that under the new circumstances knowledge is 'seen as a source of power to be used by those who control it for their own advantage rather than for the enlightenment and benefit of mankind' (Barnes, 1979: 64). He then suggests that more recently, particularly among communities in the Third World and minority groups, knowledge has been conceived as property in which it is 'regarded as … an asset possessed by an individual or a group which may be treasured but is not intended for use and which is available for sale or gift only under restrictive conditions, if at all' (Barnes, 1979: 64). Barnes provides an example of knowledge as property which is particularly apt for any discussion of Strehlow's later claims to be the owner of his extensive Collection. Barnes refers to holdings in museums as 'cultural trophies', the acquisition of which was justified 'by reference to the universal values of science' (Barnes, 1979: 65). He explains: 'The argument is, or was, that we are not impoverishing the Lapps or the Bushmen, by displaying their artefacts in our museums' but 'we are doing all mankind a service by rescuing them from destruction' (Barnes, 1979: 65). The justification for removing artefacts from their original owners and placing them in museums is based on the concept of knowledge as enlightenment, in which 'works of art and representative material objects, like knowledge itself, are sources of enlightenment' (Barnes, 1979: 65).

In a later book, Barnes expanded on his interpretation of the three categories of knowledge by discussing them in the context of India. He provides the example of a 'typical field study' in which the researcher describes the remarriage of a young widow of the dominant caste in a village (Barnes, 1990: 209). Barnes asks what type of knowledge the report of the remarriage conveys. If it is based on an enlightenment theory, it would in some sense help us understand the workings of the society and thereby 'increase our understanding of the human condition' (1990: 209). A second interpretation identifies knowledge as power whereby the remarriage of the young widow in the dominant caste is interpreted as helping to oppress the subordinate classes. A third use of knowledge relates to ownership of knowledge. Barnes asks: 'Are we invading the privacy of the young widow if we publish the fact of her remarriage?' (1990: 209).

This hypothetical example demonstrates clearly how knowledge operates according to Barnes's classifications. He notes that social sciences developed in the late eighteenth century when 'ethnographic information was perceived by those who first started to collect it as a source of enlightenment' (1990: 210). In the nineteenth century, knowledge, particularly of the 'lower classes and dependent peoples' was sought because the ruling elite believed the lower classes could not articulate their needs for themselves (1990: 210). This led during the early part of the twentieth century towards a use of knowledge as beneficent power whereby 'the knowledge gained by empirical inquiry was seen as a means for discovering how to change people's lives', usually for the better, for example, by teaching them how to build latrines, avoid alcohol or to 'stop beating their wives' (1990: 210). Barnes then suggests that after 1945 more and more people who had been the subject of ethnographic research simply refused to cooperate by withholding the information sought by outside researchers. This indicates a change in which the subjects of research began to treat knowledge of their own societies as their own private property.

Based on Barnes's three categories of knowledge, Tim Rowse suggested that Strehlow reflected each type at various times in his dealings with Indigenous people, academic colleagues and the general public. Rowse cites Strehlow's reception of knowledge from Aboriginal Elders as a sign that he believed he was a true inheritor of power that accompanied the knowledge entrusted to him. The more Strehlow entered into the world of the senior men, 'the more he qualified as the eventual successor of these donors' (Rowse, 1999: 108). Strehlow was entrusted with so much power, according to Rowse, that he experienced conflicting reactions to the Aboriginal communities among whom he was working. On the one hand, he believed that the knowledge of the traditions which had been shared with him needed to be safeguarded and preserved across the generations, but on the other hand, he believed that the young could not be trusted because 'colonial impacts had already rendered such indigenous legatees unfit for their patrimony' (1999: 108). For this reason, Strehlow regarded himself 'to be the authentic successor of his mentors' granting him not only the power that accompanied the transmission of knowledge, but also status as its rightful owner (1999: 108).

Rowse acknowledges that Strehlow also employed the knowledge he gained from Elders as a means for enlightening the Australian public about Indigenous religion, culture and society (1999: 108). As a founding member of the Australian Institute of Aboriginal Studies, Strehlow advanced the principle that conducting research possesses intrinsic value. He conveyed the knowledge he had gained through research in numerous public talks, magazine articles and pamphlets for general dissemination. Rowse notes that the problems Strehlow experienced with academic colleagues later in his career did not result so much from his reluctance to follow the enlightenment model of knowledge as it did from institutional conflicts over funding of his research and the implied attack on the integrity of his inheritance as guardian of Indigenous knowledge (1999: 109). This latter issue became evident when the Government in the late 1960s began to change its assimilationist policy and shifted towards programmes that promoted Aboriginal rights. This, according to Rowse, disempowered Strehlow, who previously had defended the integrity of Indigenous cultural values against the denigration that accompanied attempts to assimilate Indigenous people into the dominant white culture (1999: 109).

Situating Strehlow within the Three Types of Knowledge

Rowse's interpretation of the types of knowledge based on the sociological theories of J.A. Barnes helps me situate Strehlow in the contexts in which I have presented him in this book. Clearly, in so far as Strehlow employed theories consistent with the phenomenological method in the study of religion, he was following enlightenment principles of knowledge. This is implied in my argument voiced in Chapter 7 that he promoted understanding-in-depth (*Verstehen*) of Arrernte religion, culture and social organization based on an empathetic approach that interpolated the meanings of the ceremonies, songs and stories he recorded in terms that outsiders could understand. His academic books and articles became important contributions to promoting humane knowledge of Aboriginal customary ways of living in a manner consistent with the phenomenological principles advanced by Wilfred Cantwell Smith (1981: 97). My discussion and analysis of Strehlow's important writings in Chapters 3 to 6 of this book were undertaken to portray Strehlow as the champion of a method aimed at promoting understanding-in-depth of Indigenous Religions in Central Australia, or to put in terms of Barnes's classifications, as communicating his unique access to Aboriginal traditions as a means of enlightening a wide range of outside audiences.

Running alongside the commitment Strehlow demonstrated to knowledge as enlightenment was the contrary problem that Indigenous knowledge in Central Australia is almost entirely secret and regarded as the private property of the custodians of tradition. The element of secrecy appears to stand in total opposition to the principle of enlightenment creating a fundamental dilemma for the researcher who employs phenomenological methods to foster understanding of cultures that otherwise would appear bizarre, strange and permanently incomprehensible to outsiders. The researcher who uses empathy to give voice to the so-called objects of study, that is, to make them the final authority on any interpretation of their religious beliefs and practices as suggested by W. Brede Kristensen (see Cox, 2006: 108–15), confronts the problem, as in the case of the Arrernte, that they do not want to reveal their most fundamental traditions to outsiders;

to do so breaches the inviolable laws established by sacred personages when they first emerged from beneath the surface of the earth.

Indigenous Arrernte knowledge as property is also closely connected to knowledge as power, as we saw in Strehlow's discussion of the hierarchical structuring of traditional society, where the most secret songs, ceremonies and sacred objects were known exclusively to senior men and were revealed only over time to younger men as they became more mature; they were never disclosed to women or uninitiated boys. In this case, knowledge was equivalent to power, particularly in light of the overwhelming belief that the totemic ancestors had given the eternal knowledge to the Elders in a chain that had extended from generation to generation since the beginning of time. The power associated with sacred knowledge was mirrored in the social structure: it underpinned relationships within particular local totemic clans and constructed the patterns of totemic cooperation regionally through ceremonial protocols that were observed rigidly. This was the entire point of Strehlow's description of Arrernte society as personal monototemism in a polytotemic community. This model of society linked the ancient myths to current ceremonies in ways that embedded the social structure in the power of an overwhelming authoritative tradition, the knowledge of which was transmitted over time from Elders to the younger men, who when they became Elders performed the same function for the next generation.

The claim by Strehlow that the transmission of knowledge had been interrupted and irrevocably disturbed by the intervention of colonial and missionary incursions into traditional Arrernte society explains precisely why he interpreted the knowledge he gained from Arrernte Elders as evidence that he personally had replaced the next generation as the depository of secret-sacred knowledge. His extensive research during which the Elders shared with him knowledge of their most intimate sacred ceremonies, stories, songs, genealogical records, location of sacred sites and the physical sacred objects, the *tjurunga*, confirmed in his mind that he had documented in his notebooks, maps, family trees, sound recordings and films a storehouse of Arrernte religious and cultural life that otherwise would have been lost forever. As Rowse emphasized, Strehlow saw himself as the inheritor of the interrupted transmission of the authoritative tradition because, as an 'insider', the Elders entrusted him with their sacred knowledge.

The disruption in the transmission of the authoritative tradition for Strehlow changed everything and explains why, as Rowse has suggested, he fits so well into the classifications based on Barnes's three types of knowledge. In his published books and articles, Strehlow presented, as I have done in this book, knowledge of Arrernte religion and society as a means of enlightening the wider Australian and international public to foster understanding and indeed tolerance of the culture of the peoples of Central

Australia. In *Aranda Traditions* (1947), a small number of photographs of secret ceremonies and objects appear, but in *Songs of Central Australia* (1971a) no photographs are included, as a sign of respect for those who entrusted him with secret knowledge. It is evident that these two books were written in accordance with Barnes's theory of knowledge as enlightenment. On another level, as the 'owner' of the knowledge granted to him by Arrernte Elders, in place of the younger generation, which Strehlow believed was unworthy of and disinterested in the traditions of former generations, Strehlow concluded that he had the power to decide what to do with the secret knowledge that was now in his possession. In this sense, his depository of knowledge and its use corresponds to Barnes's related notions of knowledge as power and property. Towards the end of his life, Strehlow sought to centralize his Collection in the newly created Strehlow Foundation, which was to be independent from academic institutions, some of which had funded his own research endeavours. This Collection, which he regarded as his own and over which he and his wife Kathleen exercised sole power, would preserve for posterity the records of Arrernte traditions that had disappeared.

The Repatriation of Knowledge

In Chapter 8, I outlined the background to and the current efforts to repatriate knowledge through the Strehlow Collection now maintained at the Strehlow Research Centre in Alice Springs. In light of the discussion by Rowse and Barnes, we are led to ask: 'What type of knowledge is being repatriated?' Clearly, the primary aim of repatriating knowledge is not for the betterment of humanity, as in the enlightenment theory, since the term repatriation implies returning knowledge that was suppressed, interrupted or stolen by outsiders to their rightful owners. That repatriation of knowledge does not refer to enlightenment was made clear to me in an interview I held on 7 October 2013 with an Arrernte Elder at the Strehlow Research Centre in Alice Springs (Cox and Possamai, 2016: 190). The interview took place in the context of the research Adam Possamai of Western Sydney University and I were conducting, with the assistance of the local linguist David Moore, exploring 'non-religion' among Aboriginal Peoples in Australia (Cox and Possamai, 2016: 181–93). I began by asking the Elder about ancient traditions, particularly about initiation rituals, what they entailed and if they were still practised. The Elder indicated that such knowledge was secret, but if I wanted to learn about it, I should 'read about it in the books'. This was a two-edged response. In the first instance, the Elder was confirming that knowledge of initiation rituals was not something he could share because it dealt with 'secret men's business'. Clearly, this knowledge was not available to enlighten outsiders. The other side to his response suggested that the secret knowledge had been stolen and disseminated in books available to be consulted by any interested party. In this senior man's view, Indigenous Elders had been disempowered by the theft of their secret knowledge; repatriation was aimed at restoring power by returning knowledge, conceived as property, to its legitimate owners.

The secret elements within the Strehlow Collection at the Strehlow Research Centre in Alice Springs are not available for viewing or consultation by outsiders. The numerous secret-sacred objects that belonged to T.G.H. Strehlow are housed in a room and only those Indigenous leaders who can claim a legitimate right to view them are permitted into the storage area. This is true for Strehlow's films and recordings, many of his photographs and his genealogical information. It is possible for outside researchers to gain access to Strehlow's notes, private correspondence and unpublished writings, but that which is deemed to fall under the ownership of Indigenous people, including the films and recordings of their sacred ceremonies, is not available for outside researchers to consult. This part of the Collection is now intended to be used by Arrernte Elders in the process of repatriating knowledge of the ceremonies, the meanings attached to the *tjurunga*, the content of the songs and chants used in the ceremonies, the traditional attire worn during the ritual performances, location of the sacred sites and genealogical information.

Yet, the repatriation of knowledge is also restricted among Indigenous groups; each kinship-determined group is an 'outsider' with respect to information belonging to other kinship groups. The legitimate right to local knowledge is limited to those alone who can demonstrate ownership based on genealogical evidence. This, of course, is where Strehlow's detailed genealogical charts come into play in the current situation. In Chapter 8, I referred to an interview I conducted in 2015 with Phillip at his homestead outside Alice Springs. He made it clear that his visits to the Strehlow Research Centre were aimed at discovering information about his 'mob' alone. He insisted that he had no interest in interfering with the knowledge that belonged to other kinship groups. For that reason, he reiterated that he wanted to remain anonymous if I were to write about our interview; he did not want other Elders thinking he was meddling in their affairs by obtaining knowledge that did not belong to him (Interview Cox with Aboriginal Elder, Phillip, 13 October 2015). This demonstrates the continued importance of secrecy about sacred traditions in Central Australia, since knowledge wields power among its rightful owners, a power that could be misused were it to fall into the wrong hands. It is significant also that the genealogies are used to determine who are the legitimate traditional owners not only of ceremonial knowledge, but also of land, with all the practical results this implies. As we saw in Chapter 8, land claims are based on judgements about traditional owners, suggesting quite explicitly that knowledge in these cases is directly related to power.

As we have seen, Strehlow pronounced Indigenous Religion in Central Australia 'dead' because the senior men who had entrusted the knowledge of their traditions to him themselves had died making his Collection the sole link with past generations. The Repatriation of Knowledge project at the Strehlow Research Centre in one sense accepts Strehlow's claim to be the inheritor of traditions passed on to him by Elders who trusted him, but the existence of the project confirms that the transmission of the tradition did not end with Strehlow. His Collection now occupies the place of the senior men who revealed their knowledge to him as the source for transmitting knowledge to the next generation. Because Strehlow so carefully documented this knowledge, his Collection can now serve as the nexus restoring the chain of memory that has long been severed. This knowledge is no longer considered the property of Strehlow, nor is it owned by the Strehlow Research Centre or the Northern Territory Government, but it belongs to the legitimate heirs who are re-connecting with past traditions through the medium of the Strehlow Collection. Ownership in this sense does not mean that Elders can go to the Strehlow Centre and remove secret-sacred objects without properly negotiating their right to do so, but it is clear that they are regarded as the legitimate owners of the knowledge of the objects and the records preserved by Strehlow. The Strehlow Research Centre houses the material, but does not own the knowledge. The recent digitilization of Strehlow's films and recordings, however, does open avenues for making the secret information available to local kinship groups and totemic clans from whom the documentation was obtained originally. The current Repatriation of Knowledge programme at the Strehlow Research Centre clearly interprets the knowledge that is being repatriated in terms of power and property.

The Contrast between Tradition and Modernity, Pre-Modern and Modern, Pre-Axial and Axial as Applied to Indigenous Religions

The purpose of the Repatriation Programme at the Strehlow Research Centre is to return knowledge of ancient traditions to their original owners. One way to interpret this project is to insist that it entails rediscovering past ways of life and reasserting the overwhelming authority that was attached to the traditions that had been transmitted from one generation to the next stretching back in mythic terms to the beginning of time. Such knowledge, as we have seen, includes the way ceremonies were performed, the meanings of inscriptions imprinted on the sacred objects, the content of myths, songs, and chants, the location of sacred sites and genealogical information. If Strehlow was right, the aim of the Repatriation of Knowledge programme, however, cannot involve returning to traditional ways of life by re-instituting ancient customs as if they had been unaffected by outside

forces. This is because Arrernte traditions have been so disrupted by modernity that at best they can only be re-constructed and emulated, we might
say 're-invented'.

Strehlow argued that knowledge of most events he wrote about and documented had disappeared by 1960. Repatriating knowledge that has been
lost or forgotten, or as I have called it in the title of this book, 'restoring
the chain of memory', needs in this light to be analysed not as an attempt
to reinstate past authoritative traditions, which is not possible. This raises
the issue of the relationship between the traditions that are being repatriated and the current situation of Indigenous people who have experienced
radical changes in their customary ways of life under the powerful forces
of modernization. In a quite practical way, the repatriation of knowledge
project forces us to consider the theoretical implications that have been
couched in terms of the alleged dichotomy between 'tradition' and 'modernity', or as it has been discussed more recently through the intervention of
the American sociologist Robert Bellah, the contrast between pre-axial and
axial religions.

In Chapter 2, I defined religion as the transmission from generation to
generation of an overwhelming authoritative tradition. I discussed how this
socio-cultural interpretation of religion, following the secularization theory,
links the contemporary decline of religion in the West with the rise of modernity, which, following the French sociologist Danièle Hervieu-Léger, I argued
is marked by increased individualism consistent with the hegemonic influence of international capitalism. In this sense, I asserted that religion, defined
as tradition, is closely identified with authority and community, whereas the
quest for personal fulfilment, sometimes associated with 'spirituality', particularly in the Western world, is characterized by a 'pick and choose' approach in
which individuals follow whichever pathway suits them at the moment. This
theory explains the decline of religion in the West, which is being replaced
by values determined by principles of personal autonomy and the individual's
freedom of choice.

I discussed in some detail in Chapter 2 Danièle Hervieu-Léger's definition of religion as a 'chain of memory' as it applied to Indigenous societies,
specifically in terms of her own cultural setting, that of rural France. I indicated that in my concluding chapter I would return to this discussion in
light of my presentation of T.G.H. Strehlow's accounts of Arrernte Indigenous Religion and of my analysis of the repatriation of knowledge project in
Central Australia. What I called the *sine qua non* of religion and of Indigenous Religions in Chapter 2, following Hervieu-Léger, might be construed
as implying that religion is fundamentally pre-modern, a characterization
that would apply even more starkly to Indigenous Religions. This interpretation of an unbridgeable gulf between Indigenous traditions and modernity,
however, need not follow from my argument. A more historically nuanced

discussion is required to clarify why an overly rigid separation between tradition and modernity ignores the power of Indigenous agency by depicting Indigenous societies as stuck in the past, and as inevitably subject to disintegration. I am helped in qualifying what might appear as an excessively strict dichotomy between tradition and modernity based on my discussion of the *sine qua non* of religion and Indigenous Religions by two scholars who have discussed the relationship between tradition and modernity: the Israeli scholar of comparative religions, Zwi Werblowsky, in the context of secularization theory in the West, and Jacob Olupona, Professor of African Religious Traditions at Harvard Divinity School, who has analysed this theme in the context of Indigenous Religions.

In his text of the Louis H. Jordan Lectures in Comparative Religion delivered in 1974 at the School of Oriental and African Studies in the University of London, Werblowsky (1976: 17) asserted that 'from the sociological point of view modernity is not the pre-ordained grave-digger of tradition'. His justification for this comment was that modernity itself constitutes a tradition extending at least back to the seventeenth century Western Enlightenment.[1] This means that modernity, although open and fluid, 'has its own elements of tradition', but, equally, tradition possesses the characteristics of 'plasticity and malleability' (Werblowsky, 1976: 16). This is an important point when we consider that Indigenous Religions, although localized, kinship-orientated and rooted in tradition, nonetheless, respond to modernity in ways that are creative, innovative and highly adaptive. This is precisely what Werblowsky meant when he objected to the tendency to treat certain cultures 'as psychologically, socially, economically, culturally or religiously "not yet" modern, or as archaic, medieval, pre-modern' (Werblowsky, 1976: 13).

The adaptability of Indigenous Religions has been made a key point of analysis by Jacob Olupona in the introduction to his edited volume, *Beyond Primitivism: Indigenous Religious Traditions and Modernity* (2004). Like Werblowsky, Olupona associates modernity with the European Enlightenment of the seventeenth century which, he admits, has culminated in 'the secularization of Protestant Christianity, humanism, and the prominence of scientific thought in Western culture' (2004: 1). Colonialism and neocolonialism represent facets of modernity, according to Olupona, that have 'severely affected the lives of indigenous peoples at all levels – socio-economic, political, cultural and religious' (2004: 1). Olupona then poses the question which is critical to my discussion of the meaning of the

---

1. A similar point has been made by the Australian anthropologist, Peter Sutton, who prefers to use the terms 'classical' and 'post-classical' to distinguish between 'traditional' and 'contemporary' on the grounds that 'contemporary urban and rural Aboriginal people also have traditions' (Sutton, 2003: xvii).

Repatriation of Knowledge project in Central Australia: 'How static is tradition in the face of the challenges of modernity?' (2004: 2). He answers by emphasizing the adaptability of Indigenous societies through what he calls the 'cognitive efficiency' of 'traditionalists' (2004: 3), which he finds demonstrated in the 'flexibility, awareness, and coexistence of alternatives' that define, in part at least, 'the African response to modern Western mechanistic materialism' (2004: 3).

When analysed in the light of the comments of Werblowsky and Olupona, one of the most controversial analyses of the place of Indigenous Religions in the history of religions has been developed by Robert Bellah in his book *Religion in Human Evolution* (2011). In this prodigious volume, which extends over 700 pages, Bellah re-introduces the theory of the 'axial age' into the contemporary discussion of the characteristics of religion in the modern world. This book was followed a year later by a publication Bellah co-edited with Hans Joas of the University of Chicago entitled *The Axial Age and Its Consequences*, in which a key article about African Indigenous Religions appears written by Ann Swidler, Professor of Sociology at the University of California, Berkeley. Bellah and Joas introduce their book by explaining 'that in significant parts of Eurasia the middle centuries of the first millennium BCE mark a significant transition in human cultural history, and … this period can be referred to as the Axial Age' (2012: 1).

The idea of the axial age was first developed in the 1950s by the German philosopher Karl Jaspers. In his book entitled *Way to Wisdom: An Introduction to Philosophy* (1951), Jaspers observed that many of the great religious leaders and philosophers that so influenced later civilization emerged on the world scene roughly between 800 BCE to 200 CE. He explained that 'it was then that the man with whom we live today came into being' (1951: 99). He cites 'extraordinary events' that produced Confucius and Lao Tse in China; the development of the Upanishads and the rise of the Buddha in India; in Iran the dualistic philosophy of Zarathustra emerged; in Palestine the Hebrew Prophets brought their compelling moral challenge to the people of Israel; and in Greece the world witnessed the development of the high philosophy of Socrates and Plato. For want of a better term, Jaspers says, 'let us designate this period as the "axial age"' (1951: 99).

In the Introduction to *The Axial Age and Its Consequences*, Hans Joas asks what, other than the coincidence of the rise of great religious and philosophical thinkers over a period of approximately 1000 years, identifies the key change that occurred in human development at the axial point in history. Joas finds the most important element in the phrase, 'the *age of the emergence of the idea of transcendence*' (2012: 11, emphasis in original). He explains: 'A cosmological chasm between a transcendental sphere and a mundane one is then seen as the defining characteristic of axiality'. He adds that as a mode of analysis the axial age enables scholars 'to find out the tacit religious (or antireligious) assumptions in important theories of history and social change' (2012: 13). This challenge was articulated by Bellah in his 2011 volume in which he identified key evolutionary developments in the history of religion that help explain the transition from what he called 'tribal to archaic religion' (2011: 175).

The religions of tribal societies, according to Bellah, are expressed through narrative and ritual as opposed to cultures that are based on theory. In the process of evolution, 'the culture of ritual and myth' came under attack through 'antiritualism and demythologization' from 'those seeking a more universal answer to the question of meaning' (2011: 175). This corresponds to the beginning phases in the transition which Joas described as culminating in the 'cosmological chasm between the transcendent and the mundane'. Of particular interest to us is Bellah's analysis of the Walpiri people (spelled Walbiri by Bellah), who as we saw in Chapter 1 occupy territory adjacent to the Arrernte towards the northwest. Bellah explains that he has chosen to consider the Walpiri because 'Walbiri culture was among the most intact of existing Australian groups when studied in the 1950s by M.J. Meggitt and Nancy D. Munn' (2011: 146; Meggitt, 1962; Munn, 1986). Clearly, Bellah is relying on accounts of Indigenous peoples that he regards as emblematic of traditional societies that can be called 'pre-axial': localized, place-orientated and kinship directed, whose world views are characterized by mythic expressions and ritual enactments. Although Bellah (2011: 146) is not 'claiming that the Walbiri represent the ancient, unchanging, "true" Aboriginal tradition', when he discusses Walpiri society, it is apparent that he has chosen this group because he sees them as fitting into an evolutionary scheme that typifies cultures whose religious life is organized around narrative and ritual and in this sense is thoroughly pre-theoretical and hence pre-modern.

In his evolutionary scheme, Bellah identifies hunter-gatherer societies, such as the Walpiri, with egalitarianism that focussed on family or kinship relations in which 'differentiation of power and status were minimal' (2011: 174). This 'moral community', he explains, was made possible by 'mimetic and mythic' culture (2011: 177) in which natural despotic tendencies, inherited from our primate ancestors, were actively and continuously suppressed. Bellah cites the case of a people related to the Walpiri, the Pintupi, a group that always agrees 'that one will have to "listen to" fathers and mother's brothers, who have "taken care" of one since infancy' (2011: 179). However, among the Pintupi, Bellah notes, it is not primarily one's close family who exercise authority among the group, but 'elders in general, insofar as they "take care" of the younger generation by handing on to them the legacy of the Dreaming' (2011: 179). The next phase in human evolution following 'tribal' societies experienced a 'u-turn' that resulted in the end of 'the long history of egalitarianism' to be replaced by 'the rise of despotic chiefdoms and early states' (2011: 178). These societies, because they were stratified and hierarchical, developed new forms of myth and ritual that resulted in 'new understandings of the relation between cosmos, society and self' (2011: 175), culminating in what Bellah refers to as 'Archaic Religion', a phase in the progressive march of religion towards transcendence.

The contrast between the pre-axial and the axial ages among Indigenous societies is discussed at length by Ann Swidler (2012: 222–47) whose contribution to the Bellah and Joas volume analyses the Axial Age in relation to Africa by posing a fundamental question: 'What ... does it mean to say that a "civilization" is Axial or pre-Axial?' (2012: 222). Swidler clearly associates an 'Axial civilization' with 'Axial religions', by which she means the 'world' religions. She observes: 'There is no question that Africans have joined the Axial Age', a statement she confirms by reference to the 'large and ever growing number of adherents' to Christianity and Islam throughout Africa whose faith has been transformed as they were influenced increasingly by forces beyond the local, interpersonal world of the village (2012: 223). Certainly, Swidler is correct when she refers to the transformative changes occurring within African societies as a result of contact with globalizing forces including changes brought about in the realms of economics, politics, education, language and modes of communication. The notion that Indigenous societies are somehow stuck in the past or represent fossilized versions of early stages in human development has long been abandoned in intellectual discourse. Nonetheless, by identifying 'pre-Axial' with localized, kinship-orientated societies and the 'axial' with conversion of Indigenous peoples to global religions, principally Christianity and Islam, Swidler re-enforces the idea that Indigenous Religions have largely been overtaken by global institutions and by religions with universal cosmologies.

This conclusion, although correct in its emphasis on the dynamics of change affecting Indigenous societies in the modern world, is too one-dimensional, as it pits tradition against modernity, rather than, as Werblowsky and Olupona have done, describing modernity as an inheritor of its own tradition, and tradition as adaptive to the conditions imposed by modernity. I have argued elsewhere (Cox, 2000: 230–42) that Indigenous Religions are adoptive and adaptive, meaning that they possess an elasticity that allows them to respond in creative ways to outside forces. Indigenous religious practitioners, for example, frequently become Christian while retaining Indigenous identity; they become members of a universal religion and remain participants in a society that is restricted to place and kinship. They can be both Islamic, with its emphasis on a universal transcendent God, and Indigenous with its focus on ancestors. My main point is that Indigenous people are in control of their own responses to modernity, adapting their traditions to new circumstances without rejecting them altogether. Indigenous Religions function analogically as a palimpsest (i.e. the old writing is still visible under the new text that has been superimposed on the original) or, as the term is used outside its technical literary sense, as an entity with many layers of meaning. This suggests that Indigenous Religions, rather than being either global or local, universal or kinship-restricted, can be both global and local, universal and restricted to kinship, according to different settings and in various contexts. Insofar as they acknowledge the overwhelming authority of their ancestral traditions, they form a part of an Indigenous Religion; when they participate in a universal faith unrestricted by kinship, their religious life is not Indigenous. Nothing prohibits them from doing both.

The key concept in this, as I argued in Chapter 8, is agency. Indigenous people respond to modernity in ways that demonstrate choice, direction, concerted action and calculated strategies. These terms apply directly to the Repatriation of Knowledge project at the Strehlow Research Centre as Indigenous leaders take charge of their own knowledge as it was preserved in T.G.H. Strehlow's Collection. In turn, they use his Collection in ways that re-affirm Indigenous cultural values while at the same time exercising Indigenous autonomy. The Repatriation of Knowledge project is thoroughly modern, in that it involves Indigenous people in a process aimed at re-evaluating their ancient traditions in light of contemporary events and it is fundamentally traditional as Indigenous leaders transmit customary knowledge to the next generation in ways consistent with, although not always replicating, past ways of educating the young about the meaning and performance of ceremonial traditions and their kinship relations.

Implications for the Sine Qua Non of Indigenous Religions

What does the concept Indigenous agency imply for my discussion of the *sine qua non* of Indigenous Religions as I outlined it in Chapter 2? Does the idea that a person can be both-and as opposed to either-or undermine my attempt to delimit what is meant by an Indigenous religion? Does it imply that Indigenous people irrationally live in two or more worlds at the same time, keeping their differing roles separated? In some of my earlier publications on Indigenous Religions, I described Indigenous Religions as possessing multi-layered beliefs causing practitioners to maintain ideas that to a Westerner would appear contradictory (Cox, 2000: 230–42). I illustrated this by my experience working in Zimbabwe where people I interviewed responded to situations pragmatically rather than ideologically. For example, when confronted with illness, they saw no contradiction in consulting a traditional religious practitioner, an Independent Church healer, a herbalist, a Christian pastor and a Western medical doctor. Any, or all of these sources of healing, could 'work' at different times and under different circumstances, or even at the same time. This view of healing, of course, is not restricted to practitioners of Indigenous Religions; many Westerners consult a medical doctor and go to a church for prayers for healing, seeing no contradiction between the two. My point is that it is possible to hold more than one world-view at the same time, which is similar to playing different games that operate under different rules (See Cox, 1998: 91–93). This means that Indigenous people are not irrational; they know the difference between the rules of the games they are playing. They are simply following different rules of the game as Indigenous practitioners from ones when they are acting as Christians, Muslims, humanists or atheists. They can accept the overwhelming authority of a tradition that has been transmitted from generation to generation, in the case of the repatriation of knowledge movement through the medium of the Strehlow Collection, and, at the same time, exercise decision-making about how the restored knowledge is applied in modern contexts. They can do this because they possess agency; they are in control of and owners of Indigenous knowledge.

Indigenous Religions, in the terms of Robert Bellah or Ann Swidler, as pre-axial or even pre-theoretical, of course do not exist in the contemporary world, and perhaps never did. Indigenous Religions do persist, however, in living Indigenous communities, the members of which fail to see the importance of exclusive dichotomies and can live transformed lives as they re-discover their traditions and use them strategically to interact with numerous global influences that impinge on local contexts. In this sense, restoring the chain of memory has as much to do with the present and the future as it does with the past. In the dynamic responses of the Indigenous peoples of Central Australia to renewed awareness of their age-old traditions, T.G.H. Strehlow stands as a towering figure. He may not have fully understood the pivotal role his contribution would make to repatriating Indigenous knowledge nor have anticipated how significant his Collection would be to future Arrernte generations, but it is clear that his claim, which was much vilified by his detractors, to be the depository of ancient traditions has been confirmed in recent times when increasingly Arrernte leaders, family Elders and young people use his carefully documented Collection as a conduit for restoring knowledge of past traditions. This has empowered local Arrernte people to exercise Indigenous agency by taking control of and deciding how to use the knowledge that is progressively and irrevocably being repatriated to them.

The Contribution of T.G.H. Strehlow to the Contemporary Global Study of Indigenous Religions

In my 2007 publication, *From Primitive to Indigenous: The Academic Study of Indigenous Religions*, I analysed the developing academic interest in the global study of Indigenous Religions (Cox, 2007a: 8–31). Since the publication of that book, the study of Indigenous Religions has gained momentum and it is rapidly becoming an important subject in Religious Studies as well as in multi-disciplinary contexts. For example, a current project is being organized by Professor Geoffrey Davis, Former International Chair of the Association for Commonwealth Literature and Language Studies and G.N. Devy, Founder of the People's Linguistic Survey of India, who are editing a ten volume series to be published by Routledge. The series is entitled, '*Key Concepts in Indigenous Studies*'. In an email addressed to me dated 7 April 2015, Davis and Devy wrote that 'the field of Indigenous Studies has been one of the more important emerging fields of scholarship in the Humanities during the last two decades'. They note that 'leading universities in many countries have established specialized Departments of Indigenous Studies' (Personal correspondence: Davis and Devy to Cox, 7 April 2015). An example of this is located at the University of Trømso, The Arctic University of Norway, which on its website claims to be 'one of the very few in the world to offer an international Master's degree programme in comparative indigenous studies' (https://uit.no/utdanning/program/270446/indigenous_studies_-_master). Key figures in the study of Indigenous Religions at Trømso are Bjørn Ola Tafjord and Siv Ellen Kraft, who have collaborated with Greg Johnson of the University of Colorado in Boulder on the Brill *Handbook of Indigenous Religion(s)* published in 2017. Tafjord, Kraft and Johnson have developed a project on Indigenous Religions that has involved Arkotong Longkumer, Lecturer in Religious Studies at the University of Edinburgh, who in December 2016 organized a workshop on Indigenous Knowledge at Kohima, Nagaland, that also included the participation of the Africanist scholar, Rosalind Hackett of the University of Tennessee and former President of the International Association for the History of Religions (Interview Cox with Longkumer, 24 November 2016, School of Divinity, University of Edinburgh). In the United Kingdom, Graham Harvey of the Open University, continues to promote the study of Indigenous Religions, something he has been developing through a series of publications since the appearance of his groundbreaking edited volume, *Indigenous Religions: A Companion* (2000).

In Australia, initiatives have been launched at Western Sydney University by the School of Social Sciences and Psychology and at the University of Sydney in the Department of Studies in Religion. On 12 September 2016, Western Sydney University held its Inaugural Aboriginal and Torres Strait Islander Research Symposium on topics focussing on 'lived experience' and 'perspectives on research'. This was timed to follow the 2016 National Aborigines and Islander Day Observance Committee (NAIDOC) theme of 'Songlines: The Living Narrative of Our Nation', which was observed from 3–10 July 2016. The School of Social Sciences and Psychology at Western Sydney University intends to make symposia on research themes related to Inchadigenous Peoples in Australia annual events. The

Department of Studies in Religion at the University of Sydney sponsored a one-day symposium on 18 October 2013 on a theme exploring issues surrounding the category Indigenous Religions, which in 2016 resulted in the publication of the book, *Religious Categories and the Construction of the Indigenous*, edited by Christopher J. Hartney and Daniel J. Tower. In addition to leading Australian academics, such as Garry Trompf, Emeritus Professor of Religious Studies at the University of Sydney and expert on Indigenous Religions in Melanesia (Trompf, 2016: 8–37), the book contains articles by international scholars including Bjørn Ola Tafjord (2016: 138–77) and Graham Harvey (2016: 74–91), and my own submission in which I defend my restricted definition of Indigenous Religions against critics, such as Tafjord and Harvey (Cox, 2016: 38–57).

In the context of these new developments in the global study of Indigenous Religions, the importance of introducing the work of T.G.H. Strehlow to scholars working in this field around the world becomes critical. Of course, Strehlow was not unknown outside Australia, particularly among anthropologists, but his potential contribution to the study of Indigenous Religions has never been realized. He wrote informative articles in international publications, the most relevant of which for Religious Studies was his essay in the Bleeker and Widengren volume (Strehlow, 1971b: 609–28) in which he provided an overview and introduction to Aboriginal religions in Australia for scholars for whom the subject was new or outside their fields of expertise. And, as I noted in Chapter 1, Strehlow was recognized at the University of Uppsala with the award of an honorary doctorate for his research on Indigenous societies in Central Australia. Nonetheless, his works remain largely unknown among current researchers in the burgeoning field of Indigenous Religions within Religious Studies departments outside Australia.

In this book, I have described Strehlow's theoretical and empirical methodologies and classified his research findings under themes dealing with myths, rituals and social organization. I argued in Chapter 7 that the theory he employed corresponds to stages in the phenomenological method, particularly his use of the *epoché* and empathetic interpolation. By bracketing out commonly held assumptions about Indigenous Religions, he subjected the writings of Spencer and Gillen to a stinging criticism, particularly their misinterpretation of Dreamtime, which now has become almost universally associated with Aboriginal Religion throughout Australia. He was also able to show how the missionary translation of *Altjira* as God was based on a failure to understand nuances within Arrernte grammar, on the one hand, and, on the other, was the result of projecting the Christian God onto Indigenous worldviews, based partly on the notion that God nowhere had left himself without a witness (see Cox, 2014b: 195–222). By bracketing out these preconceived ideas about Indigenous Religions in Australia, Strehlow was able to look at the stories, songs and ceremonies he recorded in a fresh way and to portray the absolute centrality of totemic ancestors to the religious life of the people he studied. By making use of the technique of empathy, which was helped by his 'insider' knowledge of Arrernte culture, he was able to explain to outsiders the meaning and intent of Arrernte ceremonial and social life through the technique known as interpolation. He knew that non-Indigenous Australians, because of their overwhelmingly European background, would find many of the customs and rituals of Indigenous people bizarre, offensive or even grotesque. By interpolating Arrernte ceremonies and songs into European terms, he was able to foster understanding on the part of those who might otherwise reject them as inferior to Western values. At the same time, Strehlow did not hide the fact that traditional ways of life often entailed harsh and cruel punishments for ceremonial offences, including the death penalty. He also made it clear that ceremonies often inflicted extreme suffering on participants, as in initiation rituals or in rituals involving the spilling of blood. Strehlow's use of the *epoché* and empathetic interpolation, therefore, did not result in his romanticizing Indigenous Religions; it was intended to produce accurate descriptions of religious phenomena as free as possible from distorting and preconceived biases, while at the same time providing interpretations that would promote understanding of seemingly alien beliefs and practices by those who otherwise might maintain highly prejudicial attitudes towards them.

Strehlow's empirical methods included the scrupulous collection of data, which was documented with precision and clarity. His field notes were detailed so that any reader could trace how and where his research was conducted and what his aims were in conducting the research. He travelled vast distances, making in the process detailed maps showing the most important ceremonial sites, the tracks followed by the totemic ancestors and drawing attention to the central geographical features that were regarded as sacred embodiments of the founding ancestors. His photographs, films, recordings and transcripts of songs and chants were done with absolute precision. The testimony to his exacting empirical method of collecting data is now found in the Strehlow Collection which, I have argued, is so valuable that it occupies the place of the Elders themselves who transferred their knowledge to Strehlow and which now is providing the link between the current and the past generations. Strehlow also demonstrates how critically important it is for successful researchers to gain access to communities and in the process to win their trust. Without this, a researcher is unlikely to obtain accurate information or develop trustworthy interpretations of the data collected. Strehlow's criticism of shallow research underscores this point: promoting understanding of other cultures takes time and commitment, which Strehlow has shown requires not only sound theoretical and empirical skills, but also demands competence in local languages.

Strehlow's research was in Central Australia, primarily among Arrernte groups. His research confirms that for people living in these regions, local stories about totemic ancestors, which were tied to places on the landscape, define who they are and inform their complex kinship relations, including how marriage partners are selected. Arrernte social organization was documented in precise detail by Strehlow and portrayed in his genealogical charts, finely constructed maps, carefully designed models of totemic relations and in his detailed records of songs, chants and ceremonial performances. For the study of Indigenous Religions, I have argued that Strehlow's intensive research demonstrates that Indigenous Religions in Central Australia were restricted to the two key factors, kinship and location, which I have made central to my definition of Indigenous Religions generally. His findings also indicate that the Indigenous Religions of Central Australia, although containing beliefs in the power of the original ancestors, did not magnify these to occupy the place of a sky god, a high god or contain elements of belief in one God. The ancestors emerged from the earth at the beginning of time and they returned to the earth in the form of significant geographical features on the landscape. That these ancestors were so fundamentally intertwined with locality and kinship provides another example of how Indigenous Religions are best understood in terms of social categories rather than being confined to beliefs about supernatural beings or determined by alleged supernormal experiences.

Strehlow's descriptions of Arrernte Indigenous Religions also have implications for a sociological interpretation of religion in general. It is clear from the way in which traditions were maintained and ceremonial protocols enforced that the authority of the Arrernte way of life was rooted in age-old customary law, the knowledge of which was passed on to each new generation beginning with initiation ceremonies. Authority was invested in the Elders, who painstakingly safeguarded their secret knowledge, keeping it hidden from women, the uninitiated and outsiders. The Indigenous Religions of Central Australia, following Strehlow's analysis, precisely fit into a definition of religion as the transmission of a tradition that is invested with an overwhelming authority over members of each kinship group and totemic clan.

Strehlow's frank discussion of the decline of Indigenous Religions in Central Australia and his noting of changes that he observed over the period he conducted his research confirms that his aim was not to depict a people in the present as if they were exact replicas of the past. He recognized and documented change, even if at times he lamented the loss of the traditions he was witnessing. By studying Strehlow's writings, as outsiders we see him wrestling with the significance of disputes between Elders and younger men over the proper use of ceremonies; we see him describing the attitudes of young men who had come under the influence of white bosses and how that detracted from their respect for traditional ways of life; we see him struggling with the changes he experienced when Elders first entrusted him with their secret knowledge and how 20 years later that knowledge was largely unknown among the next generation of Elders in the line of succession. We also witness Strehlow's own changes from the time he was a young researcher to his period as Native Patrol Officer, through his time as a more senior academic when ultimately he felt estranged from many of his academic colleagues, whom he believed encouraged methods based on superficial field research that was both inadequate and self-interested. In these ways, we see that Strehlow represents a scholar who was fundamentally aware of the dynamics of historical, social and cultural change as it impinged on the traditional way of life in Central Australia and that he responded personally to these changing situations.

Finally, we find in Strehlow an academic who firmly believed in social engagement. Whether one agrees with the policies he endorsed or not, from the time he accepted the appointment as Native Patrol Officer, he became committed to providing a more humane approach to the Government's interaction with Indigenous people, and he set up a way to provide them with food supplies when they were in need. As we saw, he used corporal punishment, but this was not just to establish his authority but served as a way of using culturally accepted methods without falling into the excessive abuse of Indigenous people that was practised earlier by colonial officers and representatives of the police. Later, he became an advocate of Indigenous rights against assimilationist policies; he intervened in the case of Rupert Max Stuart, the Indigenous man accused of raping and killing a young girl in South Australia; he was consulted as the legal status of customary law in Australia was being debated. In these ways, Strehlow demonstrated that he was a socially involved scholar, not one that remained aloof or indifferent to his research subjects. His frequent public lectures and talks, as well as his pamphlets and articles written for consumption by the general public, in terms of contemporary academic jargon, demonstrated that his research had 'impact' on public perceptions of Indigenous peoples in Australia. That he regarded his Collection as a depository that served to preserve knowledge of traditions that had disappeared also supports my contention that Strehlow exemplified a scholar who balanced his commitment to serious and detailed academic research with a recognition that his research had social implications (for my general discussion of the socially engaged scholar of religion, see Cox, 2014c: 133–51).

If I apply the characteristics I have just listed that belonged to Strehlow the scholar, researcher and academic to his potential impact on the current international study of Indigenous Religions, we find that Strehlow combined a sound theoretical approach with in-depth empirical methods, which in turn helps us delimit what we mean by the term Indigenous Religions and, more generally, by religion itself. He demonstrated the inadequacy of pre-senting his findings as if they represented a perpetual 'ethnographic present' by engaging with and responding to the dynamic changes that affected the groups he was studying in Central Australia. He always understood that his research would have an impact on the peoples he was studying as well as on the general public, policy makers and on fellow academics. Reading T.G.H. Strehlow's works in-depth provides for contemporary scholars of Indige-nous Religions both an exemplary model for how research should be done while contributing significantly to our knowledge of a specific Indigenous people in Central Australia. In terms of this book, Strehlow demonstrates to students of religion that our aim is to enlighten a wide range of audiences about Indigenous Religions, while accepting that the use of this knowledge thrusts us immediately into arenas of power and involves us in questions of possession. Through this tangled web of complicated issues, introducing the work of T.G.H. Strehlow into contemporary global academic studies in Indigenous Religions offers methodological clarity and serves as a paradigm for anyone who wishes to research and write about the religious life and tra-ditions of specific Indigenous peoples in local contexts.

BIBLIOGRAPHY

Albrecht, Paul G.E. 2004. 'Friedrich Wilhelm Albrecht: An Appraisal of His Work Among Aborigines of Central Australia, Based on Personal Recollections', in W.F. Veit (ed.), *The Struggle for Souls and Science. Constructing the Fifth Continent: German Missionaries and Scientists in Australia* (Strehlow Research Centre, Occasional Paper Number 3). Alice Springs: Northern Territory Government, 111–19.

Allen, R.E. (ed.) 1990. *Concise Oxford Dictionary of Current English, Eighth Edition.* Oxford: Clarendon Press.

Anderson, Christopher. 1995. 'Politics of the Secret', in C. Anderson (ed.) *Politics of the Secret. Oceania Monograph 45.* Sydney: University of Sydney Press, 1–14.

Austin-Broos, Diane. 2003. 'The Meaning of *Pepe*: God's Law and the Western Arrernte', *The Journal of Religious History* 27(3): 311–28.

Austin-Broos, Diane. 2009. *Arrernte Present, Arrernte Past. Invasion, Violence, and Imagination in Indigenous Central Australia.* Chicago and London: The University of Chicago Press.

Australian Government, Department of Communication and the Arts. 'Indigenous Repatriation'. Available at: http://arts.gov.au/indigenous/repatriation. Last accessed 10 August 2016.

Australian Government, Department of Social Services. *Budget 2007–2008: Indigenous Affairs.* Available at: https://tinyurl.com/budget-2007-08. Last accessed 18 August 2016.

Australian Government, Department of Communication and the Arts. 'Return of Indigenous Cultural Property (RICP) Program: National Principles'. Available at: http://arts.gov.au/sites/default/files/pdfs/rics_principles.pdf. Last accessed 18 August 2016.

Australian Government, Department of Environment and Energy. 'National Heritage Places – Hermannsburg Historic Precinct'. Available at: https://www.environment.gov.au/heritage/places/national/hermannsburg. Last accessed 23 January 2017.

Barnes, J.A. 1979. *Who Should Know What? Social Science, Privacy and Ethics.* Harmondsworth: Penguin.

Barnes, J.A. 1990. *Models and Interpretations: Selected Essays.* Cambridge: Cambridge University Press.

Batty, Philip. 2014. 'The *Tywerrenge* as an Artefact of Rule: The (Post) Colonial Life of a Secret/Sacred Aboriginal Object', *History and Anthropology* 25(2): 296–311.

Baylis, Philippa. 1988. *An Introduction to Primal Religions.* Edinburgh: Traditional Cosmology Society.

Beinssen-Hesse, Silke. 2013. 'Rereading Barry Hills's "Broken Song"'. *Things German Australian Blogspot.* Available at: http://thingsgermanaustralian.blogspot.co.uk/2013/07/rereading-barry-hills-broken-song.html. Last accessed 5 July 2017.

Bellah, Robert N. 2011. *Religion in Human Evolution. From the Paleolithic to the Axial Age.* Cambridge, MA and London: The Belknap Press of Harvard University Press.

Bellah, Robert N., and Hans Joas (eds) 2012. *The Axial Age and Its Consequences.* Cambridge, MA: The Belknap Press of Harvard University.

Bergen, Penelope. 2010. 'Repatriation of Sacred Items High on Strehlow's Agenda'. *ABC*

Rural. Available at: http://www.abc.net.au/site-archive/rural/nt/content/201002/ s2821494.htm. Last accessed 10 August 2016.

Berndt, Ronald M. 1979a. 'T.G.H. Strehlow 1908–1978', *Aboriginal History* 3(1/2): 84–88.

Berndt, Ronald M. 1979b. 'Obituary. T.G.H. Strehlow, 1908–1978', *Oceania* 49(3): 230–33.

Bischofberger, Otto. 1999. 'Winthuis, Josef', in Gerald H. Anderson (ed.) *Biographical Dictionary of Christian Mission*. Grand Rapids, MI: Eerdmans, 745–46.

Capps, Walter H. 1995. *Religious Studies: The Making of a Discipline*. Minneapolis, MN: Fortress Press.

Central Land Council. n.d. 'History of the Land Rights. Available at: http://www.clc. org.au/articles/info/history-of-the-land-rights-act. Last accessed 13 January 2017.

Central Land Council. n.d. 'Kinship and Skin Names'. Available at: http://www.clc.org. au/articles/info/aboriginal-kinship. Last accessed 21 July 2017.

Central Land Council. 2003. *The Land Rights Act + Changes. Made Simple*. Alice Springs: Central Land Council.

Clarke, Geoff. 2002. 'Not Just Payback: Indigenous Customary Law', *Australian Law Reform Commission – Reform Journal* 80: 5–10, 69–70. Available at: http://www. austlii.edu.au/au/journals/ALRCRefJl/2002/2.html. Last accessed 17 January 2017.

Cohen, Hart. 2001. *Mr Strehlow's Films*. Lindfield, New South Wales: Film Australia Limited.

Cohen, Hart and Juan Salazar (co-producers). *Ntaria Heroes*. Available at: https://www. youtube.com/watch?v=k-64qnmkvsI. Last accessed 11 July 2017.

Cohen, Hart, Juan Salazar and Wendy Cowan. 'ICS Abstract. Cultural Mediation of the Visual: Knowledge Resources for Remote Indigenous Communities, 27 August 2015'. Available at: https://tinyurl.com/ics-seminar-2015. Last accessed 21 August 2016.

Cowan, James G. 1992. *The Elements of the Aborigine Tradition*. Longmead, Shaftesbury, Dorset and Rockport, MA: Element Books.

Cox, James L. 1991. *The Impact of Christian Missions on Indigenous Cultures. The "Real People" and the Unreal Gospel*. Lewiston, NY: The Edwin Mellen Press.

Cox, James L. 1992. *Expressing the Sacred: An Introduction to the Phenomenology of Religion*. Harare: University of Zimbabwe Press.

Cox, James L. 1998. *Rational Ancestors. Scientific Rationality and African Indigenous Religions*. Cardiff: Cardiff Academic Press.

Cox, James L. 1999. 'Intuiting Religion: A Case for Preliminary Definitions', in Jan G. Platvoet and Arie L. Molendijk (eds) *The Pragmatics of Defining Religion. Contexts, Concepts and Contests*. Leiden: Brill, 267–84.

Cox, James L. 2000. 'Characteristics of African Indigenous Religions in Contemporary Zimbabwe', in Graham Harvey (ed.) *Indigenous Religions: A Companion*. London and New York: Cassell, 230–42.

Cox, James L. 2006. *A Guide to the Phenomenology of Religion. Key Figures, Formative Influences and Subsequent Debates*. New York and London: Continuum.

Cox, James L. 2007a. *From Primitive to Indigenous. The Academic Study of Indigenous Religions*. Aldershot: Ashgate.

Cox, James L. 2007b. 'Secularizing the Land: The Impact of the Alaska Native Claims Settlement Act on Indigenous Understandings of Land', in Timothy Fitzgerald (ed.) *Religion and the Secular: Historical and Colonial Formations*. London: Equinox Publishing, 71–92.

Cox, James L. 2010. *An Introduction to the Phenomenology of Religion*. London and New York: Continuum.

Cox, James L. 2013a. 'The Transmission of an Authoritative Tradition: That Without Which Religion is Not Religion', in A. Adogame, M. Echtler and O. Freiberger (eds) *Alternative Voices: A Plurality Approach for Religious Studies*. Göttingen: Vandenhoeck and Ruprecht, 308–23.

Cox, James L. 2013b. 'Reflecting Critically on Indigenous Religions', in James L. Cox (ed.) *Critical Reflections on Indigenous Religions*. Farnham: Ashgate, 3–18.

Cox, James L. 2014a. *The Invention of God in Indigenous Societies*. London and New York: Routledge (originally Durham: Acumen Publishing).

Cox, James L. 2014b. 'Can Christianity Take New Forms? Christianity in New Cultural Contexts', in Paul Hedges (ed.) *Controversies in Contemporary Religion: Education, Law, Politics, Society and Spirituality*. III. *Specific Issues and Case Studies*. Santa Barbara, CA: Praeger, 195–222.

Cox, James L. 2014c. 'Phenomenological Perspectives on the Social Responsibility of the Scholar of Religion', in Abraham Kovacs and James L. Cox (eds) *New Trends and Recurring Issues in the Study of Religion*. Paris: L'Harmattan, 133–51.

Cox, James L. 2015. 'Religious Memory as a Conveyor of Authoritative Tradition: The Necessary and Essential Component in a Definition of Religion', *Journal of the Irish Society for the Academic Study of Religions* 2 (1): 5–23. Available at: https://tinyurl.com/2015-04-religious-memory

Cox, James L. 2016. 'Kinship and Location: In Defence of a Narrow Definition of Indigenous Religions', in Christopher Hartney and Daniel J. Tower (eds) *Religious Categories and the Construction of the Indigenous*. Leiden and Boston, MA: Brill, 38–57.

Cox, James L., and Adam Possamai. 2016a. 'Introduction: The Australian Census, Religious Diversity and the Religious "Nones" among Indigenous Australians', in James L. Cox and Adam Possamai (eds) *Religion and Non-Religion among Australian Aboriginal Peoples*. London and New York: Routledge, 3–23.

Cox, James L., and Adam Possamai. 2016b. 'Religion, Cultural Hybridity and Chains of Memory', in James L. Cox and Adam Possamai (eds) *Religion and Non-Religion among Australian Aboriginal Peoples*. London and New York: Routledge, 179–203.

Cox, Rupert, and Kozo Hiramatsu. 2012. 'Sounding Out Indigenous Knowledge in Okinawa', in Joy Hendry and Laara Fitznor (eds) *Anthropologists, Indigenous Scholars and the Research Endeavour: Seeking Bridges towards Mutual Respect*. London and New York: Routledge, 226–35.

Davie, Grace. 2000. 'Foreword', in Danièle Hervieu-Léger. *Religion as a Chain of Memory*. Cambridge: Polity Press, viii–x.

Edwards, Bill. 1998. 'Living the Dreaming', in Colin Bourke, Eleanor Bourke and Bill Edwards (eds) *Aboriginal Australia: An Introductory Reader in Aboriginal Studies*, 2nd edn. St Lucia, Queensland: University of Queensland Press.

Eliade, Mircea. 1958. *Patterns in Comparative Religion*. London: Sheed and Ward.

Eliade, Mircea. 1959. *The Sacred and the Profane. The Nature of Religion*. New York: Harcourt.

Eliade, Mircea. 1964. *Myth and Reality*. London: George Allen and Unwin.

Eliade, Mircea. 1973. *Australian Religions: An Introduction*. Ithaca, NY and London: Cornell University Press.

Elkin, A.P. 1974 [1938]. *The Australian Aborigines*, 5th edn. London and Sydney: Angus and Robertson Publishers.

Elkin, A.P. 1975. 'Reviews: *Songs of Central Australia*', *Oceania* 45(3): 245–47.

Fisher, Mary Pat. 2014. *Living Religions*, 9th edn. Upper Saddle River, NJ: Pearson Education, Inc.

Flood, Gavin. 1999. *Beyond Phenomenology: Rethinking the Study of Religion*. London and New York: Cassell.

Friesen, Jeff, and Steve Heinrichs (eds). 2017. *Quest for Respect: The Church and Indigenous Spirituality*. Intotemak (Special Issue).

Generation One. 'Indigenous Timeline 1970–Present – Australian Museum'. Available at: http://generationone.org.au/blog/2010/01/indigenous-timeline-1970-present-australian-museum. Last accessed 13 January 2017.

Gill, Sam D. 1998. *Storytracking. Texts, Stories, and Histories in Central Australia*. New York and Oxford: Oxford University Press.

Hall, T.W., R.B. Pilgrim and R.R. Cavanagh. 1985. *Religion: An Introduction*. San Francisco, CA: Harper and Row.

Hartney, Christopher, and Daniel J. Tower. 2016. *Religious Categories and the Construction of the Indigenous* (Supplements to Method and Theory in the Study of Religion). Leiden and Boston: Brill.

Harvey, Graham (ed.) 2000. *Indigenous Religions: A Companion*. London and New York: Cassell.

Harvey, Graham. 2016. 'Performing Indigeneity and Performing Guesthood', in Christopher Hartney and Daniel J. Tower (eds) *Religious Categories and the Construction of the Indigenous*. Leiden and Boston: Brill, 74–91.

Hawley, Janet. 1987. 'The Strehlow Collection: Preserved in Vitriol'. *Good Weekend*, 29 August, 28–34.

Hervieu-Léger, Danièle. 1999. 'Religion as Memory: Reference to Tradition and the Constitution of a Heritage of Belief in Modern Societies', in Jan G. Platvoet and Arie L. Molendijk (eds) *The Pragmatics of Defining Religion: Contexts, Concepts and Contests*. Leiden: Brill, 73–92.

Hervieu-Léger, Danièle. 2000. *Religion as a Chain of Memory*. Cambridge: Polity Press.

Hill, Barry. 2003. *Broken Song. T.G.H. Strehlow and Aboriginal Possession*. Milsons Point, New South Wales: Vintage Books.

Husserl, Edmund. 1931. *Ideas. General Introduction to Pure Phenomenology*, trans. W.R.B. Gibson. London: George Allen and Unwin Ltd.

Inglis, K.S. 2002 [1961]. *The Stuart Case*. Melbourne: Black Inc.

Jaspers, Karl. 1951. *Way to Wisdom: An Introduction to Philosophy*, trans. R. Manheim. New Haven, CT: Yale University Press.

Joas, Hans. 2012. 'The Axial Age Debate as Religious Discourse', in Robert N. Bellah and Hans Joas (eds) *The Axial Age and Its Consequences*. Cambridge, MA and London: The Belknap Press of Harvard University, 9–29.

Johnson, Greg and Siv Ellen Kraft (eds) *Handbook of Indigenous Religion(s)*. Leiden: Brill.

Jones, Philip. 2002. 'Strehlow, Theodor George Henry (Ted) (1908–1978)', *Australian Dictionary of Biography*. Melbourne: Melbourne University Press. Available at: http://adb.anu.edu.au/biography/strehlow-theodor-george-henry-ted-11792. Last accessed 20 June 2017.

Kenny, Anna. 2013. *The Aranda's Pepa: An Introduction to Carl Strehlow's Masterpiece, Die Aranda-und Loritja-Stämme in Zentral Australian (1907–1920)*. Acton, Canberra, ACT: Australian National University Press. Available at: https://tinyurl.com/ya5ez277. Last accessed 22 November 2016.

Kirby, M.D. 1980. 'T.G.H. Strehlow and Aboriginal Customary Law', *Adelaide Law Review* 7(2): 172–99.

Kirsch, Stuart. 2006. *Reverse Anthropology: Indigenous Analysis of Social and Environmental Relations in New Guinea*. Stanford, CA: Stanford University Press.

Kristensen, W. Brede. 1960. *The Meaning of Religion*, trans. J. Carman. The Hague: Martinus Nijhoff.

Krmpotich, Cara. 2012. 'Post-Colonial or Pre-Colonial: Indigenous Values and Repatriation', in Joy Hendry and Laara Fitznor (eds) *Anthropologists, Indigenous Scholars and the Research Endeavour: Seeking Bridges towards Mutual Respect*. New York and London: Routledge, 162–70.

Langton, Marcia. 2012. 'The Diaspora and the Return: History and Memory in Cape York Peninsula, Australia', in Joy Hendry and Laara Fitznor (eds) *Anthropologists, Indigenous Scholars and the Research Endeavour. Seeking Bridges towards Mutual Respect*. London and New York: Routledge, 171–84.

Latz, Peter. 2014. *Blind Moses: Aranda Man of High Degree and Christian Evangelist*. Alice Springs: IAD Press.

Loos, Noel. 2007. *White Christ, Black Cross: The Emergence of a Black Church*. Canberra: Aboriginal Studies Press.

MacFie, Adam, Mark Inkamala and Shaun Angeles. 2014. 'Abstract: Cultural Mapping Interactive Workshop: Strehlow Conference, 24 September 2014'. Available at: http://www.strehlow.co.uk/conference_2014.html. Last accessed 21 August 2016.

Mbiti, J.S. 1969. *African Religions and Philosophy*. London: Heinemann Educational Publications.

McNally, Ward. 1981. *Aborigines, Artefacts and Anguish*. Adelaide: Lutheran Publishing House.

Malik, Kenan. 2007. 'Who Owns Knowledge?' *Index on Censorship* 36(3): 156–67.

Meggitt, M.J. 1962. *Desert People: A Study of the Walbiri People of Central Australia*. Sydney: Angus and Robertson.

Moore, David C. 2008. 'T.G.H. Strehlow and the Linguistic Landscape of Australia 1930–1960', in W.B. McGregor (ed.) *Encountering Aboriginal Languages*. Canberra: Pacific Linguistics, 270–300.

Moore, David [C.]. 2016. '*Altjira*, Dream and God', in James L. Cox and Adam Possamai (eds) *Religion and Non-Religion among Australian Aboriginal Peoples*. London and New York: Routledge, 85–108.

Morton, John. n.d. 'Central Land Council. The Strehlow Collection of Sacred Objects', 1–12. Available at: http://www.clc.org.au/articles/info/strehlow. Last accessed 10 August 2016.

Munn, Nancy D. 1986. *Walbiri Iconography: Graphic Representations and Cultural Symbolism in a Central Australian Society*. Chicago, IL and London: University of Chicago Press.

National Film and Sound Archive of Australia. 'Shaun Angeles on Preservation of Remote Indigenous Collection'. Available at: https://www.youtube.com/watch?v=eUsv2dISgqs. Last accessed 15 February 2017.

Nichols, Christine Judith. 2014. '"Dreamtime" and "The Dreaming": Who Dreamed Up These Terms?' *The Conversation*. Available at: http://theconversation.com/dreamtime-and-the-dreaming-who-dreamed-up-these-terms-20835. Last accessed 31 October 2016.

Olupona, Jacob K. 2004. 'Introduction', in Jacob K. Olupona (ed.) *Beyond Primitivism: Indigenous Religious Traditions and Modernity*. New York and London: Routledge, 1–19.

O'Reilly, Karen. 2009. *Key Concepts in Ethnography*. Los Angeles, CA: SAGE Publications.

Parker, K. Langloh (aka Catherine Somerville Stow). 1905. *The Euahlayi Tribe: A Study of Aboriginal Life in Australia*. London: Archibald Constable and Co.

Platvoet, Jan G. 1992. 'African Traditional Religions in the Religious History of Humankind', in G. ter Haar, A. Moyo and S.J. Nondo (eds) *African Traditional Religions in Religious Education: A Resource Book with Special Reference to Zimbabwe*. Utrecht: Utrecht University, 11–28. Reprinted, 1993, *Journal for the Study of Religion* 6(2): 29–48.

Popkin, R.H., and A. Stroll. 1986. *Philosophy*. *Made Simple*. London: Heinemann.

Radke, D.J. 1965. 'Hermannsburg New Church'. *Lutheran Herald*, 9 October, 296–97, 299.

Radke, D.J. 1966a. 'Hermannsburg Church Nearing Completion', *Lutheran Herald*, 13 August, 228–29.

Radke, D.J. 1966b. 'Third New Church in Mission's Life of 89 Years', *Lutheran Herald*, 12 November, 330–32.

Rowse, Tim. 1992. 'Strehlow's Strap: Functionalism and Historicism in Colonial Ethnography', in Bain Attwood and John Arnold (eds) *Power, Knowledge and Aborigines*. Bundoora, Victoria: La Trobe University Press, 88–103.

Rowse, Tim. 1999. 'The Collector as Outsider – T.G.H. Strehlow as "Public Intellectual"'. *Strehlow Research Centre Occasional Paper 2*. Alice Springs: Northern Territory Government, 61–120.

Scherer, P.A. 1956. 'The New Testament in Aranda – A Linguistic Appraisal'. *Lutheran Herald*, November 24, 345–48.

Schmidt, Roger. 1988. *Exploring Religion*. Belmont, CA: Wadsworth.

Segal, Robert. 1999. 'In Defense of Reductionism', in R. McCutcheon (ed.) *The Insider/Outsider Problem in the Study of Religion: A Reader*. London and New York: Cassell, 139–63.

Sharpe, Eric J. 1986. *Comparative Religion: A History*. London: Duckworth.

Smart, Ninian. 1973. *The Phenomenon of Religion*. New York: The Seabury Press.

Smith, Wilfred Cantwell. 1959. 'Comparative Religion: Whither – and Why?', in M. Eliade and J. Kitagawa (eds) *The History of Religions: Essays in Methodology*. Chicago and London: University of Chicago Press, 31–58.

Smith, Wilfred Cantwell. 1964. *The Meaning and End of Religion: A New Approach to the Religious Traditions of Mankind*. New York: Mentor Books.

Smith, Wilfred Cantwell. 1981. *Towards a World Theology. Faith and the Comparative History of Religion*. Philadelphia, PA: Westminster Press.

Spencer, Baldwin. 1896. *Report on the Work of the Horn Scientific Expedition to Central Australia*, 4 vols. Melbourne: Melville, Mullen and Slade.

Spencer, Baldwin, and F.J. Gillen. 1899. *The Native Tribes of Central Australia*. Melbourne: Macmillan.

Spencer, Baldwin, and F.J. Gillen. 1927. *The Arunta. A Study of a Stone Age People. In Two Volumes*. London: Macmillan and Co, Limited.

Stanner, W.E.H. 2009 [1956]. 'The Dreaming', in W.E.H. Stanner, *The Dreaming and Other Essays, with an Introduction by Robert Manne*. Melbourne: Black Inc. Agenda, 57–72.

Strehlow, John. 2011. *The Tale of Frieda Keysser. Frieda Keysser and Carl Strehlow: An Historical Biography. Volume I: 1875–1910*. London: Wild Cat Press.

Strehlow, T.G.H. 1942. 'Aranda Grammar', *Oceania* 13(1): 71–103.

Strehlow, T.G.H. 1942. 'Aranda Grammar (continued)'. *Oceania* 13(2): 177–200.

Strehlow, T.G.H. 1943. 'Aranda Grammar (continued)'. *Oceania* 13(4): 310–61.

Strehlow, T.G.H. 1943. 'Aranda Grammar (continued)'. *Oceania* 14(1): 68–90.

Strehlow, T.G.H. 1943. 'Aranda Grammar (continued)'. *Oceania* 14(2): 159–81.

Strehlow, T.G.H. 1944. *Aranda Phonetics and Grammar. Oceania Monographs No. 7.* Sydney: Australian National Research Council.

Strehlow, T.G.H. 1947. *Aranda Traditions.* Melbourne: Melbourne University Press.

Strehlow, T.G.H. (trans) 1956. *Ankatja Arandauna Knatiwumala: Testament Ljatinja* (Bible. New Testament. Aranda). Adelaide: Lutheran Press in Cooperation with the British and Foreign Bible Society in Australia.

Strehlow, T.G.H. 1957. 'Thoughts of a Translator'. *Lutheran Herald*, January 12, 4–5.

Strehlow, T.G.H. 1958. *Dark and White Australians.* Adelaide: Aborigines Advancement League of South Australia.

Strehlow, T.G.H. 1962a. 'Aboriginal Language, Religion, and Society in Central Australia'. *Australian Territories* 2(1): 4–11.

Strehlow, T.G.H. 1962b. 'Aboriginal Australian Languages and Literature', *Hemisphere: An Asian-Australian Magazine* (August): 2–7.

Strehlow, T.G.H. 1963. 'Commentary', in W.E.H. Stanner and Helen Sheils (eds) *Australian Aboriginal Studies. A Symposium of Papers Presented at the 1961 Research Conference of the Australian Institute of Aboriginal Studies.* Melbourne: Oxford University Press, 248–51.

Strehlow, T.G.H. 1964. 'Personal Monototemism in a Polytotemic Community', in Elke Haberland, Meinhard Schuster and Helmut Straube (eds) *Festschrift für Ad. E. Jensen.* 2 vols. Munich: K. Renner.

Strehlow, T.G.H. 1965. 'Culture, Social Structure, and Environment in Aboriginal Central Australia', in R.M. Berndt and C.H. Berndt (eds) *Aboriginal Man in Australia.* Sydney: Angus and Robertson, 121–55.

Strehlow, T.G.H. 1966. *The Sustaining Ideals of Aboriginal Societies.* Adelaide: Aborigines Advancement League of South Australia.

Strehlow, T.G.H. 1969. 'Mythology of the Centralian Aborigine', *The Inland Review* 3 (11 June/August): 11–15.

Strehlow, T.G.H. 1970. 'Geography and the Totemic Landscape in Central Australia: A Functional Study', in Ronald M. Berndt (ed.) *Australian Aboriginal Anthropology: Modern Studies in the Social Anthropology of the Australian Aborigines.* Nedlands, Western Australia: University of Western Australia Press, 92–140.

Strehlow, T.G.H. 1971a. *Songs of Central Australia.* Sydney: Angus and Robertson.

Strehlow, T.G.H. 1971b. 'Religions of Illiterate People: Australia', in C.J. Bleeker and G. Widengren (eds) *Historia Religionum, vol. II.* Leiden: Brill, 609–28.

Strehlow, T.G.H. 1978a. *Central Australian Religion. Personal Monototemism in a Polytotemic Community.* Australian Association for the Study of Religions. Special Studies in Religions Series, volume 2. Bedford Park, South Australia: Flinders University.

Strehlow, T.G.H. 1978b. *Aboriginal Religion.* Adelaide: The Strehlow Research Foundation (pamphlet no. 4, vol. 1, June 1978). (Now held at the Strehlow Research Centre, Alice Springs. Box A: T.G.H. Strehlow. Articles by Title).

Strehlow, T.G.H. 1999. 'Aranda Regular and Irregular Marriages'. *Strehlow Research Centre Occasional Paper* 2: 1–44.

Strehlow, T.G.H. 2015 [1969]. *Journey to Horseshoe Bend, with an Afterword by Philip Jones.* Artarmon, New South Wales: Giramondo Publishing Company. (Originally published in 1969, Sydney: Angus and Robertson Ltd).

Strehlow Research Centre. 2000. 'The Strehlow Story'. *Information Sheet No. 2.* Alice Springs: Strehlow Research Centre.

Sutton, Peter. 2003. *Native Title in Australia: An Ethnographic Perspective*. Cambridge: Cambridge University Press.

Swain, Tony. 1985. *On 'Understanding' Australian Aboriginal Religion*. Bedford Park, South Australia: Australian Association for the Study of Religions.

Swain, Tony. 1993. *A Place for Strangers. Towards a History of Australian Aboriginal Being*. Cambridge: Cambridge University Press.

Swidler, A. 2012. 'Where Do Axial Commitments Reside? Problems in Thinking about the African Case', in Robert Bellah and Hans Joas (eds) *The Axial Age and Its Consequences*. Cambridge, MA: The Belknap Press of Harvard University, 222–47.

Tafjord, Bjørn Ola. 2013. 'Indigenous Religion(s) as an Analytical Category'. *Method and Theory in the Study of Religion* 25(3): 221–43.

Tafjord, Bjørn Ola. 2016. 'Scales, Translations, and Siding Effects: Uses of *Indigena* and *Religion* in Talamanca and Beyond', in Christopher Hartney and Daniel J. Tower (eds) *Religious Categories and the Construction of the Indigenous*. Leiden and Boston: Brill, 138–77.

Theology and Religious Studies UK. 'About TRS'. *TRS News*. Available at: http://trs.ac.uk/about-trs/. Last accessed 7 April 2017.

Tremlett, Paul-François. 2008. *Religion and the Discourse on Modernity*. New York and London: Continuum.

Trompf, Garry W. 2016. 'Reflections on Indigeneity and Religion', in Christopher Hartney and Daniel J. Tower (eds) *Religious Categories and the Construction of the Indigenous*. Leiden and Boston: Brill, 8–37.

Turner, Victor W. 1985. 'Liminality, Kabbalah and Media'. *Religion* 15: 205–17.

Turpin, Myfany. n.d. 'Aboriginal Languages', Central Land Council website. Available at: http://www.clc.org.au/articles/info/aboriginal-languages. Last accessed 24 May 2017.

Tylor, E.B. 1913. *Primitive Culture. Researches into the Development of Mythology, Philosophy, Religion Art and Culture*, 5th edn. London: John Murray.

UNESCO. 'Text of the Convention for the Safeguarding of the Intangible Cultural Heritage'. Available at: http://www.unesco.org/culture/ich/en/convention. Last accessed 21 August 2016.

van der Leeuw, Gerardus. 1938. *Religion in Essence and Manifestation*, trans. J.E. Turner. London: George Allen and Unwin Ltd.

van Gennep, Arnold 1960 [1908]. *The Rites of Passage*. London: Routledge and Kegan Paul.

Veit, Walter F. 2004. 'Contributor Biographies', in W.F. Veit (ed.) *The Struggle for Souls and Science. Constructing the Fifth Continent: German Missionaries and Scientists in Australia*. (Strehlow Research Centre, Occasional Paper Number 3). Alice Springs: Northern Territory Government, 214–16.

Waardenburg, Jacques. 1978. *Reflections on the Study of Religion*. The Hague: Mouton Publishers.

Werblowsky, R.J. Zwi. 1976. *Beyond Tradition and Modernity. Changing Religions in a Changing World*. London: University of London, The Athlone Press.

Wolfe, Patrick. 1991. 'On Being Woken Up: The Dreamtime in Anthropology and in Australian Settler Culture', *Comparative Studies in Society and History* 33(2): 197–224.

Archival Sources

Lutheran Archives, Adelaide: Strehlow, T.G.H. 'One Hour Before Sunset'. Public Talk, given in the Mawson Theatre, University of Adelaide, on 16th June, 1954 at 8 p.m. by Mr. T.G.H. Strehlow at 8 p.m. UELCA, FRM, no. 67 (Dr Lohe's Files), 1932–1966. T.G.H. Strehlow folder 1950–1966.

Lutheran Archives. Adelaide. Strehlow, T.G.H. 'The Central Australian "Man-Making" Ceremonies with Special Reference to Hermannsburg, Northern Territory'. 11th August 1977. LCA, FRM, no. 13.

Strehlow Research Centre, Alice Springs. Strehlow, T.G.H. 1978. 'In the Beginning', *Journal of the Anthropological Society of South Australia* 16(8). Citation from Strehlow's typed version. SRC Box A. T.G.H. Strehlow. Articles by title.

Interviews

James Cox with Phillip (pseudonym for Indigenous Arrernte Elder). Alice Springs: 13 October 2015.

James Cox with Steve Bevis (independent researcher). Alice Springs: 13 October 2015.

James Cox with Arkotong Longkumer, 24 November 2016, School of Divinity, University of Edinburgh, Scotland.

Private Correspondence

Davis and Devy to Cox, 7 April 2015

Hart Cohen with James Cox, 8 September 2016

Newspapers

Lutheran Herald, 9 October 1965, 296–97, 299.

Lutheran Herald, 13 August 1966, 228–29.

Lutheran Herald, 12 November 1966, 330–32.

Alice Springs News, 30 September 2016.

Websites

http://arts.gov.au/indigenous/repatriation

https://tinyurl.com/budget-2007-08

https://tinyurl.com/budget-2007-2008-gov-au

https://tinyurl.com/places-aranda

http://generationone.org.au/blog/2010/01/indigenous-timeline-1970-present-australian-museum

http://www.clc.org.au/articles/info/history-of-the-land-rights-act

https://www.environment.gov.au/heritage/places/national/hermannsburg

http://www.clc.org.au/articles/info/strehlow: 4

http://arts.gov.au/indigenous/repatriation

https://tinyurl.com/dss-gov-au-budget-2007-08

https://tinyurl.com/ics-events-seminars-2015

http://www.unesco.org/culture/ich/en/convention

http://www.strehlow.co.uk/conference_2014.html

https://www.youtube.com/watch?v=k-64qnmkvsI

http://www.clc.org.au/articles/info/aboriginal-kinship

https://www.youtube.com/watch?v=eUsv2dISgqs

https://uit.no/utdanning/program/270446/indigenous_studies_-_master

INDEX

www.ingramcontent.com/pod-product-compliance
Lightning Source LLC
Chambersburg PA
CBHW050805270326
41926CB00025B/4542